THE NATURAL RELIGION

The
Natural Religion

BY THE
REV. VERNON STALEY,
AUTHOR OF "THE CATHOLIC RELIGION," ETC.

WITH A PREFACE BY THE
REV. J. R. ILLINGWORTH, M.A.,
BAMPTON LECTURER, 1894.

"In proportion as Christianity is professed and taught in the world, Natural Religion is thus distinctly and advantageously laid before mankind, and brought again and again to their thoughts, as a matter of infinite importance."
—Bishop Butler, *Analogy* ii. i. § 11.

New Edition, Revised and Enlarged.
Completing the 15th Thousand.

WIPF & STOCK · Eugene, Oregon

Wipf and Stock Publishers
199 W 8th Ave, Suite 3
Eugene, OR 97401

The Natural Religion
By Staley, Vernon
ISBN 13: 978-162032-380-9
Publication date 7/15/2011
Previously published by Mowbray, 1896

PREFACE.

GREAT additions have been made, within the last few years, to our knowledge of the older religions of the world; not only of the great ones, whose records are in books, like those of India, China, Persia, Babylon, and Egypt; but also of the earlier and ruder creeds, whose fragments survive, like fossils, embedded in the strata of rustic or savage custom, folklore, poetry, and myth. These discoveries have given rise to what is called the science of religions, the science which compares and classifies the various phases of religious belief, with a view to reconstruct, as far as possible, the spiritual history of our race. But the facts of history are one thing, and their interpretation is another; the same events looking very different, when differently viewed: and as men never differ more than over questions of religion, we find very opposite conclusions drawn from the same religious facts. Hence there is still great variety of opinion about much in the religion of the past. One theory, however, there is,—one misinterpretation, as we must call it of the facts,—

against which we cannot too strongly protest. It is the view which regards religion as discredited by the rudeness of its earlier forms; arguing that what arose amid gross and savage superstition, is still only a superstition, however gracefully refined. Now, granting it to be true, though this is far from certain, that the rudest forms of religion are the earliest, the theory in question precisely inverts the true significance of such a fact. In other things we see this plainly enough. When a man rises by his merit in the world,—as once a peasant became pope,—we judge his earlier by his later, not his later by his earlier state. We do not say, 'This shows the pope to be no more than a pretentious peasant,' but, 'This shows that even a peasant may be a potential pope.' And, indeed, the general principle was laid down by Aristotle once for all. 'The true nature of a thing,' he said, 'is whatsoever it becomes, when the process of its development is complete.' It is strange, therefore, that we should still see attempts to explain away moral restrictions, as being derived from savage systems of taboo; and religious doctrines as, in like manner, survivals of irrational fetichism. As long, however, as such attempts are made, they need contradiction; and it is the object of the following pages to present, in a popular form, the converse and more reasonable view of religious history; according to which we interpret the lesser by the light of the larger creed; and, in so doing, are enabled to recognize, even in the lowest forms of faith, far more truth than the mere antiquarian can possibly perceive.

But while Christianity thus helps us to interpret what is commonly called natural religion, natural religion, in its turn, bears witness to the need for, and truth of Christianity. It shows us the constitutional religiousness of man; his universal, or almost universal, belief in gods and their relation to men, in prayer, in forms of worship, in sacramental union with the divine life, in sacrifice as an instrument of propitiation and of praise. And all these are the instinctive needs to which Christianity appeals. While further, if we view the religions of the past with sympathy,—with a spiritual, and not merely with a critical eye,—they will be seen to be strangely prophetic of the greater faith that was to come. For they are full of aspirations, hopes, forebodings, which were never solved and satisfied till Christianity arose: while many of their customs, symbols, rites, and even phrases were taken up by the Christian Church, often with a curious exactness; but clothed, in the process, with such new meaning, and inspired with such new life, as makes us feel that there at last, and only there, they have found their goal; in the universal—the catholic—religion.

Both these aspects of natural religion—its relative truth, and its prophetic tendency, together with their fulfilment in the Christian creed—are traced in the following work. And though, of course, it will not be expected that different minds should exactly agree upon the details of so large a subject, I am sure that the line here adopted is one which meets a need, and a serious need of the day. For, with every advance of science, men need to be reminded of the lesson which past experience should have taught us once for all: that however much new knowledge may modify our previous ways of thinking, all new knowledge, fairly faced, will prove ultimately Christian.

J. R. ILLINGWORTH.

AUTHOR'S PREFACE.

IN the first chapter of Bishop Butler's great work are found the following words, which fairly state the main idea of this book: "What is natural, as much requires and presupposes an intelligent agent to render it so, i.e., to effect it continually, or at stated times; as what is supernatural or miraculous does to effect it for once. And from hence it must follow, that persons' notion of what is natural, will be enlarged in proportion to their greater knowledge of the works of God, and the dispensations of His Providence. Nor is there any absurdity in supposing, that there may be beings in the universe, whose capacities, and knowledge, and views, may be so extensive, as that the whole Christian dispensation may to them appear natural, i.e., analogous or conformable to God's dealings with other parts of His creation; as natural as the visible known course of things appears to us."[1]

It is the author's endeavour to show that the truths of the Christian religion—the doctrines

[1] *Analogy*, i. i. § 31.

of the Holy Trinity, the Incarnation, the Atonement, the Resurrection, the Church, the Life to come, in short, the whole Christian Economy, are in the truest sense of the word *natural:* that they are as fixed, settled, and ordered, by the will of God, as are the laws of heat, light, or electricity: that the source from which all things natural or supernatural proceed, is one and the same.

The author hopes that this work may be found of use to various classes of persons:

(1) To those who as yet find themselves unable to accept the truths of Christianity;

(2) To those whose faith has been disturbed by the widespread unbelief in the supernatural in religion, and who are tempted to doubt the truth of the Christian revelation;

(3) To those who desire to know the foundations upon which that revelation primarily rests.

He has endeavoured to give a comprehensive view of the main arguments for the Christian position, in as simple a manner as the subject permits. In encountering difficult words or terms, the reader is desired to refer for their meaning to the Glossary at the conclusion of the volume. He ventures to suggest that the work should be read through from beginning to end, in order that the progressive argument may be allowed its full force and effect; and that,

Author's Preface.

after such perusal, the reader should proceed to study in like manner his former work, *The Catholic Religion*, to which the present work is intended as an introduction.

The author desires to express his sincere thanks to the Rev. Canon Gore, and the Rev. A. J. Harrison, for help in drawing up the syllabus of the work: to the Rev. Canon Bodington, the Rev. Canon Carter of Clewer, the Rev. G. S. Cuthbert, and the Rev. J. R. Illingworth, for valuable help in revising the proofs. In gratefully acknowledging this assistance, he desires to state that he alone is responsible for the positions maintained in this work; and that, on certain points, his views have not been fully shared by all the persons named. He begs to tender his thanks to the Rev. the Hon. James Adderley, Messrs. Longmans, Green and Co., Messrs. Macmillan and Co., Mr. John Murray, and the Society for the Promotion of Christian Knowledge, for their kind and ready permission to make extracts from works of which they severally own the copyright.

In cases of quotation from the Holy Scriptures, the Revised Version has in every instance been followed. The quotations from Bishop Butler's *Analogy* are taken from The Right Hon. W. E. Gladstone's edition of that writer's Works, printed at the Clarendon Press, Oxford, 1896. The quotations from Pascal's *Thoughts* are drawn from the translation of Mr. C. Kegan Paul, published by Messrs. George Bell and Sons, 1895.

V. S.

South Ascot.
March, 1896.

PREFACE TO THE SECOND EDITION.

THE Second Edition of this work is practically a reprint of the First Edition with a considerable amount of enlargement. A Synopsis of Contents has been supplied. On page 237, will be found an added note on the term 'Person' as applied to the Holy Trinity: on page 327, an added note on the Miracles of the Old Testament—an admirable passage from the Duke of Argyll's *Philosophy of Belief*. The author has added to the Appendix a chapter on Inspiration, which he trusts may be of use as a reasonable answer to some prevalent objections raised against the authority and trustworthiness of the Bible, and as a rectification of certain popular misconceptions concerning the purpose of the Sacred Volume.

V. S.

Inverness,
June, 1903.

SYNOPSIS OF CONTENTS.

INTRODUCTION.

	PAGE
What is natural religion?	3
No antagonism between natural and supernatural religion	4
Relation of supernatural to natural religion	4–5
The fundamental truths of Christianity consistent with natural religion	6–8

BOOK I.

Part First.

THE EVOLUTION OF THE BELIEF IN GOD.

CHAPTER I.

GOD SEEN IN NATURE.

i. Derivation of the term *natural religion*	11–12
No religious system traced out by unaided reason	13–14
ii. Belief in the superhuman universal	14–15
iii. The earliest form of natural religion expressed in the worship of nature	15–16
The conception of superhuman beings a later development	16
Relation of natural religion to a primeval revelation	17–18

	PAGE
iv. Primeval revelation lost or obscured to mankind at large	18
Source of man's earliest ideas concerning God	18–20
Note on the office of nature in leading man to perceive God	21

CHAPTER II.

GOD SEEN IN MAN.

Desire in early times to discover the infinite and divine in man	23
i. The immortality of the soul	24
ii. Ancestor-worship	25–27
iii. Hero-worship	27–28
iv. Anthropomorphism	28–30
Note on Anthropomorphism	31–32
v. The use of myth and illusion	32
Myth a vehicle of approach to God	32–35
Illusions rectified by experience	35–36
Myths and illusions the evidence of effort in man's search for God	36–37

CHAPTER III.

THE PERSONALITY OF GOD.

Development of belief in a Personal God	39
Truth may be revealed by imperfect methods	40
i. The disclosure of a Personal God awaited man's fitness to receive it	41
What is meant by *personality*	41–42
Man's recognition of the Personality of God dependent on a recognition of his own personality	43–44
The argument for the existence of a Personal God stated—	
ii. Creation implies a Creator possessing personal attributes	44–46
iii. God higher than man and therefore Personal	46–48
iv. Human affection unsatisfied until it rests in a Personal God	48–51

Part Second.

PROOFS OF THE EXISTENCE OF GOD.

CHAPTER I.

THE PLACE OF EVIDENCE IN CONFIRMING BELIEF IN GOD.

Importance of the subject	55
i. The appeal to reason not absolutely convincing	56
Faith is moral not absolute certainty	56
'God sensible to the heart not to the reason'	57–58
ii. Belief in God intuitive	58
Intuitive belief in God confirmed by evidence	59–60

CHAPTER II.

THE EXISTENCE OF GOD ATTESTED BY THE GENERAL CONSENT OF MANKIND.

Belief in a God or gods universal	63
i. Alleged exceptions considered	64–65
True form of the argument	66
ii. The objection that belief in God owes its origin to Fetichism and Polytheism examined	66–67
Revelation the record of how man has risen from lower to nobler ideas of God	68–69
iii. The weight to be attached to universal consent	70
Note on alleged exceptions to the general consent of mankind in the belief in the existence of God	71–72

CHAPTER III.

THE EXISTENCE OF GOD ATTESTED BY THE CONSIDERATION OF THE UNIVERSE.

The general unity in nature points to one author	75
Attempted explanation of the world by natural causes	76

i. The First Cause	77–78
ii. Secondary causes	78–81
iii. Evolution	81–84
Note on Evolution	84–86
iv. Origin of Life and Mind —	
(1) The origin of Life	86–88
Note on the origin of Life	88
(2) The origin of Mind	88–91
Note on the origin of Mind	91–92

CHAPTER IV.

The existence of God suggested by the presence of design in nature.

Design in nature suggests the unity o' its author	95
i. Order in nature	96–97
ii. Adaptation in nature	98–102
iii. Natural selection	102–108
Cumulative force of the proofs of God's existence	108–109

Part Third.

THE MORAL NATURE OF GOD.

CHAPTER I.

God a moral being.

Problem to be discussed	113
i. Characteristics of man's moral nature	114–117
ii. Origin of the moral law	117–119
Note on the testimony of conscience to God	119–120
iii. Need ul qualifications for the recognition of God as a Moral Being	120–122

Synopsis of Contents.

	PAGE
iv. Absence of such qualifications delayed the revelation	123
Summary	124–125

CHAPTER II.

THE PROBLEM OF MORAL EVIL.

'Unde malum et quare?'	127–128
i. The answer of Dualism	129–130
ii. What is involved in the idea of moral evil	130–133
iii. The probability that moral evil would arise in free agents	134–136
iv. Is the toleration of moral evil reconcilable with the righteousness and power of God?	136–138
The Incarnation the recognition of the divine responsibility for the permission of moral evil	138–139

CHAPTER III.

THE PROBLEM OF PHYSICAL EVIL.

Conjectures as to the origin of physical evil	141–142
Physical evil in relation to the lower animals—	
i. No evidence that the animals were ever exempt from pain and death	143–145
ii. Animal suffering not necessarily purposeless	145–146
iii. The intensity of animal suffering a matter of conjecture	146–148
iv. Considerations on the mitigation of pain	148–150
v. The animals look neither before nor after	150–151
Physical evil in relation to the human race—	
i. Death, but not all pain, amongst mankind the direct result of sin	152
ii. Human pain preventive and corrective	153–154
iii. Higher use of pain to purify and elevate character	154–156
The bearing of the doctrines of the Incarnation and a future life on physical evil	156–158

BOOK II.

THE REVELATION OF GOD.

THEOLOGY, NATURAL AND SUPERNATURAL ... 161–163

CHAPTER I.

THE REVELATION OF GOD.

The expectation of God's Self-disclosure ...	165–166
i. Revelation not a sudden act, but a continuous and progressive process	167
The relation of Christianity to earlier systems of religion	167–169
ii. The Christian revelation the climax of God's Self-disclosure, and made when mankind was prepared to receive it	170–172
iii. The vehicles of God's revelation—	
(1) nature	172–173
(2) man	173–174
(3) prophets	174–175
(4) the Jews	175–176
(5) Christ the revelation of God ...	176–180
Note on the relation of Christianity to other religions	180–181

CHAPTER II.

THE PERSON OF CHRIST THE EVIDENCE OF THE CHRISTIAN REVELATION.

Jesus Christ the evidence of the Christian revelation	183
i. Jesus Christ an historical Person	183–184
Experience lead the first believers to accept Him as divine	184
Note on the apostolic testimony	185–186
ii. The Gospels, as the record of the life of Christ, had no share in the first spread of belief in Him	186
Genuineness of the gospels as historical records	187
Note on the genuineness of the gospels ...	188–189

Synopsis of Contents.

	PAGE
iii. Christ the subject of His revelation	189–191
iv. Evidences of the truth of the divine claims of Jesus Christ	191
I. The characteristics of Jesus Christ as the Teacher—	
(1) His unconsciousness of any moral defect	192–194
(2) His conscious authority	194–195
(3) His self-assertion	195–199
II. The characteristics of the teaching of Jesus Christ—	
(1) The morality of His teaching	199–201
(2) The adaptability of His teaching to human needs	201–203
III. The influence of Jesus Christ—	
(1) His influence in the progress of the world	203–205
(2) His influence upon individuals	205–208
(3) His influence beyond the circle of the Christian world	208–209
IV. The existence of the Church of Jesus Christ	209–211
V. The supernatural elements in the life of Jesus Christ—	
(1) The expectation of the miraculous in His life	212–215
(2) Consideration of the miracles of which He was the subject	215
The Virgin-birth	215–220
The Resurrection	220–225
Note on the cumulative character of the evidence for the divine claims of Christ	225–226

CHAPTER III.

BELIEF IN THE HOLY TRINITY THE RESULT OF THE CHRISTIAN REVELATION.

Jesus Christ disclosed—
  i. The doctrine of the Holy Trinity 229–231

	PAGE
ii. essentially a Christian doctrine	231–233
iii. a reasonable doctrine	233–235
Note on the reasonableness of the doctrine of the Trinity	235–237
Note on the term 'person' as applied to God	237

CHAPTER IV.

THE REVELATION OF THE FATHER.

Man naturally regards God as his Father	239
The Christian revelation supplements this natural belief	239–240

I. The relation of God to man—

i. Christ disclosed the love of God to man	240–241
ii. ,, interpreted pain and sorrow	241–242
iii. ,, revealed God's love for individuals	242–243
iv. ,, disclosed God's particular providence	244–245
v. Objections to God's providence examined	246–247
vi. A belief in God's providence does not imply that He approves all He tolerates	248
vii. Conclusion	248–249

II. The relation of man to God—

i. The Incarnation disclosed man's true dignity	250–251
ii. Prayer the privilege of the children of God	251–252
iii. Objections to the practice of prayer examined	253–255
iv. The influence of prayer on human character	255–257

III. The relation of man to his fellows—

The brotherhood of the human race a result of belief in the Fatherhood of God	257–258

CHAPTER V.

THE REVELATION OF THE SON.

By sin man is estranged from God as his Father ... 261

I. The removal of the penal consequences of sin—

  i. God in Christ interposed to save man from the eternal consequences of sin ... 262–264
  ii. Objection to the doctrine of the Atonement examined ... 264–266
  iii. Christ offered Himself not only as our substitute but also as our representative ... 266–268
  iv. Summary ... 269
  v. Reasonableness of the doctrine of Atonement ... 269–271
  vi. Verification of the doctrine in human experience ... 271–272

II. The destruction of the power and habit of sin—

  What Christ did *for* us He works *in* us ... 273
  i. Christ's deliverance of mankind from original sin ... 273–277
  Note on original sin ... 277–278
  ii. Christ's deliverance of mankind from actual sin ... 278–281

CHAPTER VI.

THE REVELATION OF THE SPIRIT.

The manifestation of the Spirit a gradual process ... 283

i. In the development of the organic world a new cause or power came into action at certain stages ... 283–285

This new cause or power attributed to the presence of the Spirit of God as the Life-Giver ... 285–286

The operation of the Spirit in the moral sphere ... 286–287

		PAGE
ii.	The manifestations of the Spirit's presence reached their climax in the Incarnation ...	287–288
iii.	The revelation of the Spirit the completion of God's Self-disclosure	289
	The effect of the advent of the Spirit ...	289–290
iv.	The Spirit came to abide amongst men ...	290
	The higher level of life attained in Christian times attributed to Christ's gift of the Spirit	290–291
v.	Christ the Life: the Spirit the Life-Giver ...	291–292

CHAPTER VII.

THE REVELATION OF THE CHURCH.

	The Church the extension of the Incarnate Life of Christ	295–296
	"Grace and truth came by Jesus Christ" ...	296
	The Church the divine society to which Christ entrusts the treasures of grace and truth for the benefit of mankind ...	296
	The Spirit the Agent in the application of grace and truth	296–297
i.	The Church the sphere of grace	297–301
ii.	,, ,, the organ of truth	301–303
	The idea of the Church reasonable and satisfactory	303–304

CHAPTER VIII.

THE REVELATION OF THE LIFE TO COME.

	Man's universal belief in a future life verified by Christ	307–308
i.	The resurrection and ascension of Christ the pledge of man's immortality	308–309
	A future life necessary for the reward of virtue and the punishment of vice ...	309–310
ii.	Man's future state determined by character...	310–311
	The hope of a future life a stimulant to moral effort	312
iii.	Conduct and character influenced by a right faith	312–313

APPENDIX.

MIRACLES.

	PAGE
The Christian revelation sometimes rejected as involving belief in miracles	317
I. Objections to miracles examined—	
(1) 'Miracles do not happen now'	317–318
(2) ' ,, are against natural law'	318–321
II. The rationale of miracles—	
(1) New forces produce new effects	321–324
(2) The miracles of the New Testament	324
(3) ,, ,, Old Testament	325–327
Note on the miracles of the Old Testament	327–328
(4) The moral purpose of miracles	328–332
Note on the moral purpose of miracles	332–333
III. Conclusion—	
Summary of the argument	333–335

INSPIRATION.

Erroneous ideas concerning the basis of Christianity	337–339
i. The relation of Christianity to the New Testament—	
Christianity not primarily derived from the New Testament	339–340
The first spread of Christianity due to living teachers	340–341
The function of written documents	341–342
The statement 'Christianity is based on the Bible' a perversion of historical facts	342
ii. The inspiration of the Bible—	
The Church not committed to the theory of verbal inspiration	343
The truer view of inspiration stated	343–347
Biblical inaccuracies admitted	347

Synopsis of Contents.

	PAGE
Inspiration not given to teach natural science	347-348
The use of allegory	348-349
,, ,, primitive traditions	350-351
Conclusion of the argument	351-352
Declaration on Inspiration	352-354

GLOSSARY	355
INDEX TO AUTHORS	362
GENERAL INDEX	364

Introduction.

"Christianity is a republication of natural religion. It instructs mankind in the moral system of the world : that it is the work of an infinitely perfect Being, and under His government ; that virtue is His law ; and that He will finally judge mankind in righteousness, and render to all according to their works, in a future state. And, which is very material, it teaches natural religion in its genuine simplicity ; free from those superstitions, with which it was totally corrupted, and under which it was in a manner lost. Revelation is further, an authoritative publication of natural religion, and so affords the evidence of testimony for the truth of it."—Butler, *Analogy*, ii. 1, §§ 5, 6.

INTRODUCTION.

A BLACKFOOT Indian once described the difference between his own religion and that of the white man in the following words: "There are two religions given by the Great Spirit, one in a book for the guidance of the white men who, by following its teachings, will reach the white man's heaven; the other is in the heads of the Indians, in the sky, rocks, rivers, and mountains. And the red men who listen to God in nature will hear His voice, and find at last the heaven beyond."[1] Now that religion which the Indian described as being in the head and heart of man, in the sky, rocks, rivers, and mountains, may be termed natural religion. Natural religion has its foundation in nature—in human nature and in that world around us which is believed to be the revelation of God. Natural religion, or universal religion as it may be called, is the perception of the Infinite and His laws—however rude such a perception may be—which is found amongst savage races, apart from a special or an authenticated revelation, such as is presented to man in Holy Scripture and Christian tradition. In our own day, natural

[1] *The Indians, whence came they?* McLean, 1889, p. 301.

religion has been contrasted with supernatural or revealed religion properly so called. It is the object of this work to show that there is no antagonism between natural religion and supernatural religion; but, on the contrary, that they form one whole, the latter being the outcome or development of the former, just as the flower is the outcome or development of the bud, or the full-grown man of the little babe.

It is to the failure to base supernatural religion on natural religion, that much of the doubt and unbelief of modern times may be traced. "There may be," says Professor Max Müller, "other reasons for this omnipresent unbelief, but the principal reason is, I believe, the neglect of our foundations, the disregard of our own bookless religion, the almost disdain of natural religion."[1] And the same writer goes on to add, "What our age wants more than anything else is natural religion. Whatever meaning different theologians may attach to *supernatural religion*, history teaches us that nothing is so natural as the supernatural. But the supernatural must always be *super-imposed* on the *natural*. Supernatural religion without natural religion is a house built on sand, and when, as in our days, the rain of doubt descends, and the floods of criticism come, and the winds of unbelief and despair blow, and beat upon that house, that house will fall, because it was

[1] *Natural Religion*, p. 570.

not founded on the rock of bookless religion, of natural religion, of eternal religion."[1] St. Augustine's words are worthy of record, as bearing upon the necessary relation of supernatural religion to natural religion: "That thing itself which now is called the Christian religion was amongst the ancients, neither was it wanting from the beginning of the human race up to the time when Christ Himself came in the flesh, then the true religion, which already existed, began to be called the Christian religion."[2] Thus, supernatural religion does not ignore or do away with natural religion, it educes, supplements, stimulates, and perfects it. The spiritual order grows out of, and follows the natural order: the supernatural pre-supposes the natural. The divine and supernatural in religion implies the recognition and the permanence of the human and natural. Natural religion is thus to be regarded as the necessary prelude to, and preparation for supernatural religion.[3]

[1] *Natural Religion*, pp. 571, 572. [2] *Retract.* i. 13. 3.
[3] "Grace does not abolish nature, but it perfects and supplies the defect of nature."—St. Thomas, *Summa*, 1°. 1. 8. ad 2. et q 2. 2. et T.

"Christianity is a religion in addition to the religion of nature ; it does not supersede or contradict it ; it recognizes and depends on it, and that of necessity : for how possibly can it prove its claims except by an appeal to what men have already? be it ever so miraculous, it cannot dispense with nature ; this would be to cut the ground from under it ; for what would be the worth of evidence in favour of a revelation which denied the authority of that system of thought, and those methods of reasoning, out of which

It is the writer's purpose to endeavour to present the positive elements of natural religion in such a way as may be 'understanded of the people,' and, further, in such a manner as to lead to the acceptance of the truths revealed by supernatural religion. It is his earnest desire to present supernatural religion in such a form as to commend itself to every man's conscience. He has before his mind the case of one who, putting away all prejudice and bias, is willing to be led by the path of reason, observation, and experience. "We are told that all knowledge, in order to be knowledge, must pass through two gates, and two gates only: the gate of the senses, and the gate of reason. Religious knowledge also, whether true or false, must have passed through these two gates. At these two gates, therefore, we take our stand."[1] Supernatural religion rests mainly upon authority—the authority of Jesus Christ, the Holy Scriptures, and Christian tradition. But there are many in our day who, for various reasons, are unable to accept this authority; and who need leading and persuading by reasonable methods to the

---

those evidences necessarily grew?"—Newman, *Grammar of Assent*, p. 383.

"In the application of Christianity to the sanctifying of human character we are for ever bound to insist that the human character in its most fundamental nature is meant to be developed, not overthrown, by supernatural grace."—Gore, *Dissertations on the Incarnation*, p. 285.

[1] Max Müller, *Hibbert Lectures*, 1878, p. 220.

Introduction.

acceptance of the authority upon which the divine revelation of supernatural religion primarily rests.

"It is a very old saying, that we never know a thing, unless we know its beginnings. We may know a great deal about religion, we may have read many of the sacred books, the creeds, the catechisms, and liturgies of the world, and yet religion itself may be something entirely beyond our grasp, unless we are able to trace it back to the deepest sources from whence it springs."[1] It is our purpose to begin at the beginning, and to trace the stages which lead to the acceptance of the fundamental truths of Christianity; and to deal with these truths on the principles of natural reason, historical fact, observation, and experience.

Such fundamental truths are:

> Belief in God.
> Belief in Jesus Christ.
> Belief in the Holy Ghost.
> Belief in the Holy Catholic Church.
> Belief in the Life to come.

It will be our aim to show that these main articles of the Christian Faith, and the duties which they imply, are consistent with natural religion. We shall strive to prove that Christianity is no worn out creed, the outcome of

[1] Max Müller, *Hibbert Lectures*, p. 220.

past superstition or ignorance, fading away in the light of common sense and scientific research; but the greatest fact of history and experience, a sublime and satisfactory reality.

BOOK I.

Part First.

The Evolution of the Belief in God.

"He left not Himself without witness, in that He did good, and gave you from heaven rains and fruitful seasons, filling your hearts with food and gladness."—*Acts* xiv. 17.

"There is religion in everything around us, a calm and holy religion in the unbreathing things of nature, which man would do well to imitate. It is a meek and blessed influence, stealing in, as it were, unawares upon the heart; it comes quickly, and without excitement; it has no terror, no gloom in its approaches; it does not rouse up the passions of man; it is fresh from the hands of its Author, glowing from the immediate presence of the Great Spirit which pervades and quickens it."—*Ruskin*.

CHAPTER I.

GOD SEEN IN NATURE.

IT is an old rule, and a good rule too, that, before discussing any given subject, the terms about to be used should be clearly defined. We are about to treat of natural religion. What do we mean by *religion*, and what do we mean by *natural religion?*

i.

There is no perfect agreement as to the precise derivation of the word *religion*. St. Augustine and other high authorities derive the word from the Latin verb *religare*, which means 'to hold back,' 'to bind up,' 'to fasten.' Others, again, hold that it is derived from the verb *relegere*, which means 'to gather up again,' 'to take up,' 'to consider,' as opposed to *negligere*, 'not to take up,' 'to leave unnoticed,' 'to slight,' 'to neglect.'[1] "People were called religious," wrote Cicero, "from *relegere*, because they went over again, as it were, and reconsidered carefully whatever referred to the

[1] See Max Müller, *Hibbert Lectures*, pp. 11, ff.

worship of the gods." If we adopt the first derivation, *religion* signifies the restraint, or the bond, which binds man to God: if we adopt the second, the word signifies the consideration, or reverence for God and divine things.

The adjective *natural* is derived from the Latin word *natura*, which, in its turn, comes from the verb *nasci*, 'to be born.' *Natura* means 'nature,' 'the course' or 'order of things.' *Natural* signifies, therefore, that which is according to the law of our birth, according to nature, derived from nature, or dictated by nature. That which is natural is that which is born in us, or which grows within us in the ordinary course or order of things, and is suggested by them. On the other hand, the adjective *supernatural* denotes that which is above, beyond, or higher than that which is merely natural: it may be contrasted with *natural*, but never opposed to it. The term *natural* is opposed only to *unnatural*.[1]

---

[1] "Let us not leave it unnoticed that every sort of energy results from one of three distinguishable causes: one sort of energy proceeds from natural power; another from the perversion of the natural habit; the third represents an elevation or advance of the nature towards what is higher. Of these the first is and is called natural; the second unnatural; the third supernatural. Now the unnatural, as its name implies, being a falling away from natural habits and powers, injures both the substance itself and its natural energies. The natural proceeds from the unimpeded and naturally cogent cause. But the supernatural leads up and elevates the natural energy and empowers it for actions of a more perfect order, which it would not have been able to

God seen in Nature.

Natural religion is therefore the natural bond between man and God, or the reverence for God which is born in us, or which is taught by the natural world around us. Thus, we may consider natural religion both as an inherited instinct, and as a possession acquired by contact with the world of nature. In this latter sense, natural religion may be defined as the sum of knowledge of things superhuman, which the human mind may discover by the use of its ordinary faculties, and the ordinary methods of scientific investigation.

But, whilst we speak thus, we must guard ourselves by adding that we have no grounds for asserting that a religion of any kind, however rudimentary, has been fashioned by the unassisted reason of man. "When religion of some sort is said to be *natural*," wrote Cardinal Newman, "it is not meant that any religious system has been actually traced out by unaided reason. We know of no such system, because we know of no time or country in which human reason *was* unaided. Scripture informs us that revelations were granted to the first fathers of our race, concerning the nature of God and man's duty to Him; and scarcely a people can be named, among whom there are not traditions, not only of the

---

accomplish so long as it remained within the limits of its own nature."—Leontius of Byzantium, qu. by Gore, *Dissertations*, p. 277.

existence of powers exterior to this visible world, but also of their actual interference with the course of nature, followed up by religious communications to mankind from them. The Creator has never left Himself without such witness as might anticipate the conclusions of reason, and support a wavering conscience and perplexed faith. No people (to speak in general terms) has been denied a revelation from God, though but a portion of the world has enjoyed an authenticated revelation."[1] We may with greater safety regard natural religion as, in some sense or degree, partaking of the character of a revelation in embryo—a revelation from without made to man in his natural state, in contrast to supernatural religion which implies 'an authenticated revelation.'

ii.

The natural reverence for superhuman powers, which implies belief in a God or gods, is universal in all rational beings, in all ages, in all places. "As long as we know anything of the different races of mankind, we find them always in possession of something that may be called religion, . . . out of the sum total of human beings now living on this earth, those who are ignorant and those who deny the existence of any supernatural beings

[1] *University Sermons*, ii.

God seen in Nature.

form a mere vanishing quantity."[1] But of this universal consent of mankind to the existence of a God or gods we must speak later.

We use the expression 'a God or gods' advisedly, for it would be inaccurate to say that mankind has always believed in a Personal God, the Maker and the Ruler of the universe. Such a belief, as we are about to show, was only reached by slow degrees, as men were able to receive and act upon it. It is truer to fact to say that an universal belief in things, powers, or persons, superhuman or supernatural, has never been wanting from the very dawn of the history of our race. In other words, the religious instinct in some shape or other is natural to man; it is born in him, it grows with his observation of the world around him, and he cannot get rid of it, do what he will.[2]

It is of the evolution, or development of this religious instinct, of which we are now about to speak.

iii.

The earliest form of natural religion with which we are acquainted, has its roots in the acknowledgment of some power or powers

[1] Max Müller, *Natural Religion*, p. 222.
[2] "The recognition of God is said to be innate in us, in so far as we are able without difficulty to perceive that God exists by the principles innate in us."—St. Thomas, Opusc. super Boeth. *de Trin.*

To man's instinctive belief in the divine, we shall refer later.

superior to man. It found its expression in the worship of the objects of nature—the heavens, the earth, the sun, the moon, the stars, fire, water, trees, mountains, rivers, and even animals. When a savage looks for the first time upon a machine in motion, he comes to the conclusion that it lives, but he does not at once rise to the belief in the maker or designer of the machine. For mankind at large, it was even so at the beginning.

The conception of a superhuman being or beings for long ages remained dark and undeveloped. The conception of a God or gods assumed its earliest form in the reverence shewn to things of sense—the forces and creatures which surrounded man in the world of nature, till at last 'it threw off the husk, and disclosed the ripe grain'—the Personal God of revealed religion. Thus the idea of superhuman beings was only slowly evolved. "I have no hesitation in saying," writes Professor Max Müller, "that, so far as our knowledge of ancient religions reaches at present, they do not support the opinion that religion began anywhere with the general concept of superhuman beings. . . . Religious thought began with the naming of a large number of clearly marked and differentiated beings, such as Sky, Dawn, Thunder, Lightning, Storm, Mountains, Trees, etc., and that the concept of superhuman beings arose afterwards."[1]

[1] *Natural Religion*, pp. 129, 130.

There are good reasons for believing that this rudimentary form of natural religion was not its earliest form, but a falling away from a higher primeval revelation. In this view, the truth would be that the original religious instinct of man went astray, fastening upon wrong objects of worship. The conclusion that the higher stages of natural religion were only reached after a protracted period, during which primitive man worshipped stocks and stones and four-footed beasts and creeping things, is hardly so probable as the view which regards such a worship as a degradation of an earlier and purer system.[1] This is the view corroborated by St. Paul in the Epistle to the Romans, where he speaks of those who "changed the glory of the incorruptible God for the likeness of an image of corruptible man, and birds, and of four-footed beasts, and creeping things."[2]

During the long prehistoric period of man's existence, he lived in a savage, rude, and uncivilized state. But we must remember that primitive man was not quite on the same

---

[1] "The moral and spiritual degeneration of races is an important fact in history, and acts immediately upon the religious conceptions; and we may safely infer that it was equally active in prehistoric ages. And consequently when we meet with petty, grotesque, absurd, obscene, horrible objects and forms of worship, there is a reasonable presumption that they are largely due, not to original limitation of intellect, but to gradual moral deterioration and distortion."
—Illingworth, *Bampton Lectures*, vi. pp. 159, 160.

[2] i. 23.

moral plane as the modern savage. The latter represents "the remnant of humanity that has failed to progress, the other must have contained in himself the germ of all the progressive peoples. A man may have high thoughts amidst very low surroundings."[1] To say that man was from the first barbarous, does not necessarily imply that he was immoral.

iv.

Granting that God originally imparted a clear revelation of Himself to man in his first state, history teaches that, for the race at large, this revelation, if not altogether lost, had become so dim as practically to involve a new beginning in the acquirement of religious knowledge.[2] The early ideas of mankind in general concerning God, appear to have grown out of a natural instinct, influenced by the simplest perceptions of the senses — touch, taste, smell, sight, and hearing. Man found himself

---

[1] Illingworth, *Bampton Lectures*, vi. p. 146.

[2] The author must not be understood to throw any doubt upon the accuracy of the account of man's early state, given in the opening chapters of Genesis. Admitting that account to be true, all that can be said is—

  i. That the original communications of God to man were interrupted by man's sin.

  ii. That if the tradition of a primeval divine revelation was handed on through individuals, it became lost to the vast majority of mankind.

  iii. That whilst further special divine communications were granted to individuals, and later to one nation, they were denied to the world at large.

surrounded by objects which did not lie wholly within the grasp of those senses, and which thus appeared to his mind as embodiments of the infinite. The sky overhead was lost to view as it met the horizon, but thoughts would arise as to what lay beyond the limits of sight. The clouds drifting along, or gathering blackness as the prelude to terrible storms, the flashing lightning and the rolling thunder, the rain and the dews, must one and all have been things of inconceivable wonder. The wind, which "bloweth where it listeth, and thou hearest the voice thereof, but knowest not whence it cometh, and whither it goeth," must have appeared as a mysterious power, exciting continual astonishment. The dawn seemed to be infinite in its far-reaching splendour. The sun, as a living ball of fire, rose and set with unfailing regularity, shedding light and warmth upon the earth; and to the unscientific mind the question would sooner or later present itself, Whence comes it, and whither doth it go? The moon, with its changing phases, the countless stars, now visible, now invisible, appeared alive with mysterious motion. Man stood at the base of high mountains, whose summits were wreathed and lost to view in clouds, and upon which the very sky seemed to rest—but what was beyond them? The rivers, now fertilizing the plains, now swelling into disastrous floods, sped on before his eyes; but the whole river could never be taken in at a glance—whence came they, and whither were they going? The sea, with its waves and tides, its peaceful calms or raging tempests, was full of mystery. Man stood beneath the lofty trees, which lived and grew and changed their foliage and yielded their fruit, whose roots lay buried out of sight, and whose branches towered high above his head—whence came their life and power of growth and fruitfulness? Wild beasts, which no man could capture or tame, ferocious and destructive to human life, must have struck terror into the hearts of men. All these and such like things in the natural world had, to the uninformed mind of primeval man, strange elements of infinity and mystery; and what was more natural than that man, in the early stages of his mental development, should have regarded them as gods, or as veils hiding their presence. In short, the recognition of something in all such like natural objects and things beyond the range of the senses, was to primitive races the first step to the perception of the unknown, the infinite, the divine—of God.

> "A voice is in the wind I do not know;
> A meaning on the face of the high hills
> Whose utterance I cannot comprehend.
> A something is behind them: that is God."
>
> George McDonald, *Within and Without*, Bk. i.

Note on the Office of Nature in leading man to perceive God.

"Man could never have framed a name for God, unless nature had taken him by her hand, and made him see something beyond what he saw, in the fire, in the wind, in the sun, and in the sky. He spoke of the fire that warmed him, of the wind that refreshed him, of the sun that gave him light, and of the sky that was above all things, and by thus simply speaking of what they all *did* for him, he spoke of agents behind them all, and, at last, of an Agent behind and above all the agencies of nature."—Max Müller, *Anthropological Religion*, p. 188.

"God has created the heavens and the earth and the sea, and has most wondrously and beautifully adorned all nature, that men may see in it their mirror and their pattern. And the visible world is as it were one great holy book, full of pictures, and parables, and analogies, and other instructive things. All the things we see have their own beautiful and deep meanings.

"The beautiful white clouds, the rosy sunset, the storm-winds, the soft breezes laden with the fragrance of the flowers on a spring morning, the summer sun glowing like a fiery sea, and the silent sparkling of the stars on a winter night, the mighty thunder, and the gentle chirping of the cricket on the hearth; all these things mean more than we can hear with our ears or see with our eyes.

"And the dark mountain forest, and the tall oak-trees, the poplars by the stream, the hawthorn hedges, the vineyards and the cornfields, the wild flowers and the clover fields, the friendly violet and the fragrant rose; all these are not there only for our use and pleasure; they are the letters of a wonderful secret writing, written by God Himself, and the thoughts of God lie concealed in them.

"And the deer, with its gentle eyes, the nightingale in the wood, the toad in the mossy ditch, the stag-beetle and the blind-worm, the tiny insects dancing over the stagnant water; yes, these and all other creatures, small and great, are not sent into the world only to eat and drink, and grow, and be eaten by other creatures; they are living letters in the book of the Creator. The Lord God inscribed them upon the table of the earth before man came there, that when he came he might begin at once to learn and spell them."—Alban Stolz, *The 'Our Father,'* pp. 69, 70.

"The gods are come down to us in the likeness of men."—
Acts xiv. 11.

"Anything which transcends the ordinary, a savage thinks of as supernatural or divine: the remarkable man among the rest. The remarkable man may be simply the remotest ancestor remembered as the founder of the tribe; he may be a chief famed for strength and bravery; he may be a medicine-man of great repute; he may be an inventor of something new; and then, instead of being a member of the tribe, he may be a superior stranger bringing arts and knowledge; or he may be one of a superior race gaining predominance by conquest. Being at first one or other of those, regarded with awe during his life, he is regarded with increased awe after his death; or the propitation of his ghost develops into an established worship."—Herbert Spencer, *Sociology*, p. 440.

"We see how, starting from different points, the deepest thinkers in every part of the world suspected in man something more than the body, something not mortal, soon something immortal; something not merely human, soon something superhuman, divine, and infinite."—Max Müller, *Anthropological Religion*, p. 387.

CHAPTER II.

GOD SEEN IN MAN.

IN the previous chapter we have seen how, at the dawn of history, external nature came to be regarded by man as the veil or organ of the infinite and divine. It is true that this conception of a God or gods was of the most imperfect and elementary character: but still it was there, and it largely prepared the way for higher and truer ideas, as men became capable of receiving them. We are now to trace the next stage of its development.

From very early times there is distinct evidence of the desire to discover something not merely human but superhuman, something infinite and divine, in man. As religious ideas grew and became more formed, the divine came to be sought for and recognized, not only in nature external to man, but also in nature within man. In other words, from seeing the infinite in *nature*, the mind passed on to see the infinite in *man*. When man had discovered God without, he would naturally look for God within.

i.

The Immortality of the Soul.

If man was part of the natural world, he knew that he was more than a tree or mountain. As the crown of created things, he was conscious of something within, which raised him high above all other natural objects. That something was what, in popular language, we know as the soul—the invisible and immaterial part of man, as distinguished from the visible and material body. Under the idea of *soul*, we commonly include the breath or life, the passions good or bad, the organ of reason, thought, or will, the immortal element in man. From very early times there appears to have existed a belief in the immortality of the soul.[1] If it is too much to say that this belief was universal amongst primitive races, it was certainly widespread, being closely connected with, and in fact implied by, the reverence shewn to departed ancestors, and 'heroes.'

---

[1] See Max Müller, *Natural Religion*, pp. 155, 156; *Anthropological Religion*, p. 187; also De Quatrefages, *Human Species*, p. 482.

"From the commencement of the Neolithic period downwards, there is abundant proof that man had ideas of a future state of existence. . . . Throughout the whole Neolithic period we find objects buried with the dead which were evidently intended for use in a future life." —S. Laing, *Modern Science and Modern Thought*, pp. 165, 200. According to Mr. Laing's calculation, the Neolithic period in Europe may be reckoned as covering a period of 10,000 years. See Ibid. p. 136.

ii.

Ancestor-Worship.

Man would naturally reflect upon his origin, and from thence pass on to the thought of his father, and forefathers, or some more remote ancestor. It is not difficult to see the connection, which sooner or later would arise between such a distant progenitor and the Father of all men. It was only a question of throwing the mind back far enough, and, in the end, arriving at the belief in an universal Father, the Father of all fathers, the Author of all men. Professor Max Müller has pointed out that among the Zulus, for example, the term 'great great-grandfather' has been used as the name of God.

There were then, as there ever have been, 'giants in the earth in those days,'—individuals who surpassed the common run of men in stature or in beauty, in physical strength or in mental power, in courage in war or in skill in the chase. The memory of these great ones, living in the world of spirits, must have been handed down to succeeding generations, and they would be naturally treated with special reverence.[1] By

---

[1] "You asked me to put down in writing a remarkable tradition that I heard from the lips of a great Maori chief, whose son had disgraced himself by telling a lie, and whose paternal feelings were struggling to excuse his son, as if it did not much matter. I asked him whether he, though a heathen, had not just the same instinctive feelings about truthfulness as we Christians had. He said, 'To tell a lie great is the fault; that is the thought of a chief from *the other side of time.*'"—*Private Letter* from Bishop Abraham.

a very natural and simple transition, the mind of primitive man would pass on from a belief in the immortality of these remarkable ancestors, to the conception of an Immortal Being— One infinitely great and powerful. Thus, the reverence shown to ancestors would pave the way for recognition and worship of the Universal Father of all men.

In the words of Professor Max Müller, " The Infinite has been discovered, not only behind the phenomena of nature, but likewise behind man, taking man as an objective reality, and as the representative of all that we comprehend under the name of mankind. Something not merely human, or very soon, something superhuman was discovered at a very early time in parents and ancestors, particularly after they had departed this life. Their names were preserved, their memory was honoured, their sayings were recorded, and assumed very soon the authority of law, of sacred law, of revealed truth. As the recollection of fathers, grandfathers, great-grandfathers, and still more distant ancestors became vaguer and vaguer, their names were surrounded by a dim religious light. The ancestors, no longer merely human, approached more and more to the superhuman, and this is never very far removed from the divine.

" Offerings, similar to those that had been presented to the gods of nature, were tendered likewise to the ancestral spirits, and when the very natural question arose, who was the ancestor of all ancestors, the father of all fathers, the answer was equally natural,—it could only be the same father, the same creator, the same wise and loving ruler of the universe who had been discovered behind the veil of nature."[1]

iii.

Hero-Worship.

Closely connected with, though in some measure differing from, the idea of reverence for ancestors and remarkable men, is what is known as hero-worship. The 'heroes' were mythical beings, supposed to be neither gods nor men—intermediate beings, the offspring of the gods and men. This hero-worship was chiefly the product of the Greek mind. In the idea of the 'heroes' we have a mingling of the human and the divine, and of the transition of the human into the divine. The 'heroes,' after having lived on earth as ordinary mortals, were after death supposed to be admitted to the society of the gods, and eventually came to be regarded and worshipped as gods. This process, known as the deification of 'heroes,' though altogether fanciful in its origin, may have helped towards the discovery of something divine in man. The belief in the 'heroes' affords but further evidence of the natural desire to discover something God-like

[1] Max Müller, *Physical Religion*, pp. 2, 3.

or divine in man, and undoubtedly had an important part in preparing the way for the recognition and worship of the One True God.

iv.

Anthropomorphism.

A very common objection against belief in a Personal God has been founded on the fact that He has been regarded as a magnified man. "The lions, if they could have pictured a god," wrote Xenophanes, "would have pictured him in fashion like a lion; the horses like a horse; the oxen like an ox;" and it is urged that, with no more justification, man inevitably pictures Him as a superior man. In the Old Testament, God is constantly described as clothed in human form, and as possessing human attributes. We read of the hand, the arm, the eye, of God; of His forgetting or remembering, of His repenting, loving or hating. This mode of thought and speech is named *anthropomorphism*, a term which signifies the conception of God under human form. The adjective *anthropomorphic* means 'man-like.'

'The instinctive tendency of rational beings is to express the unknown in the terms of the known, the unfamiliar in terms of the familiar.' If gods were conceived from the very first as agents, they would naturally be regarded as exalted human agents, and consequently described in human terms. We have seen how primitive man rose from the contemplation of himself and his fellows to the perception of God. When we consider this, it was only to be expected that he would first conceive of Him as a superior or supreme man. In the natural world man knew of nothing greater than himself, and therefore it was inevitable that he should frame his earliest ideas of God from human experience. All science is, in the strictest sense of the term, as anthropomorphic as theology; because all knowledge is limited by human experience, controlled by human thought, and expressed in human form of speech. "Without ' anthropomorphism ' every science remains barren, and its results are inconceivable to our minds."[1] All our thoughts and feelings on any subject must necessarily be anthropomorphic, because we who think and feel are human. It is from our intense realization of our existence as human beings, that our conceptions of the Supreme Being are so truly human. "Belief in a Personal God means nothing else than belief in One who acts towards us as persons act, and therefore to whose action human analogies may be applied."[2]

Theology teaches that God is ' without body, parts, or passions;' but this is merely a negative description of God. "What would re-

[1] Curteis, *Boyle Lectures*, p. 33.
[2] Illingworth, *Bampton Lectures*, v. p. 125.

main," writes Professor Max Müller, "if man deducted from his early conceptions or rather imaginations of God everything that we call body or shape, everything that we call parts or distinguishable elements, everything that we call passions, not only wrath and indignation, which are so often ascribed to God, but likewise pity and love, which are passions in the true sense of the word, but which we can never separate from our human ideal of the Godhead?"[1] Such a being would be to ordinary minds a dumb and blind idol, not the living and loving God. We may in theological language deny that God has body, parts, and passions, such as we have, but we could never form any conception of Him without human phraseology. We believe that God is a Spirit, but as human beings we have no language in which to describe the being and actions of a spirit, unless we have recourse to human terms.

Thus man, being what he is, and arriving at the perception of God in the way he did, the objection we are considering loses all its force, and becomes a positive argument in favour of the point assailed. The whole proceeding of anthropomorphism is as intensely natural, and true to fact, as it is inevitable. It is in full accordance with what we should have expected from the nature of the case.

[1] *Anthropological Religion*, p. 26.

NOTE ON ANTHROPOMORPHISM.

"All our knowledge is vitiated by this fundamental flaw of its anthropomorphic origin, the conceptions of our science are all direct descendants of the grossest anthropomorphisms of primitive savages, who naïvely and uncritically ascribed whatsoever they felt, and whatsoever seemed natural to them, to the world outside them. . . . What conceivable meaning can be attached to the reproach that a conception is anthropomorphic? Anthropomorphic means partaking of the nature of man, and what human reasoning can fail to render the peculiarities of the human reason? . . . Surely it is too plain for words that *all* our thought and all our feeling *must be anthropomorphic.*"—*Riddles of the Sphinx*, by a Troglodyte, pp. 60, 61, 144, 145.

"If by anthropomorphic you mean subject to the conditions of human consciousness, then indeed, religion, like everything else that is human, must be anthropomorphic. But it does not follow that because all our consciousness is subject to limitations, all the objects of our consciousness are limited also. Whether that it be true in itself or not, it does not follow from the admission of our own limitation. If it did, it would also follow that man could never be conscious of anything in any sense greater than himself."—Harrison, *Problems of Christianity and Scepticism*, 2nd Ed. p. 108.

"The mere fact that we are men shows that our ideas of God must be anthropomorphic, though it does not follow that that of which we have ideas is anthropomorphic also.

"Mr. H. 'The Church affirms that God is without body, parts, or passions.'

"Mr. L. 'No such thing! At the chapel I attended I was taught that God was just what I should call a very big man!'

"Mr. H. 'Do you really mean that?' I, at least, have never been so taught. I have often heard sceptics sarcastically remark that the Bible says man was made in the image of God, and man returns the compliment by making God in *his* image, but I was not prepared to find there was so much ground for the statement.'

"Mr. L. 'Well, so it is. But do you mean to say your Church does not teach that?'

"Mr. H. 'Assuredly it does not.'

"Mr. L. 'I always thought it did, and that it taught also that to cast any doubt on it was at least to imperil the soul's salvation.'

"Mr. H. 'I cannot answer for individuals, but there is no such teaching in the authorized creeds.'

"Mr. L. 'Then there are many passages in the Bible which you ought to expunge to make it fit your teaching.'

"Mr. H. (smiling). 'That is a keen thrust. But you are too much of an evolutionist not to see that any revelation must be gradual. Language is not only allowable, but necessary, in its lower stages, which would be unnecessary and unallowable in the higher stages. Besides, figurative language has a recognized place in all literature, and I very much doubt if any Jew ever understood the words to which you refer as implying that God had literally hands, etc.'"—Harrison, *The Church in Relation to Sceptics*, 1892, pp. 337, ff.

v.

The use of Myth and Illusion.

A further objection has been raised as to the methods whereby man, in the earlier stages of his development, arrived at a belief in God. The influence, and a very strong influence too, of myth and illusion is clearly to be recognized in man's first discovery of God. It is urged that the acquirement of a knowledge of God by such imperfect methods is impossible.

It is readily granted that myth—ennobling and elevating, not debasing and degrading myth—was, at one time in the history of our race, an avenue by which God permitted man to approach Him. Myth is thus to be regarded as a human vehicle of approach to God, rather than the medium of a Divine revelation. In myth, the human element largely predominates. Man's use of myth was but a rude and imperfect effort in his search after God—a feeling after

God seen in Man.

Him, if haply he might find Him. The truth is not so much that God employed myth in order to make Himself known to man, as that man used myth in order to find God. When man, at the dawn of the world, saw God in the sun, moon, and stars, in the storm and lightning, and other forces of nature, he undoubtedly founded his belief upon myth. But "a myth," as Mr. Gore so well says, "is not a falsehood; it is a product of mental activity, as instructive and rich as any later product, but its characteristic is that it is not yet distinguished into history, and poetry, and philosophy. It is all these in the germ, as dream and imagination, and thought and experience, are fused in the mental furniture of a child's mind. . . . Myths are the preface and germ of positive history and philosophy and dogmatic theology."[1]

[1] Lux Mundi, *The Holy Spirit and Inspiration*, 11th Ed. pp. 356, 357.

Myth is not another name for falsehood, a myth is "a form of expression, an infantile way of looking at things, the stammering language of babes and sucklings from which praise has been perfected. . . . The myth is the embodiment of the thoughts of man in his youth about the phenomena which a more scientific age learns later to distinguish into doctrines about God, the soul, the world."—Cobb, *Origines Judaicæ*, pp. 9, 10.

"In the *mythus*, the truth, and that which is only the vehicle of the truth, are wholly blended together: and the consciousness of any distinction between them, that it is possible to separate the one from the other, belongs only to a later and more reflective age than that in which the mythus itself had birth, or those in which it was heartily believed."—Archbp. Trench, *Notes on the Parables*, 11th Ed. p. 5.

"It is highly erroneous to speak, as is often done, of myth and history as two opposites which exclude any third

The objection to a true knowledge of God being acquired by means of illusion, is well answered in the words of Mr. Illingworth. It is admitted at the outset, that "the phenomena of dreams, and storms, and sunshine, and animal activity, were the agencies, through which man's spiritual sense was first consciously awakened, the first objects on which, infant-like, it tentatively fixed. . . . It would seem to be a necessity of human progress, that man should regard the immediate objects of his apprehension, or pursuit, as ends in themselves, ultimate ends; whereas, in fact, when once attained they turn out to be only relative ends, means to other objects, greater and grander than themselves, and, by contrast with those greater things, unreal. Hence, as has been often pointed out, man is always educated by illusions.

"Now since this principle of development through illusion is thus a natural necessity, and pervades even the most civilized life, we should expect it to operate more powerfully still among ignorant and uncultured races. The method of evolution need not discredit the result

possibility."—Goldziker, *Mythology among the Hebrews*, p. 22.

To the myths of primitive man we may apply the words of F. D. Maurice—"Visions they were, but visions which came to men concerning the dreadful realities of their own existence. They were visions of the night, but by them men had to steer their vessels and shape their course; without them all would have been dark."—*The Religions of the World*, p. 127.

evolved. And the feeling after God need be no less veracious a guide, for having first sought to find Him among the objects of His creation—sun, moon, stars, tempests, memories of the beloved dead. But illusion of this kind is utterly distinct from delusion. An illusion is an inadequate conception; a delusion is a false one."[1]

We begin life with illusions: from the very first our bodily senses are the victims of illusion, in regard to the common objects with which we find ourselves surrounded. The earth, for example, appears to be a level plain; we soon learn that it is a globe. The sun seems to rise and set; as we know more, we are convinced that it does neither one nor the other. The

[1] *Bampton Lectures*, iii. pp. 77, 78.
"What is the theological imagination of early times? It is essentially this—that man transports himself into nature—endues the great objects or powers of nature with human feeling, human will—and so prays and worships, and hopes to propitiate, and to obtain aid, compassion, deliverance. Well, this primitive imagination is *in the line of truth*. We begin with throwing a man's thought there into nature; we purify and exalt our imaginary being; we gradually release him from the grosser passions of mankind. We are, in fact, raising ourselves above the domination of those grosser passions; and as we grow wise and just, we make the good wise and just, beneficent and humane. Meanwhile science begins to show us this goodly whole as the creation of one Divine Artificer. And now we recognize, not without heart-beatings, that God is indeed not man, but that He has been educating man to comprehend Him in part, and to be in part like Him. . . . Man *dreamt* a god first. But the dream was sent by the same Power, or came through the same law, that revealed the after-truth."— W. Smith, *Thorndale*, v. ii. § 6.

moon appears to be hundreds of times larger than a distant star; whilst the reverse is really the case. The stars overhead seem to us no larger than the sparks of fire which fly up the chimney; science teaches that they are, at least many of them, larger than our sun. That which at a distance appears to be oval, we find from a nearer view to be circular. The apparently stationary object moves, the apparently moving object turns out to be stationary. As life goes on experience comes to our aid, correcting, adjusting, or modifying our early illusions.

Many of the greatest discoveries have been made by the use of arguments, or founded upon premisses, which fuller light has shown to be seriously imperfect or illusive. Inadequate conceptions are necessarily illusive, but not necessarily delusive: they may contain the germ of great truths but imperfectly grasped. It was surely to be expected that the dawning of religious belief in the minds of rude and savage peoples, would be associated with crude and simple notions of the world, and of the God who made it. But we may rest assured that the methods which God adopted, in leading primitive man to belief in Him, were the best and only methods possible under the circumstances. The early search for God in nature and in man, that first "seeking God, if haply men might feel after Him, and find Him,"[1] was partial and

---

[1] Acts xvii. 27.

clumsy; still it was an effort in the right direction, and along the true line: and we may believe that God recognized the reality of the effort, and answered it.

> " And those illusions which excite the scorn
> Or, more, the pity of unthinking minds—
> Are they not mainly outward ministers
> Of inward conscience?—with whose service charged
> They came, and go, appeared, and disappear,
> Diverting evil purposes, remorse
> Awakening, chastening an intemperate grief,
> Or pride of heart abating."
>
> Wordsworth, *Excursion*, Bk. iv.

"It is from the intense consciousness of our own real existence as persons, that the conception of reality takes its rise in our minds: it is through that consciousness alone that we can raise ourselves to the faintest image of the supreme reality of God. . . . That which I see, that which I hear, that which I think, that which I feel, changes and passes away with each moment of my varied existence. I, who see, and hear, and think, and feel, am the one continuous self, whose existence gives unity and connection to the whole. Personality comprises all that we know of that which exists: relation to personality comprises all that we know of that which seems to exist. And when, from the little world of man's consciousness and its objects, we would lift up our eyes to the inexhaustible universe beyond, and ask, to whom all this is related, the highest existence is still the highest personality; and the Source of all Being reveals Himself by His Name, I AM."—Mansel, *Bampton Lectures*, iii. pp. 61, 62.

"If God be in reality only the spirit or life of the universe, how can He provoke the yearnings of the soul, or how satisfy its aspirations? How can He be the object, whether of religious homage or of religious trust? How can we yield love, obedience, worship to a mere torrent of existence that flows onwards inexorably beneath our feet?"—Liddon, *Some Elements of Religion*, p. 62.

CHAPTER III.

THE PERSONALITY OF GOD.

THE idea of One Supreme Personal God was one which man took long ages to conceive. It is of the development and acceptance of this idea that we are now about to speak. Hitherto, we have traced the gradual growth of the belief in God from crude and humble origins. We have followed step by step the desire to explain that in nature which lay beyond the grasp of the senses; we have seen further, how the reverence for departed ancestors and mythical beings, led man onward in his search for the True God. Man's belief, in the early stages of his development, was, as we have seen, of the most vague and elementary description. It was the natural result and outcome of his belief in the forces of nature personified, deified heroes, fabulous beings, family, tribal, and national gods, gods of the various departments of nature, the arts, or war. But up to this point, although much had been gained in a right direction, the idea of God as the Supreme Personal Being had not as yet been conceived.

What we have to remember is, that all these primitive ideas afford overwhelming evidence of man's determined effort and persistent desire to find God. If the methods were faulty, the end achieved was not necessarily a delusion. The question of the origin of any religious belief is on a different line from the question of its truth or falsehood. The truth arrived at is one thing; the method by which it is arrived at is another thing. To describe the clumsy steps, the frequent falls, the wanderings from the right path, the retracing of wrong steps, the circuitous route, whereby a lost child has found its way home, has little to do with the fact that the child has reached home in the end. That the lost child should find its father, it matters not how, that is the point.

We may here pause to enquire why God has permitted such faulty methods of approach to Him. The answer appears to be, Because man was, up to the time of which we are speaking, both intellectually and morally unable to receive a more perfect and direct revelation of God: but ot this we shall speak later. And, further, we may be assured that if such a perfect and direct revelation had been made, man, as he then was, would not have recognized it.

i.

Belief in God as a Personal Being was the goal to which all the early efforts of man were

The Personality of God. 41

slowly and surely tending. The revelation of God as a Personal Being was but waiting man's fitness and ability to receive it. The revelation was only delayed until a needful preliminary on man's part was fulfilled. God could not reveal Himself as a Person, until man had realized his own personality. The order of a natural development must necessarily be observed. We have already seen how important a part man's recognition of his immortality played, in preparing the way for belief in an Immortal God. It was even so in the case of his personality. Until man recognized his own personality, he was unprepared to recognize the Personality of God.

But, before we proceed further, let us pause to enquire what is meant by personality? When we speak of a man possessing a strong or commanding personality, we are not using the word in its first and proper meaning. Personality, strictly speaking, does not signify the possession of strong characteristics, which lift a man above his fellows; but the possession of a separate, self-identical, and conscious existence. The term 'personality' includes the ideas of individuality, identity, and self-consciousness. Every one has personality in this stricter meaning, and it is with this meaning that we shall henceforth use the word. Personality is that within which pertains to every member of our race, making each member of that race man. Personality is that which lies at the centre of man's being, and from which all his thoughts and actions radiate. By personality we are to understand that within each human being which we speak of as 'I.'[1] When a man has realized, 'I am myself and no one else, and I have always been myself and no one else,' he has acknowledged his personality. In the words of Bishop Butler, "Every person is conscious, that he is now the same person or self he was as far back as his remembrance reaches: since when anyone reflects upon a past action of his own, he is just as certain of the person who did that action, namely, himself, the person who now reflects upon it, as he is certain that the action was at all done."[2] The idea of personality is realized when a man

---

[1] "Personality is the unifying principle, or, to use a more guarded expression, the name of the unity in which all a man's attributes and functions meet, making him an individual self.

"I think, therefore I am—Thought, that is to say, is the evidence of its own reality, and of the real existence of its thinker, the individual man.

"My sense of personal identity irresistibly compels me to regard myself as one and the same being, through all changes of time and circumstance, and thus unites my thoughts and feelings of to-day with those of all my bygone years."— Illingworth, *Bampton Lectures*, i. pp. 6, 20; ii. p. 29.

A person is "a thinking, intelligent being, that has reason and reflection, and can consider itself as itself, the same thinking thing in different times and places."—Locke, *Works*, Vol. i. Ch. 27, § 9.

Locke defined personal identity as "the sameness of a rational being."—Ibid.

See also Footman's *Reasonable Apprehensions*, 3rd Ed. pp. 66, 67.

[2] Diss. i. *of Personal Identity*, § 10.

The Personality of God.

can say, 'I am a conscious being, therefore in that consciousness, I have a personal existence.'

We are, in describing personality, trying to define that which defies definition. We cannot, strictly speaking, define personality, for the simple reason that we cannot place ourselves outside it. We are conscious of possessing personality, if we cannot fully explain it. It will perhaps help to a clearer understanding of the idea of personality, if we think of something which has no personality. Take, for example, heat. Heat is an impersonal thing; that is to say, it has no individual being, it cannot reflect upon itself, it is unconscious of its own power, it cannot determine its own action, it is an instrument, not an agent. By a person, then, we are to understand an individual being, possessing continuous self-consciousness, continuous identity, intelligence, self-determination.

The recognition of human personality, as we have said, has been a slow process. A savage has a very indistinct realization of personality. In the history of our race, the perception of persons, as distinct from things, has been a matter of gradual development. And we find that man's recognition of his own personality has run on parallel lines with his recognition of the Divine Personality—a Personal God. " Belief in the personality of man, and belief in the personality of God, stand or fall together.

The Personality of God.

A glance at the history of religion would suggest that these two beliefs are for some reason inseparable. Where faith in the Personality of God is weak, or is altogether wanting, as in the case of the pantheistic religions of the East, the perception which men have of their own personality is found to be, in an equal degree, indistinct. The feeling of individuality is dormant."[1] The conscious recognition of self must ever precede the intelligent perception of God as a Personal Being.[2] 'If you will believe in God, look within.' And when we do thus look within, what do we find? We find the most real thing in all the world—our own personality.

ii.

The argument for the existence of a Personal God may be considered thus. "Amidst the mysteries, which become the more mysterious the more they are thought about," writes Mr. Herbert Spencer, "there will remain the one absolute certainty, that we are in the presence of an Infinite and Eternal Energy from which all things proceed."[3] We are not now about to argue on behalf of the existence of God, from

---

[1] Fisher, *The Grounds of Theistic and Christian Belief*, p. 1.

[2] "Man's belief in a personal God, from whatever source it is derived, must obviously be interpreted through his consciousness of his own personality."—Illingworth, *Bampton Lectures*, iii. p. 54.

[3] *Nineteenth Century*, Jan. 1884.

The Personality of God. 45

the necessity of a First Cause, this we shall do later, but for the existence of a *Personal* God. It is the Personality, not the Existence of God, of which we are now thinking. We cannot conceive of the world as we know it, or of man as we know him, coming into being spontaneously. Creation implies a creator: the question is, what is the nature of the creator and author of the universe? Is the existence of the universe due to the presence of a mere impersonal energy, possessing neither mind, intelligence, nor will? Do all things owe their origin to a blind unreasoning force, or to a Being possessing reason and self-determination—to a mere mechanical agency, or to a Supreme Rational Agent? These are questions which we may safely leave to the verdict of our reason. That reason rebels against the notion that the universe has for its author an irrational, irresponsible, impersonal energy, destitute of mind, will, and purpose. The idea is unthinkable.

But if the Author of the world is One, who exercises energy, who possesses intelligence, reason, will, He must be a Person. The idea of infinite eternal energy at work in the world is undoubtedly grand, but that of a Personal Being who is infinite, eternal, and energizing is grander, and it is more intelligible also. The wonderful revelations of science, which this century has witnessed, when rightly considered, drive us more and more to the conclusion that behind nature and behind man is the presence of an Infinite Mind, a Personal Author. It seems impossible to avoid the conclusion that, as the designer and upholder of the universe, God must of necessity have a personal existence.[1]

iii.

In the second place, man's recognition or realization of his own personality leads naturally to a belief in a Personal God. The idea of personality is inextricably bound up with all our highest and noblest notions of God. In the whole range of our observation of the universe, nothing is greater than human personality: it is the highest and most intense form of creaturely existence. Its attribute of self-consciousness, or mind, as we commonly call it, is far greater than matter; that is, not greater in bulk or quantity, but in power or quality. Its attribute of self-determination, or will, as we commonly call it, is greater than any other known power. It is the possession of personality, with its attributes of mind and will, which raises man head and shoulders above

---

[1] "If it is absolutely certain, as Mr. Herbert Spencer assures us, that behind the veil of visible phenomena there is 'the presence of an Energy,' which is 'Infinite, Eternal, and from which all things proceed,' reason suggests at least, if it does not demand, the additional attribute of intelligence and will; and intelligence and will imply personality."—MacColl, *Christianity in relation to Science and Morals*, 4th Ed. p. 13.

The Personality of God.

the most powerful of the lower animals,[1] and makes him greater by far than the most subtle forces of nature. For example, one of the greatest and most subtle forces of nature is electricity; but compare electricity with human mind, and its inferiority in the scale of creation is at once apparent. Electricity is an impersonal agency: mind implies a rational agent, which asserts itself in making electricity its instrument. But if there be no personality in God, it follows that there is a perfection in man which is wanting in God; and thus it would come to pass that personal man is superior to an impersonal God. 'Over a free and living person, nothing short of a free living person can have higher authority.' The most elementary idea of God is the perception of One who is infinitely greater in the scale of being than man—of One higher than the highest in His own creation. We may therefore conclude that human personality implies and demands the Divine Personality. In other words, we may believe that God possesses the attributes which we know under the names of intelligence and will, in short, that He is a Person. "Perfect Personality is in God

[1] "It is the fact of *personality* which distinguishes the self-conscious moral being from the beasts that perish. . . . The sharp line is drawn, not (only) between organic and inorganic, living and dead, but between man as the embodiment of *personality* and all other created beings as void of personality."— Aubrey L. Moore, Essays Scientific and Philosophical, *Theology and Law*, pp. 234, 235.

only, to all finite minds there is allotted but a pale copy thereof." [1]

iv.

Connected with our conception of human personality is the idea of social intercourse. The word 'person' would lose much of its deepest signification, if we failed to include in it the capacity for loving intercourse with others. A person is an individual, but an individual with relations to other individuals. A person is one who can not only reflect on his own existence, and exercise self-determination, but one who can also enter into communication with other persons by the exchange of thought and affection. Hitherto we have spoken only of two of the attributes of human personality, thought and will. But there is a third attribute to which we must now refer, that of desire or love. Love demands an object upon which to spend itself. Love without one to love is but an unsatisfied desire. Love, too, demands a return of love. And the highest love seeks the highest object of love, in the return of love from that object. Man's love for nature and his fellow-men may satisfy the craving for affection up to a certain point, but only to a certain point. 'We needs must love the highest when we see it,' but that highest is not to be found in man, but in God. All human love is more

Lotze, *Microcosmus*, 4th Ed. Vol. ii. Bk. ix. Ch. iv. p. 688.

or less imperfect, and however faithful it may be, before long a separation must come—one will be tåken and the other left. Human love, beautiful as it is, can never completely satisfy the deep yearning of the human heart, with its capacity for infinite love. There remains the void which One alone can fill, and that One is the Infinite and Personal God. "The religious mind," says Lotze, "is led to apprehend the Supreme Good under the form of a Personal God, both by humility and by the longing to be able to reverence and love."[1] "As the hart panteth after the water brooks, so panteth my soul after thee, O God."[2] "Thou hast made us for thyself, and our heart can find no rest until it rests in thee."[3]

Thus the possession of human personality, the home of affection, leads us to the feet of the Personal God, in whom this affection can find

---

[1] *Microcosmus*, Vol. ii. Bk. ix. Ch. iv. p. 676.

"The ordinary doubts as to the possibility of the personal existence of the Infinite, have not made us waver in our conviction. But in seeking to refute them, we have had the feeling that we were occupying a standpoint which could only be regarded as resulting from the strangest perversion of all natural relations."—Ibid. p. 685.

"Man demands not only satisfaction for the intellect in the postulate of a First Cause, from which all things proceed; he demands satisfaction for his affections and conscience as well. For man is not an intellectual being only; he is a being endowed with affections and a sense of right and wrong. He bestows love, and he demands it in return."— MacColl, *Christianity in relation to Science and Morals*, p. 26.

[2] Ps. xlii. 1.

[3] St. Augustine, *Confessions*, i. 1.

complete rest and satisfaction. If God was but blind force, or eternal energy, we might dread Him, but we could not love Him. "No man," says the Duke of Argyll, "can worship a ball of fire, however big; nor can he feel grateful to it, nor love it, nor adore it, even though its beams be to him the very light of life."[1] An impersonal God would be incapable of either receiving or returning love. Love, in the deepest meaning of the word, is altogether a personal thing.[2] It is saturated with the idea of personality; for love is a personal expression towards a personal object capable of accepting and requiting that expression—a personal search for a personal being able to

---

[1] *Unity of Nature*, p. 309.

[2] "We have various desires, and each of them conducts us into a different kind of connexion with other persons. We may be more passive and receive sympathy from them, or more active and exercise influence over them. We may desire to share with them our pleasures, or our perplexities, or our work, or to exchange with them social amenities or intellectual ideas. And in all these ways they may represent ends to us, but still, in a sense, only partial ends; satisfying, that is, some one class of our desires, some one mode of our activity, some one department of our complex being. But we instinctively seek more than this. We require to find in other persons an end in which our entire personality may rest. And this is the relationship of love. Its intensity may admit of degrees, but it is distinguished from all other affections or desires, by being the outcome of our whole personality. It is our very self, and not a department of us, that loves. And what we love in others is the personality or self, which makes them what they are. We love them for their own sake. And love may be described as the mutual desire of persons for each other as such; the mode in which the life of desire finds its climax, its adequate and final satisfaction."—Illingworth, *Bampton Lectures*, ii. pp. 37, 38.

reward that search, a personal finding and a personal being found.

We have thus traced the steps whereby man, recognizing his own personality, and the attributes of that personality, must logically arrive at the belief that God is a Personal Being.[1]

---

[1] "Personality marked man from the first as a being destined for communion with, and free imitation of God. Personality enables man to be receptive of a message and a call from God. It confers on each possessor of it an absolute dignity and worth. . . . Man is great, not merely because he thinks and can recognize moral relationships and obligations; but chiefly because he was created for union with God; and was destined to find blessedness and perfection in Him alone. Christianity therefore rates highly the worth of the individual; and her task is to develop each human personality—to bring each into contact with the Personality of God."—R. L. Ottley, in Lux Mundi, *Christian Ethics*, p. 472.

Part Second.

Proofs of the Existence of God.

"Our belief in a Personal God is based upon an instinct, or instinctive judgement, whose universal or practically universal existence is a fact of historical experience, and which we do not find that adverse criticism is adequate to explain away. Consequently, when we come to consider the various evidences, arguments, proofs by which this belief is commonly supported, we must remember that these are all attempts to account for, and explain, and justify something which already exists."—Illingworth, *Bampton Lectures*, iv. p. 81.

"Belief in God is not a science, but a virtue. . . . It is after the heart knows Him, that the reason also seeks Him. It everywhere seeks for Him, and for traces of Him in nature, in history, in the mind itself. It is the most exalted employment of man's mind, and the chief proof of its dignity, to follow up these traces of divinity, that the understanding may attain that certainty which the heart already intuitively possesses."—Luthardt, *The Fundamental Truths of Christianity*, p. 47.

"The proofs of the existence of God would never have been drawn out by so many of the clearest and most powerful of the minds of all ages, if there had not been in all these minds that innermost conviction that 'God is,' which forms the basis and substratum of all religions."—Ellicott, *The Being of God*, p. 17.

CHAPTER I.

THE PLACE OF EVIDENCE

IN CONFIRMING

BELIEF IN GOD.

HITHERTO, we have been occupied in the consideration of man's instinctive belief in God. By this we mean that perception of God which is natural to man, and which rests primarily neither upon external testimony nor proof. Starting from this preparatory idea or consciousness of God, which we have already traced out, we are about to approach what are generally known as the proofs of His existence. It must be admitted that there is no subject which demands more careful and patient study, than that of the general evidence by which, apart from a special or authenticated revelation, belief in God is supported. It will be our endeavour in the following chapters to set forth, briefly and concisely, the main arguments upon which belief in the existence of God is based. They are three in number, namely:

1. The general consent of mankind.
2. The existence of the universe.
3. The presence of design in nature.

Of the testimony or evidence known as the moral argument, we shall treat later.

i.

Whilst the appeal will be made to reason, it is well to say at the outset, that this appeal cannot be regarded as absolutely convincing. In the ordinary acceptation of the word, it may be granted that there is no absolutely convincing proof of God's existence. It may be doubted if any actual demonstration of the existence of a Divine Being can be adduced. Water cannot rise above its source; and absolute proof implies an appeal to something higher and more certain than that which is to be proved. Belief in God is belief: and in belief there must necessarily be the element of trust. Faith is not of the nature of absolute certainty, but rather of the nature of strong conviction or high probability,[1] leading on to moral certainty. The voice of faith is, 'I am morally convinced,' not 'I am absolutely sure:' 'I cannot actually demonstrate, but I feel reasonably certain.'

In belief, there is more of heart and will, than

[1] "Probability is the very guide of life."—Butler, *Analogy*, Introd. § 4.

of reason.[1] If faith is reasonable, as it must be,[2] it is faith nevertheless. "The heart," as Pascal says, "has its reasons, which reason knows not, as we feel in a thousand instances. . . . It is the heart which is conscious of God, not the reason. This then is faith; God sensible to the heart, not to the reason"[3] "The truths of religion, dealing with things unseen and with our relation to them, can never be the subject of scientific test, or form the premisses of a strictly logical conclusion. There

[1] "Reason is not the only attribute of man, nor is it the only faculty which he habitually employs for the ascertainment of truth. Moral and spiritual faculties are of no less importance in their respective spheres even of everyday life; faith, trust, taste, etc., are as needful in ascertaining truth as to character, beauty, etc., as is reason. Indeed we may take it that reason is concerned in ascertaining truth only where *causation* is concerned; the appropriate organs for its ascertainment where anything else is concerned belong to the moral and spiritual region. . . . Belief is neither made nor marred by the highest powers of reasoning, apart from other and still more potent factors."—Romanes, *Thoughts on Religion*, pp. 112, 138.

Mr. Romanes has a striking passage in which he describes his mental state previous to his restoration to belief—"I have been so long accustomed to constitute my reason my sole judge of truth, that even while reason itself tells me it is not unreasonable to expect that the heart and the will should be required to join with reason in seeking God (for religion is for the *whole* man), I am too jealous of my reason to exercise my will in the direction of my most heart-felt desires."—Ibid. p. 132.

[2] "It is not pride in reason to try and know, nor can reason without being false to itself, submit to that which is not true, nor is there any, even the most sacred region, where it is inconsistent with reverence to ask the question, Why?"— Aubrey L. Moore, Essays Scientific and Philosophical, *The Pride of Intellect*, p. 253.

[3] *Various Thoughts*, pp. 306, 307.

may be inward conviction of truths which cannot be proved. I cannot prove, but I have felt."[1] Few, if any, have been convinced of God's existence by the mere force of logic. "God is not comprehended by investigation, but by imitation," says Cardinal Hugo.[2] Moral likeness to God, as we shall show later, has much to do with belief in Him. The heart and the will must co-operate with the reason in the search after God. "God chooses rather to sway the will than the intellect. Perfect clearness would be useful to the intellect, but would harm the will."[3]

ii.

Again, intuition has much more to do with the foundations of belief than evidence. "An intuitive conviction of the existence of God," as Luthardt so well says, "dwells within the human mind. We can by no means free ourselves from the notion of a God. We cannot think of ourselves, we cannot think of the world, without involuntarily connecting therewith the idea of God. Our thoughts hasten past the visible and the finite towards a supreme, invisible, infinite Being, and cannot rest till they have attained their goal. We are obliged to think of God. Consciousness of God is as essential an element of our mind as

[1] *Ellen Watson*, p. 35.
[2] *on Eph.* v. 1.
[3] Pascal, *Proofs of the Christian Religion*, p. 207.

consciousness of the world, or self-consciousness. The idea of God is a deep necessity of the mind. 'When the mind rises, it throws the body upon its knees.' "[1] Belief in God does not primarily rest upon the force of the proofs of His existence. They are 'attempts to account for, and explain, something which already exists,' viz., man's instinctive belief in God. These proofs are of value in establishing what Tertullian described as 'the testimony of the soul naturally Christian;' or, to use the words of St. John Damascene, 'the knowledge of the existence of God which is sown in all men naturally of itself;' or, in the language of Cicero, that 'certain anticipation of the gods,' which all men have, 'even without being taught.' The special work of arguments, such as we are about to state, is to establish the truth of that which is already felt instinctively—to strengthen the faith which both anticipates and confirms the conclusions of reason.[2] Whilst reason may succour or restore a feeble or shattered faith, it cannot orginate faith. It is to those, in whose hearts the feeling and the consciousness of the existence of a

---

[1] *Fundamental Truths*, p. 44.

[2] "All proofs together can and ought only to serve to explain and confirm that which, before all proof, lived and expressed itself in every human heart."— Van Oosterzee, *Christian Dogmatics*, p. 242.

"It would be against reason itself to suppose that God can be known by reason; He must be known, if knowable at all, by intuition."—Romanes, *Thoughts on Religion*, p. 146.

Divine Being has already found a home, that argument and proof most effectually appeal. Thus, argument can never take the place of faith: its use is to justify the belief which has been already, however partially, accepted. In short, logical proof is only convincing, when it finds the previous disposition to believe, already existing in the heart. "He that cometh to God must believe that He is, and that He is a rewarder of them that seek after Him."[1]

But, in saying this, there is no intention to underrate the great force of the arguments we are about to state. When taken together, and carefully examined, they possess a cumulative power, which it requires a positive effort of the mind to resist. "The truth of our religion," said Bishop Butler, "like the truth of common matters, is to be judged of by all the evidence taken together."[2]

[1] Heb. xi. 6.   [2] *Analogy*, ii. vii. § 62.

"If you go round the world, you may find cities without walls, or literature, or kings, or houses, or wealth, or money, without gymnasia, or theatres. But no one ever saw a city without temples and gods, one which does not have recourse to prayers, or oaths, or oracles, which does not offer sacrifice to obtain blessings or celebrate rites to avert evil."—Plutarch, *adv. Coloten Epicureum.*

"There is no people so wild and fierce, as not to know that they must have a god, although they may not know what sort of a god it should be."—Cicero, *de Leg.* i. 8.

The notion of God is "the public and universal reason of the world. No age so distant, no country so remote, no people so barbarous, but gives a sufficient testimony of this truth. When the Roman eagle flew over most parts of the habitable world, they met with atheism nowhere; but rather by their miscellany deities at Rome, which grew together with their victories, they showed no nation was without its god. And since the later art of navigation improved hath discovered another part of the world, with which no former commerce hath been known, although the customs of the people be much different, and their manner of religion hold small correspondency with any in these parts of the world professed, yet in this all agree, that some religious observances they retain, and a Divinity they acknowledge. So much of the creed hath been the general confession of all nations, 'I believe in God.' Which were it not a most certain truth grounded upon principles obvious unto all, what reason could be given of so universal a consent? Or how can it be imagined, that all men should conspire to deceive themselves and their posterity?"— Bp. Pearson, *Exposition of the Creed*, Art. i.

CHAPTER II.

THE EXISTENCE OF GOD

ATTESTED BY THE

GENERAL CONSENT OF MANKIND.

WE will now proceed to state the argument for the existence of God, derived from the General Consent of Mankind in the recognition of religion. The general belief in the existence of a God or gods is common to all religions; and, broadly speaking, no nation or tribe is to be found destitute of a religion of some kind or other. "As yet," writes Professor Max Müller, "no race has been discovered without some word for what is not-visible, not-finite, not-human, for something superhuman, and divine. . . . To my mind the historical proof of the existence of God, which is supplied to us by the history of the religions of the world, has never been refuted, and cannot be refuted."[1]

[1] *Anthropological Religion*, pp. 90, 92.

i.

It may be granted that amongst some savage tribes, the religious instinct does not lead to anything beyond a reverence for the spirits of departed ancestors.

> The dead chief's ghost
> A shadow cast
> Across the roving clan.

It is possible too, if not actually proved, that amongst some degraded races, even this rudimentary belief in the supernatural is wanting. These insignificant exceptions, if in reality there are such exceptions,[1] have been urged as an objection to the proof of God's existence to be derived from the general consent of mankind.

This objection, if it possesses any force at all, is founded on a misapprehension of what is meant by the general consent of mankind in the truth of God's existence. The argument from the general consent of mankind, is not based upon the assertion that a belief in a God or gods is inseparable from the human mind. There may be tribes so low in the mental scale, that no perception of the superhuman exists in the mind. If such tribes exist, this absence of belief may but represent the depth of their degradation from a higher state of intelligence. The belief in the superhuman and divine may once have existed, and gradually have become extinct. And it is to

[1] See Note, p. 71.

be noted that where such belief has been lost, it is capable of being revived. "The Caffres, when first discovered, had no name for or idea of God: but certain old men dimly remembered having, in their youth, heard of 'Morimo' (or, rather 'Molimo'), 'the One above.' The first step taken by missionaries among them was to revive the fast-disappearing traces of this belief; and the name 'Molimo,' so nearly lost, is now the recognized Christian Caffre name for God."[1] It is noteworthy and deeply significant that, in the case of a few barbarous tribes which appear to possess no belief in the supernatural, this absence of belief is accompanied by an utter lack of mental culture. Again, in the case of atheists, we have an example of persons who have argued themselves out of a belief in God, and so have got rid of that belief. But, putting aside the case of professed atheists, we may safely affirm that no instance is to be discovered of a race of men, which has reached any degree of mental development, destitute of the belief in a God or gods of some kind or other. The absence of belief in the superhuman or the divine, is the invariable accompaniment or result of a lack of all interest in the problems of the universe. The belief in a God or gods is undoubtedly 'persistent and indestructible in the mass of mankind.'

[1] *Butler's 'Analogy,' and Modern Thought*, by Dr. Eagar, p. 70.

The true form in which to state the arguments for the existence of God from the general assent of mankind, is as follows:—"On the presentation of certain problems of life, the normal human reason refers the answer to some form of Theism.[1] The form varies according to the mental and moral characteristics of the worshipper: the belief established is not ineradicable. But the tendency is so marked, that, at some period in their history, all races capable of appreciating the problems in question have been Theists: and, when apparently eradicated, the belief tends to re-appear. 'When religion goes out of the door, superstition flies in at the window': atheism never forms a permanent resting-place for human nature."[2]

ii.

An objection has been raised, which is supposed to weaken the force of the appeal to the common belief of mankind in the existence of God. It is based upon the assertion that all religious beliefs owe their origin to Fetichism,[3] i.e., the attributing life to inanimate

---

[1] "The most simple and intelligible mode of using the word *Theism* is to denote by it belief in a personal God, the Creator and Moral Governor of the universe."—*The Being of God*, p. 32.

[2] *Butler's 'Analogy' and Modern Thought*, pp. 78, 79.

[3] "The idea conveyed by Fetichism is the very lowest form of barbarous superstition and belief in the preternatural; a notion of weird influence attaching to natural objects as the means of propitiating witchcraft and demoniacal malice.

objects. The next stage is said to be Polytheism; by which is signified the belief in, and the worship of more gods than one—the fetich being distinguished from the inanimate object, and regarded as a supernatural being, connected at first in some way with that object. By a further progression the last stage is reached, and belief is centred in One God, with or without inferior spirits under His control. And thus, says the objector, Monotheism, or the belief in a Supreme Being, is at last reached.[1] The objection, in short, runs thus— Your belief in a Supreme God is but the gradual outcome of the worship of stones, and trees, and the ghosts of distant and savage ancestors; and, since it is based upon superstition and falsehood, it cannot be worthy of acceptance in an enlightened age.

Fetichism at times seems to raise itself to something like belief in the unity of the Deity, and the responsibility of man; but in every other respect its history is a dismal picture of the deep degradation into which unaided human nature is sure to fall."—Blunt's Dictionary of Doctrinal and Historical Theology, pp. 285, 286. Art. *Fetichism*.

[1] "There is strong reason for thinking, that the earliest religious system constructed by any given race of men must have been a Monotheistic one, and that the later Polytheistic forms, which the religions of some races have assumed, have been in every case the result of a debasement or degeneration of their original belief."—Ibid. p. 570. Art. *Polytheism*.

As we have said before, the degraded systems of religion current amongst savage and barbarous tribes, may be but the overlaying of an earlier and purer revelation. In which case, the evolution of religion represents the process of freeing this primitive revelation from the degradation which had overtaken it, or reviving it where extinguished.

We freely admit that such a development may have taken place, whilst we deny the force of the objection founded upon it. The supposition that the belief in God rests wholly upon some clear-cut revelation, made suddenly to the world at large at a given time, utterly unconnected with the crude, imperfect, and even superstitious beliefs of primitive races, cannot be entertained. The history of revelation is but the continuous record of how God has raised men, by slow and gradual steps, from lower to nobler and more perfect ideas concerning Himself—first to Elohim, The Almighty; then to Jehovah, The Personal Self-Existent; and then, through the Incarnation, to the acknowledgment of the Triune God of Christianity.[1] As we have already seen, to trace the origin of an idea to its source, however humble that source may be, does not necessarily imply that such an idea is false. "Things are what they are, quite irrespectively of how they came to be. The truth of astronomical discoveries is not affected by the fact, that the faculty which makes them could not formerly count four."[2] Savages lived on human flesh, before they discovered

---

[1] "A progressive revelation, such as the Jewish, may adopt for its present use the highest imperfect moral standard of the age, as embodied in particular rules and precepts, and may yet contain an inner movement and principle of growth in it, which will ultimately extricate it as a law out of the shackles of a rudimentary stage."—J. B. Mozley, *Ruling Ideas in Early Ages*, p. 222.

[2] Illingworth, *Bampton Lectures*, iv. p. 110.

the use of proper food; they multiplied wives, before they were taught truer ideas of the marriage-state. The use of proper food, and the higher ideas of marriage, are not to be discredited, because they are the out-growth of savage and degrading customs. It may be urged, with much show of reason, that cannibalism and polygamy are but the degradation of earlier and purer ideas. If this be so, the argument would not be affected; for the process of restoration would be that of a gradual evolution from the base to the noble. The beauty of the flower is not to be depreciated, because once its life lay hidden in the unsightly root, buried in the dark. Because religion has been associated with dark and debasing superstitions, it is not therefore proved to be false. The history of religious belief is true to a natural law, the law of growth, development, and purification, such as, from the nature of the case, was to be expected. Behind all the ignorant and unformed beliefs of barbarous races, some idea of the invisible, the superhuman, the divine, is ever to be found. The evolution of the true belief in One Supreme God, has been the clearing of this universal idea from what was false and imperfect. The truth of the evolution of religious belief remains the same, whether we regard false and imperfect ideas of God as man's original possession, or as a falling away from higher and truer conceptions of Him.

iii.

Accepting as true the broad statement that a belief in God is the common-sense of all men, what weight, in proving God's existence, may we attach to such an universal consent? To such a question, we reply in the words of Bishop Ellicott, "It certainly raises in every candid mind a strong presumption in favour of a belief in the existence of God, and especially in favour of that form of belief which seems to be the highest development of the idea, viz., that of a Supreme Being who is alike the Creator of the universe, and its Moral Ruler and Governor. Such a presumption it undoubtedly raises. And such a presumption in such a matter seems to carry with it consequences of the gravest kind, and of the highest possible moment. And the chief of these consequences is this,—that no one who feels that such a presumption is really raised can be morally justified in putting the whole matter aside, and in declining to enter further into the momentous question. To feel the real strength of the presumption, and not to test the considerations to which the strength is to be ascribed is to fail, and grievously to fail, in a serious duty to ourselves and to the highest interests of our whole moral nature."[1]

[1] *The Being of God*, pp. 47, 48.

NOTE ON ALLEGED EXCEPTIONS TO THE GENERAL CONSENT OF MANKIND IN THE BELIEF OF THE EXISTENCE OF GOD.

The statement that an universal belief in a God or gods exists, has been challenged on the ground that races have been discovered, possessing no such belief in any superior power whatever. One such instance is named by Mr. Darwin in the account of his first voyage in the *Adventure*, but in this, as in similar cases, closer acquaintance with the tribe in question has led to a different opinion. The difficulty of communicating with savages on such a mysterious subject as religious belief is very great. It is therefore unsafe to base any conclusion upon a slight intercourse with such races. Upon this question Bishop Ellicott remarks, "It is still the practice of the hasty traveller to trust to a few loose enquiries, and, on the strength of answers to imperfectly framed questions, to describe as atheistic, wild tribes, of which the uttermost, perhaps, that could possibly be said would be, that they did not appear to have definite ideas on the subject of a personal God. And even this, probably, on fuller enquiry and with an improved knowledge of the language, would have to be very considerably modified. It must be added, too, that even in cases where enquiries have been made of a more exact kind, with a competent knowledge of the language of those of whom enquiry was made, and with every manifestation of a patient desire to arrive at their true religious sentiments, the attempt to elicit trustworthy information has constantly failed, from the reserve which those most fitted to give answers have not unnaturally shown, in the matters of their religion, towards the alien and the foreigner."—*The Being of God*, pp. 43, 44. See Boedder's *Natural Theology*, p. 65, where the testimony of the eminent anthropologist, Mr. Tylor, is given supporting Bishop Ellicott's statement.

The testimony of St. Clement of Alexandria is important as giving an account of the beliefs of races known in the third century. He says, "All nations, whether they dwell in the East, or on the remotest shores of the West, in the North, or in the South, have one and the same rudimentary apprehension of Him by whom this government (of the world) has been established."—*Strom.* Lib. v. n. 260.

The verdict of the eminent writer, M. De Quatrefages, whose opinion as that of an agnostic may be considered quite impartial, is worthy of record —" Obliged, in my course of instruction, to review all human races, I have sought atheism in the lowest as well as in the highest. I have nowhere met with it, except in individuals, or in more or less limited schools, such as those which existed in Europe in the last century, or which may still be seen at the present day. . . . We nowhere find either a great human race, or even a division however unimportant of that race, professing atheism."—*The Human Species*, pp. 482, 483.

The case of Buddhism is quoted as that of a religion which has no Deity. It is true that a Buddhist has no Intelligent or Personal God, His place being occupied by various elements. But Buddhism was derived from Brahminism, in which a belief in God had its place. It was the corruption of the earlier religion which gave rise to a reaction, under which the idea of a Personal God was eliminated. Moreover the Buddhist, whilst ignoring the idea of a Personal Deity, appeases the hunger of his heart by the unconscious worship which he pays to the deified founder of his religion. Buddha then is in practice the substitute for God that the human heart dimly requires and demands. Thus, we may fairly consider it to be proved, that, in the words of Lactantius, a belief in a God or gods has for its support " the testimony of peoples and nations that differ not in this one particular"; or, as Bishop Pearson more clearly puts it, " The notion of God is the public and universal reason of the world." We may in this matter confidently hold with St. Augustine, that " the judgment of the whole world is safe."

"I questioned the earth, and it said, 'I am not He;' and all that is in it confessed the same. I questioned the sea and the depths, and the creeping things which have life, and they replied, 'We are not thy God, seek above us.' I questioned the blowing winds, and the whole air with its inhabitants replied, 'I am not God.' I questioned the heavens, sun, moon, stars; 'Neither are we,' say they, 'God whom you seek.' And I said to all those things which stand about the doors of my flesh, 'Ye have told me of my God, that ye are not He; tell me now something of Him.' And they cried out with a loud voice, 'He made us.'"—St. Augustine, *Confessions*, x. 6.

"Looking out upon the universe around it, the mind seeks for its productive cause. . . . What cause, what force, preceded and brought into existence this universe? All the causes with which we come in contact here, are, as we term them, second causes; but they point to a cause beyond themselves, to a cause of causes, to a supreme all-producing Cause, Itself uncaused, unoriginated."—Liddon, *Some Elements of Religion*, pp. 51, 52.

"Neither materialists, nor evolutionists, nor pantheists are bold enough to give an explanation of the origin of the present world, without supposing an eternal *something*, either 'Matter,' or the 'Unknown,' or the so-called 'Absolute,' or the pure 'Ego,' or the 'Idea' of Being, or the 'Will,' or the 'Unconscious.'"—Boedder, *Natural Theology*, p. 35.

CHAPTER III.

THE EXISTENCE OF GOD

ATTESTED BY THE

CONSIDERATION OF THE UNIVERSE.

IN the last chapter we saw that the best common-sense of our race, or, in other words, the general consent of mankind, can be claimed in support of a belief in God. We now pass on to consider the second of the great arguments for the existence of God—the argument derived from the Consideration of the Universe. How far does serious attention to the universe lead towards the belief, that it owes its origin and continuance to the existence and power of God?

In the first place, we need to state that the latest and greatest discoveries of science tend to show, that an essential unity or oneness pervades the various departments of the material world. This fact gives a strong presumption that the natural order of things owes its origin to a single primal force or being. There is, in short, a general unity in nature, which leads us to refer its beginning and permanence to one author.

When we seriously think of it, it is inconceivable that the universe in general, and our world in particular, is eternal. Reason demands that the universe had a beginning, however remote that beginning was. There is within us an instinctive desire to trace all things back to their origin or cause. This desire is part of our mental outfit, and is active in every mind possessed of any degree of intelligence. In the early stages of man's career, he strove to satisfy this inborn curiosity, by attributing the existence and movements of natural objects to the immediate action of 'spirits of the air, and the woods, and the waters, smiling through the sunrise, and frowning in the storm.' And it is commonly urged by unbelievers in God, and in His providence, that the progress of knowledge has led to the substitution of natural causes for such supposed and fanciful agencies. Where mankind, in his infancy, regarded the thunder as the voice of God, the gathering of the storm-clouds as the assembling of His armies, or the lightning as His arrows; science now teaches that such things may be traced to atmospheric disturbances, which, in their turn, are due to natural causes, and so on in endless sequence.[1]

But granting the scientific truth of all this, two great questions arise—

Who or what set these natural causes going?

[1] See Illingworth, *Bampton Lectures*, iv. p. 85.

Who or what provides that such causes and effects should continue?

i.

The First Cause.

The admission that such secondary or natural causes exist, only throws the question further back. The demand for the First Cause still remains to be satisfied. A child's solemn question, Whence came I? is not finally answered by the reply, Your father begat you. A further question is only suggested, Whence came my father? The child's enquiry is thrown further back, and its solution postponed. Reason demands something which shall give a satisfactory account of the phenomena of nature, without giving an account of itself. The instinctive craving for information concerning the origin of things cannot rest content, until it arrives at the ultimate cause of all other causes—the original and underived cause, the primal independent cause, the uncaused cause. The natural demand of reason refuses to be silenced, until it gets back to something self-moved, self-determined, the fountain-head of all causation, the originating source of all things.

That there must be such a First Cause, is, to every rational mind, an inevitable and unavoidable conclusion. The recognition of an uncreated Author of all things is the common-sense of all scientific thought. "No one," writes Mr. S. Laing, "with the least knowledge of science can maintain that it can ever be demonstrated that everything in the universe exists of itself, and never had a Creator."[1] Mr. Herbert Spencer gives it as his opinion that "amidst the mysteries, which become the more mysterious the more they are thought about, there will remain the one absolute certainty, that we are ever in the presence of an Infinite and Eternal Energy, from which all things proceed."[2]

ii.

Secondary Causes.

"Everything that *happens* has a cause. The same happening has always the same cause. It is only familiarity with this great fact that prevents universal wonder at it."[3] Not only must the universe have had a beginning, and therefore an uncreated Source or Author, but there must also be some efficient cause for its continuance. "The originating principle," says Bishop Ellicott, "be that what it may, must be able not only to originate, but to maintain in full efficiency, what is originated. If it

[1] *Modern Science and Modern Thought*, p. 71.
[2] *Nineteenth Century*, Jan. 1884.
"It is more credible that matter was made by God, because He is all-powerful, than that the world was not made by God; because nothing can be made without mind, intelligence, and design."—Lactantius, *Divine Institutes*, Bk. ii. Ch. 9.
[3] Romanes, *Thoughts on Religion*, p. 126.

gives the first start, it must be also able to maintain all consequent movements, and initiate all changes and adaptations that may be needed to secure stability and permanence."[1]

What, then, is the energy or force which keeps the universe going? To what power or person are we to attribute the existence of secondary causes, — the cause of causes? "God is still grudged His own universe, so to speak, as far and as often as He can possibly be. Men have always committed the fallacy of concluding that if a phenomenon has been explained in terms of natural causation, it has thereby been explained *in toto*—forgetting that it has only been explained up to the point where such causation is concerned, and that the real question of ultimate causation has merely been thus postponed."[2]

---

[1] *The Being of God*, p. 69.
[2] Romanes, *Thoughts on Religion*, pp. 122, 123.

"The hypothesis, or fundamental postulate, in question is, *If there be a personal God, He is not immediately concerned with natural causation.* It is assumed that *qua* 'first cause,' He can in no way be concerned with 'second causes,' further than by having started them in the first instance as a great machinery of 'natural causation,' working under 'general laws.' . . . Provided only we lay aside all prejudice, sentiment, etc., and follow to its logical termination the guidance of pure reason, there are no other conclusions to be reached than these, namely, (*a*) That if there be a personal God, no reason can be assigned why He should not be immanent in nature, or why all causation should not be the immediate expression of His will. (*b*) That every available reason points to the inference that He probably is so. (*c*) That if He is so, and if His will is self-consistent, all natural causa-

It is a false idea to think that there must be something inexplicable and miraculous about a process of nature, in order to its being divine. It is a false idea to assume that directly some natural effect has been traced to a natural cause, it has thereby ceased to be ascribable to God. No reason exists why secondary causes should not be attributed to the continuous action of God, as the Prime and Efficient Cause.

We see motion everywhere around us: whence is all this motion, and what is its cause? We reply, that motion implies will behind it, and that energy or force is the action of will. And, when we consider that the energy, force, or motion displayed in nature is uniform and not erratic, that the same causes always produce the same effects, all this seems to point irresistibly to the action of an Infinite Rational Will. And is it not therefore perfectly reasonable to suppose, that secondary causes owe their force and persistence to a Divine Mind, a Supreme Will; and to believe that all causation, be it primary or secondary, proceeds from that Mind and Will? Action and agency imply actor and agent, as much as the existence of the universe implies a Creator. The belief in God, as the Cause of all motion, is a reasonable belief.

tion must needs appear to us 'mechanical.' Therefore (*d*) that it is no argument against the divine origin of a thing, event, etc., to prove it due to natural causation."—Romanes, *Thoughts on Religion*, pp. 120, 121.

> O God, Creation's secret Force,
> Thyself unmoved, all motion's Source,
> Who from the morn till evening's ray,
> Through all its changes guid'st the day.

God's creative act is not that of the watchmaker, who, having made a watch, sells it to a customer, never sees it again, and has nothing more to do with it. It is rather the action of the watchmaker, who, having made the watch, and set it going, keeps it in his own hands, winds it up regularly, protects it from injury, cleans and repairs and regulates it from time to time, and keeps it going. 'The home of the creature is the hand of the Creator.' There is no action of any creature independent of the Divine Will. "Every being that acts is in the exercise of its action dependent upon an influence proceeding from God Himself, and thus He is the cause of all actions of active beings."[1]

iii.

Evolution.

The labours of Mr. Darwin and other scientific men, if they have not already absolutely proved, have greatly tended to establish the truth of the process known as Evolution.[2]

---

[1] Boedder, *Natural Theology*, p. 369.

[2] "Evolution means 'unfolding,' and the simplest illustration of what is meant by evolution is *growth*. When a seed is sown and germinates, and develops according to natural law, or when the chick comes out of the egg and grows to maturity, we have there a familiar instance of evolution."—Aubrey L. Moore, in Oxford House Papers, Second Series, *Evolution and Christianity*, pp. 149.

By evolution, we mean the supposition that the universe as it now is, and all the infinite variety of species of animals, and classes of plants found on our planet, have been ultimately derived and gradually developed from a few primary varieties.[1] The doctrine of evolution, if finally established, will explode the idea conveyed by the term 'special creation,' or 'the carpenter theory' of the universe. The theory, formerly largely held, that everything in nature was planned by itself, without connection with what preceded it, or what followed it, is being rapidly abandoned as unscientific, and therefore untrue. If the truth of evolution be demonstrated, as in all probability it will be, it will be quite as noble a conception of God to believe that He created a few original forms, and then, by His Almighty Power, proceeded through the agency of nature to develop them into other higher and more complex forms, as to believe that in every variation or species we are to recognize His original creative act. The doctrine of evolution in no wise disposes of the need of the working of the Divine Energy. It makes the presence of the Divine Energy a greater necessity. Given a book, the ultimate problem is, how did it come to be a book? A book is evolved out of paper, type, and a

---

[1] "I believe," wrote Mr. Darwin, "that all animals are descended from at most only four or five progenitors, and plants from an equal or lesser number."—*Origin of Species*, p. 424.

printing press; but in admitting this, we have not done away with the need of an author, or of man's agency in making the paper, in putting together the type, and working the printing press. Thus, as Mr. Aubrey Moore says, "If evolution has won from the unknown law of primary creation much which it has transferred to the more familiar law of evolution," yet, it "has done nothing to explain Creation."[1]

In reference to the doctrine of evolution, we may apply the words of Mr. Romanes—" Logically regarded the advance of science, far from having weakened religion, has immeasurably strengthened it. For it has proved the uniformity of natural causation. The so-called natural sphere has increased at the expense of the 'super-natural.' Unquestionably. But although to lower grades of culture this always seems a fact inimical to religion, we may now perceive it is quite the reverse, since it merely goes to abolish the primitive or uncultured distinction in question. It is indeed most extraordinary how long this distinction has held sway, or how it is the ablest men of all generations have quietly assumed that when once we know the natural causation of any phenomenon, we therefore know all about it— or, as it were, have removed it from the sphere of mystery altogether, when, in point of fact,

[1] Essays Scientific and Philosophical, *Creation and Creatianism*, p. 72.

we have only merged it in a much greater mystery than ever."[1]

NOTE ON EVOLUTION.

"The Doctrine of Evolution, rightly conceived, has for its subject-matter not the changes exhibited by the organic world only, but also the changes which went on during an enormous period before life began, and the changes which have gone on since life rose to its highest form, and man, passing into the associated state, gave origin to the endlessly varied products of social life. It has for its subject-matter the entire cosmic process, from nebular condensation down to the development of picture-records into written language, or the formation of local dialects; and its general result is to show that all the minor transformations in their infinite varities are parts of the one vast transformation, and display throughout the same law and cause—that the Infinite and Eternal Energy has manifested itself everywhere and always in modes ever unlike in results but ever like in principle."—Herbert Spencer, *Nineteenth Century*, Nov. 1895. p. 757.

"The first point in which evolution is popularly supposed to come into collision with Christianity is in the matter of *Creation*. The first words of the Bible are, 'In the beginning God created the heaven and the earth.' The first words of the Nicene Creed are, 'I believe in God, the Father Almighty, Maker of heaven and earth, and of all things visible and invisible.' How can we believe in evolution and creation too? The answer here is a very simple one. If by creation we mean original or primary creation, the calling into being of something which was not, evolution has nothing in the world to do with it. Evolution only tells us how different forms came from some one form already in existence. If all the known forms of animal and vegetable life could be traced back by evolution to a speck of protoplasm; if the difference between living and not living could some day be transcended, and life in all its forms could be shown to have come from what we now call dead matter; if the whole visible world could be known to have been evolved from a primeval mist;—of the origin of that primeval mist evolution can tell us nothing. And if God created it, He would still be the Creator of the world. There can, therefore, be no collision here, if we understand what we are talking about.

[1] *Thoughts on Religion*, p. 124.

the Consideration of the Universe. 85

And all evolutionists admit this. Mr. Darwin says, 'The theory of evolution is quite compatible with the belief in a God.' 'The mystery of the beginning of all things is insoluble by us.' Professor Tyndall says, ' Evolution does not solve—it does not profess to solve—the ultimate mystery of this universe. It leaves, in fact, that mystery untouched.' Herbert Spencer says, 'The production of matter out of nothing is the real mystery.' And Professor Clifford in the same way says, 'Of the beginning of the universe, we know nothing at all.' Those, then, who believe, as Christians do, that God is the Creator of heaven and earth hold a view which, whether it is true or not, touches a question on which evolution is wholly silent ; so that, as Professor Huxley puts it, ' Evolution does not even come into contact with Theism considered as a philosophical doctrine.'

"Christianity is in no way committed to the belief that all the species of plants and animals were created at once in the beginning of all things.

    (i.) There is no vestige of such a belief in the Creeds of Christendom.

    (ii.) It is not in the Bible, though it has often been read between the lines of *Genesis*.

"What the Bible reveals is that there is nothing which is not God's creation, nothing which has life and being independently of Him. It does not attempt, and does not profess, to teach us science."—Aubrey L. Moore, in Oxford House Papers, Second Series, *Evolution and Chrisitianity*, pp. 152, 153, 156.

"Evolution, whatever be its extent, is not a cause, or even a force, but a *method*, which might be the path, either of a voluntary cause, or of a blind force, and has nothing to say to the controversy between them."—Martineau, *Study of Religion*, Vol. i. p. xiv.

" Supposing this improved science should turn for us into a certainty, the belief that with blind inherent necessity the yet formless chaos of the infant world steadily advanced in perfection, till it reached the point where the production of man became inevitable ; would the outlook into an infinite distance, that science seems to shun, then be closed for it ? If it could make men comprehend how, first of all, the solid earth-crust and the skiey spaces of the atmosphere were separated from the fiery ball of vapour ; how each stage of this separation gave occasion for new effects of the elective affinities of the elements ; how then, in the favourable circumstances supplied by the blind necessity of nature, the first germ of a plant or of an animal came into being, still simple and rude in contour, and with little aptitude for significant development; how, finally, under happy conditions, to which this low stage of life conduced, organic existence gradually improved, lower species were in the course of countless ages developed into higher ones, till at last man appeared, not in the image of God, but as the final link in this chain of necessary events—if science could make all this comprehensible, what more would it have accomplished, than to have driven back the marvel of immediate creation to an earlier point in past time, at which infinite wisdom infused into unsightly chaos the boundless capacity for regular development? By the long array of graded stages of evolution, through which it traced the development of the chaotic *prima materia*, it would but have enhanced the splendour and variety of scenes, in whose outward pomp our admiring fancy could revel; but it would have given no more sufficient explanation of the wondrous drama as a whole, than does that modest belief which cannot conceive of living species as coming into being, save by the direct creative will of God. So a decision about these points, as far as science will ever be able to give one, we must quietly wait to receive from its impartial love of truth. Whichever way of creation God may have chosen, in none can the dependence of the universe on Him become slacker, in none be drawn closer."—Lotze, *Microcosmus*, Vol. i. Bk. iii. Ch. v. pp. 373, 374.

iv.

The Origin of Life and Mind.

If reason teaches that the material world had a beginning, and therefore owes its origin to a First Cause, there are two other beginnings to be accounted for—Life, and Mind. No theory of evolution or derivation can satisfactorily account for the origin of life, and mind.

(1) *The Origin of Life.*—That Life, like everything else in our world, had a beginning, it is impossible to deny. If we cannot conceive of

the Consideration of the Universe. 87

the material world as self-originating, much less can we do so in the case of life. There exists a gulf between matter endowed with life and matter lacking life, which no scientific knowledge based on experience can ever hope to bridge over. The efforts of science to account for the origin of life by spontaneous generation, have entirely failed. The unanimous verdict of all scientific men who have studied the question of the origin of life is, 'life from life.' "Of the causes that have led to the origination of living matter, it may be said that we know absolutely nothing. . . . There is not a shadow of trustworthy evidence that anything of the kind (viz., of the derivation of life from inorganic matter) does take place or has taken place, during the period within which the existence of the earth is recorded."[1] Professor Allman, in his *Address to the British Association*, stated that "No one has ever yet built up one particle of living matter out of lifeless elements," and that "Every living creature has its origin in pre-existent living matter." Mr. St. George Mivart says, " That there is an absolute break between the living world and the world devoid of life, is what scientific men are now agreed about."[2]

Science declares with unhesitating voice that life ever proceeds from life; and if we only push the enquiry back far enough, we arrive at the inevitable conclusion that life owes its origin to

[1] Huxley, in Encyclopædia Britannica, Art. *Biology*.
[2] *Origin of Human Reason*, p. 10.

One who ever had Life in Himself—the Self-Existent and Eternal God. The old familiar question, Which came first, the hen or the egg? can only be satisfactorily answered by saying, Whichever came first, owed its life and productiveness to the First Cause of all life.

NOTE ON THE ORIGIN OF LIFE.

"It is as certain," says Mr. S. Laing, "that all individual life, from the most elementary protoplasm up to the highest organism Man, originates in a minute or embryo cell, as it is that oxygen and hydrogen combined in certain proportions make water. But if we try to go back one step further, behind the cell, we are stopped. In the inorganic world we can reason our way beyond the microscopic matter to the molecule, and from the molecule to the atom, and are only arrested when we come to the ultimate form of matter, and of energy, out of which the universe is built up. But, in the case of life, we are stopped two steps short of this, and cannot tell how the cell containing the germ of life is built up out of the simpler elements.

"Many attempts have been made to bridge over this gulf, and show how life may originate in chemical compounds, but hitherto without success. Experiments have been made which, for a time, seemed to show that spontaneous generation was a scientific fact, i.e., that the lowest forms of life, such as bacteria and amœba, really did originate in infusions containing no germs of life; but they have been met by counter experiments confirming Harvey's *dictum*, ' Omne animal ex ovo,' or all life proceeds from antecedent germs of life, and the verdict of the best authorities, such as Pasteur, Tyndall, and Huxley is, that spontaneous generation has been 'defeated along the whole line.' . . . On the whole, therefore, we must be content to accept a verdict of 'Not proven' in the case of spontaneous generation, and admit that as regards the first origin of life, science fails us, and there is at present no known law that will account for it."—*Modern Science and Modern Thought*, pp. 84, ff.

(2) *The Origin of Mind.*—There is yet another beginning, which can be accounted for only on

the supposition of the agency of a First Cause—the origin of self-conscious Mind. "The Darwinian theory," says Mr. Alfred Russel Wallace, "even when carried out to its extreme logical conclusion, not only does not oppose, but lends a decided support to, a belief in the spiritual nature of man. It shows us how man's body may have been developed from that of a lower animal form under the law of natural selection; but it also teaches us that we possess intellectual and moral faculties which could not have been so developed, but must have had another origin; and for this origin we can only find an adequate cause in the unseen universe of Spirit."[1] Should science ultimately succeed in demonstrating that man has been gradually evolved from some highly organized ape, or more remotely, as Professor Drummond argues, from a fish,[2] the origin of the human mind would still remain to be explained. "The ultimate origin of mind is as inscrutable a mystery as the origin of life."[3] "I have nothing to do with the origin of the mental powers," wrote Mr. Darwin, "any more than I have with that of life itself."[4] The chasm between mind and matter, is as fixed as that between life and matter.[5]

[1] *Darwinism*, Ch. xv. p. 478.
[2] See *The Ascent of Man*, Ch. ii.   [3] Ibid. p. 155.
[4] *Origin of Species*, p. 191.
[5] "I know nothing, and never hope to know anything, of the steps by which the passage from molecular movement to states of consciousness is effected."—Huxley, in *Contem-*

"We are taught," says Mr. Balfour, "that the successive developments of species have not been along one main channel, but in countless branching streams, like those that intersect the delta of some great river. We also know that at some point or other on the way towards the development of a higher intelligence all these streams but one have been checked. The progenitors of man, and they alone, would seem to have hit off the precise line of flow, which could produce an Aristotle or a Newton."[1] That 'the progenitors of man should have hit off this precise line of flow' without the aid of an external creative agent, is unthinkable. How, then, did mind in man originate? The only reasonable answer which can be seriously made to such an enquiry is, that as life comes from Life, so mind comes from Mind—that the human mind is the product of the Divine Mind, the creation of a Personal and Intelligent Being.

---

porary Review, 1871. "The two things are on two utterly different platforms, the physical facts go along by themselves, and the mental facts go along by themselves."—Clifford, *Fortnightly Review*, 1874.

"It is all through and for ever inconceivable that a number of atoms . . . shall be other than indifferent as to how they are disposed and how they move, how they were disposed and how they were moved, how they will be disposed and how they will be moved. It is utterly inconceivable how consciousness shall arise from their joint action."—Du Bois-Raymond, *Ueber die Grenzen des Naturerkennens*, p. 42.

The above quotations are taken from Professor Drummond's *Ascent of Man*, p. 158.

[1] *The Religion of Humanity*, p. 21.

Thus, in conclusion: If we repeat the question, Whence comes the material universe, whence did it spring, by what power is it continued and sustained: What is the origin of life and mind, how did they begin to be? The reasonable and satisfactory answer is, The material universe owes its origin and continuance to One Supreme Cause, Himself uncaused: the life and mind of man owe their origin to One All-powerful Will, the Mover of all motion, to an Intelligent Mind, the Source of all self-consciousness—the Living and Personal God.

NOTE ON THE ORIGIN OF MIND.

It is, of course, not denied that the lower animals have a rudimentary form of mind, "but only that height of mind which men have, and which evolution would never look for in any living thing but man. An evolutionist would no more expect to find the higher rational characteristics in a wolf or a bear than to unearth the modern turbine from a Roman aqueduct.

"The enormous distance travelled by the mind of man beyond the utmost limit of intelligence reached by any animal is a puzzling circumstance, a circumstance only equalled in strangeness by another—the suddenness with which that rise took place. Both facts are without a parallel in nature. Why, of the countless thousands of species of animals, each with some shadowy rudiment of a mind, all should have remained comparatively at the same dead level, while man alone shot past and developed powers of a quality and with a speed unknown in the world's history, is a question which it is impossible not to raise."—Drummond, *The Ascent of Man*, pp. 166, 190.

"As animal consciousness is related to human self-consciousness, so exactly is animal will to human free-will, animal intelligence to human reason, animal sign-language to rational grammatical speech of man, constructive art of

animals to true rational progressive art of man. In every
one of these the resemblance is great, but the difference is
immense, and not only in degree but also in kind."—Le
Conte, *Evolution*, 2nd Ed. p. 324.

"The special faculties" possessed by the human race,
"clearly point to the existence in man of something which
he has not derived from his animal progenitors—something
which we may best refer to as being of a spiritual essence or
nature, capable of progressive development under favourable
conditions. On the hypothesis of this spiritual nature, superadded to the animal nature of man, we are able to understand much that is otherwise mysterious or unintelligible in
regard to him, especially the enormous influence of ideas,
principles, and beliefs over his whole life and actions. . . .
Thus we may perceive that the love of truth, the delight in
beauty, the passion for justice, and the thrill of exultation
with which we hear of any act of courageous self-sacrifice,
are the workings within us of a higher nature which has
not been developed by means of the struggle for material
existence."—Wallace, *Darwinism*, Ch. xv. p. 474.

That eminently scientific thinker, Mr. Romanes, has said
that "the differences that unquestionably do obtain between
the mind of the highest ape and the mind of the lowest
savage, are many and immense." But even should this
chasm be eventually bridged over, and if it should be ascertained that mind in man is only different in degree, and not
in kind, from mind in the lower animals; if it should be
ascertained that human mind is derived or developed from
animal mind; the fact would not affect the argument stated
above. The origin of mind would still remain to be accounted for, the chasm between mind and matter would still
be there. "In what manner the mental powers were first
developed in the lowest organisms, is as hopeless an enquiry
as how life itself first originated."—Darwin, *Descent of Man*,
p. 66.

"Shall the potter be counted as clay; that the thing made should say of him that made it, He made me not; or the thing framed say of him that framed it, He hath no understanding?"—Isaiah xxix. 16.

"There cannot be design without a designer; contrivance, without a contriver; order, without choice; arrangement, without anything capable of arranging; subserviency and relation to a purpose, without that which could intend a purpose; means suitable to an end, and executing their office in accomplishing that end, without the end ever having been contemplated, or the means accommodated to it. Arrangement, disposition of parts, subserviency of means to an end, relation of instruments to a use, imply the presence of intelligence and mind. . . . The marks of *design* are too strong to be gotten over. Design must have had a designer."—Paley, *Natural Theology*, Ch. ii. 23.

"How could blind elements, not having in themselves any principle of direction, have been able to find stable and constant combinations, and that indefinitely? All *design* supposes a designer."—Janet, *Final Causes*, p. 177.

"What time this world's great workmaister did cast
To make all things such as we now behold,
It seems that He before His eyes had plast
A goodly patterne, to whose perfect mould
He fashioned them as comely as He could,
That now so fair and seemly they appear;
As nought may be amended anywhere.

That wondrous patterne, wheresoe'er it be,
Whether in Earth, laid up in secret store,
Or else in Heaven, that no man may it see
With sinful eyes, for fear it to deflore,
Is perfect beauty."—*Spenser.*

CHAPTER IV.

THE EXISTENCE OF GOD

SUGGESTED BY THE

PRESENCE OF DESIGN IN NATURE.

WE are now to consider the argument for the existence of God suggested by the evidence of Design in Nature. We are to enquire how far marks of contrivance and final aims in nature, may be claimed as proof of the Being of a purposeful Creator.

As the consideration of the existence of the universe leads to the conclusion that it owes its origin to a Single Cause, so likewise the recognition of purpose and design in nature tends to prove the Unity of God. In other words, if the former argument conducts to belief in One God as the Originator of the universe, the latter argument conducts to belief in One God as the Shaper and Disposer of that universe. We hope to show the high probability that the universe has been designed from beginning to end by an Intelligent Being.

i.

Order in Nature.

When we look out upon the universe, the most striking characteristic which presents itself to the mind is that of Order or Law. 'Whether we gaze upwards to the heavens, or view the succession of phenomena on earth, the conception of order, silent, certain, and majestic, is at once called up.' All the most recent discoveries of science unanimously and unhesitatingly proclaim, that order and law bear undisputed rule in the natural world—that order and law have been inextricably woven up with, and worked into, the very structure of the universe. Science teaches that 'there is nothing useless, nothing meaningless in nature, nothing due to caprice or chance, nothing irrational or without a cause, nothing outside the reign of law.' Order is the first law of the natural world.

If the universe is under the reign of law and order, it is law and order which results in harmony and progress. It is the interweaving of these things in one great whole, which affords such a strong presumption that the universe proceeds from One All-powerful and Intelligent Mind.

A heap of printers' type, lying in confusion on the ground, suggests neither order nor mind; but when we find the type set up letter by letter in regular order, and when the book is produced which conveys the thoughts of its author, we at once recognize the action of mind. "How is it," asks Mr. Romanes, "that all physical causes conspire, by their united action, to the production of a general order of nature? It is against all analogy to suppose that such an end as this can be accomplished by such means as those, in the way of mere chance or 'the fortuitous concourse of atoms.' We are led by the most fundamental dictates of our reason to conclude that there must be some cause for this co-operation of causes. . . . We are thus, as it were, driven upon the theory of Theism as furnishing the only nameable explanation of this universal order. That is to say, by no logical artifice can we escape from the conclusion that, as far as we can see, this universal order must be regarded as due to some one integrating principle; and that this, so far as we can see, is most probably of the nature of mind. At least it must be allowed that we can conceive of it under no other aspect. . . . It is enough to take our stand upon the broadest general fact that Nature is a system, and that the order observable in this system is absolutely universal, eternally enduring, and infinitely exact. . . . In my opinion no explanation of natural order can be either conceived or named other than that of intelligence as the supreme directing cause."[1]

[1] *Thoughts on Religion*, pp. 67, 71, 72.

ii.

Adaptation in Nature.

But beyond order, harmony, and progress, there is a further characteristic of the natural world to be noticed—that of Adaptation of means to fulfil certain ends. Adaptation, beautiful and endless, is found everywhere in the organic world. The adjustment of organs to their appointed work, the adaptation of means to ends, is one of those 'open secrets in nature,' which the advance of science has so conclusively proved. The study of nature is ever most fascinating, and it is the recognition of adaptation which makes it so. As examples of such adaptation in nature, the following facts will serve by way of illustration. They might be multiplied indefinitely.

The plumage of the ptarmigan, without any effort on its own part, becomes white as snow in winter, and mottled and tinted like the ground in autumn. The markings of the young unfledged plover exactly resemble the beach pebbles amongst which it hides. The colour of the stoat, which is ruddy brown in summer, changes in winter, in snow regions, into a beautiful white. This change takes place in direct association with a lower temperature: not only does a new white fur appear, but persistent dark hairs may change. Thus, by the provision of nature, the ptarmigan, and the young plover escape notice; whilst the stoat is able to approach its prey in winter unobserved. The fur of the cat, and other animals, is cast in the summer, when the temperature is highest and the risk of taking cold slight: it is at its thickest in the winter, when the cold is greatest. The larva of the male stag-beetle, in its chrysalis state, builds up a larger case than is needed for its body, in order to provide room for its horns which develop later. We cannot believe that the larva has any knowledge of its future form of existence. The butterfly lays its eggs on the very leaves upon which its future progeny like most to feed. Thus, the food of the new comers, in their weakest state, is ready to hand the moment they emerge into life as caterpillars. The butterfly, too, places its eggs on the underside of the leaves, where they will be protected from rain, and the sight of their enemies. The butterfly does not feed upon the food of its offspring, neither does it see the result of its provision for their welfare. The wall-wasp, common in this country, digs a hole in walls, and stocks it with paralysed grubs and caterpillars, and amongst these an egg is laid. Thus, the offspring, when it awakes to life, finds itself surrounded with appropriate food during the early days of its existence. The Indian form of the insect 'mantis' resembles an orchid-like flower in shape and colour. By this provision smaller insects, upon which it feeds, are deluded into approaching near enough to be captured. Mr. A. R. Wallace describes the 'mantis' as "a living trap, baited in the most alluring manner to catch the unwary flower-haunting insects."[1] The wood-pecker feeds upon insects lodged chiefly in decaying trees. In order to find its food, nature has supplied it with a bill, straight, hard, and angular, by which it is enabled to bore into the wood, and reach the cell of its prey. But when the cell is reached, how is the insect to be extracted? It is done by means of the bird's tongue, which is of extraordinary length, and tipped with a barbed hook or needle. By a movement of lightning swiftness the insect is speared, and withdrawn from its retreat.

"The pairing time with birds, as everyone knows, occurs in the spring. With reptiles this is also the case; but among mammals each species has a season peculiar to itself, every separate month being selected by one or other, and invariably adhered to. It might seem that no law governed these various dates, but their very variety is the proof of an underlying principle. For these dates show that each animal in each particular country chooses that time of the year to give birth to her young when they will have the best chance of surviving—that is to say, when the climate is mildest, food most abundant, and the prospects of life on

[1] *Darwinism*, Ch. viii. p. 212. The whole of this most fascinating chapter is worthy of careful perusal.

the whole most favourable. The dormouse thus brings forth its young in August, when the nuts begin to ripen; and the young deer sees the light just before the first grass shoots into greenness."[1]

Let us survey another department of the universe, the solar system, and the place of our planet in that system. The earth, upon which we live, is subject to two influences in its journey round the sun. Its swift movement through space gives rise to a strong tendency to wander from its appointed path. This catastrophe is averted by the attraction of the sun upon the earth. If this attraction ceased, the earth would promptly fly off into space to its destruction. So wonderfully are these two influences balanced, that the earth preserves its proper course.

A consideration of such like facts suggests to a thoughtful mind the question, How did all these marvellous adaptations—their harmony, beauty, and usefulness—originate? How have they come about? Can the idea be seriously entertained that all these wondrous adaptations in nature are the result of chance? Can it be even imagined that all these striking adjustments owe their continuance, century by century, year by year, to mere haphazard? Is there not, in the words of Paley, "an extreme difficulty or rather impossibility of conceiving this immense and

[1] Drummond, *The Ascent of Man*, pp. 381, 382.

wonderful universe, as the result of blind chance or necessity?"

What reasonable explanation is to be given of all the contrivances and mechanisms, which we meet with in such astonishing profusion in nature, so manifold in variety, so amazing in perfection? Who, we ask, has endowed animals with instincts and habits so marvellously adapted to the fulfilment of necessary ends? Who has so exquisitely balanced the mutually counteractive laws of centripetal and centrifugal force, to which we have referred, and given the heavenly bodies "a law which cannot be broken"? Who, but One possessed of intelligent Mind, boundless Power, and infinite Wisdom? May we not reasonably say with Bacon, "I had rather believe all the fables in the legend, and the Talmud, and the Alcoran, than that this universal frame is without a Mind,—than that an army of infinite small portions, or seeds unplaced, should have produced this order and beauty without a Divine Marshal."[1]

iii.

Natural Selection.

It now remains to examine an objection, which is supposed to overthrow the conclusion

[1] *of Atheism.*

John Stuart Mill was of opinion that "it must be allowed that in the present state of our knowledge, the adaptations in nature afford a large balance of probability in favour of creation by intelligence."—*Three Essays on Religion*, pp. 172, 174.

the Presence of Design in Nature. 103

which has been drawn from the presence of design or final aims in nature. This objection is based upon the doctrine known as derivation, or natural selection of species. It is admitted that nature, on every side, abounds in instances of adaptation and adjustment to future requirements and final ends, too intricate to explain: but it is assumed that all this is the result of caprice and chance. This objection has been concisely stated thus—" If a hundred varying organisms came by chance into existence, and ninety-nine of them, being ill-adapted to their surrounding circumstances, perish and are forgotten, the single one which is better adapted to its environment, and therefore survives, will appear to owe to purposeful design what is really due to accidental variation. And if we could conceive this process of natural selection, by survival of the fittest, to have operated exclusively throughout the universe, the result would be an appearance of design without its reality, and the argument from final causes would vanish."[1] In other words, it is held, that the various adaptations and contrivances met with in nature, owe their existence to no creative acts of God, but are the results of a long series of natural causes. This long series of natural causes is named Natural Selection.[2]

[1] Illingworth, *Bampton Lectures*, iv. p. 94.
[2] "There are many difficulties in the way of our recognizing natural selection as the sole cause of even organic develop-

The doctrine of natural selection, and that of organic evolution (i.e., the unfolding and growth of original germs in organisms) are frequently supposed to be one and the same thing. But this is not the case. "Were," says Mr. Herbert Spencer, "the theory of natural selection disproved, the theory of organic evolution would remain."[1] Natural selection may be regarded as the method by which organic evolution has reached its greatest perfection. Natural selection is the handmaid of evolution: it has chiefly operated in guiding and modifying the processes of organic evolutions in directions which otherwise they might not have taken: it is the account which evolution gives of the chief method whereby the present order of species has been arrived at.

The question which evolution raises is not whether the species at present existing were originally created by God, or came into being independently of Him; but whether they were directly created at first, or by gradual stages.[2]

---

ment; while the possibility of its ever accounting for the mechanical and chemical properties of inorganic matter, that already 'manufactured' material, as it has been called, out of which organisms are developed, is, to say the least, extremely doubtful. And, even if all this ground should be one day occupied by natural selection, the original variability of matter, not to mention matter itself, would still remain to be explained. Natural selection acts by selecting variations, and the variations must exist before they can be selected."—Illingworth, *Bampton Lectures*, iv. p. 95.

[1] *Nineteenth Century*, November, 1895.

[2] "According to special creation, forms of life are produced by the will of God, having, indeed, the minutest

Were the various classes of animals and plants, as we now know them, independently created, or have they been derived or developed by gradual processes from primary species? The answer of evolution is, They have been derived and developed from a few original and simple forms. When we ask, How has the work of evolution been accomplished? we get the reply of science—The species have been developed to a considerable extent by means of natural selection, working through the struggle for life, and the survival of the fittest. Now, as we said before, the objection to the proof of the existence of God from the presence of design in nature, is founded upon the assumption that natural selection is purely a product of natural law, independent of any origination, purpose, assistance, or control of God.

analogies to one another, and yet having no relation to one another. According to evolution, species are not merely created by God, but created by Him according to a method which relates each species with the rest, and explains their analogies, like family likenesses, by a common ancestry."—Aubrey L. Moore, *Science and the Faith*, p. 173.

"Even if a doctrine of evolution should in time be accepted as scientifically, and so theologically certain, such a doctrine would not be inconsistent either with that belief in the original act of creation which is essential to Theism, or with 'the recognition of plan and purpose in the number and variety of animated beings.' 'Evolution,' from a Theistic point of view, is merely our way of describing what we can observe of God's continuous action upon the physical world; and because the phrase seems tacitly or poetically to invest the universe with a power of self-unfolding, it does not follow that the question of an Intelligent Creator and Ruler is thereby decided in the negative by those who employ it."—Liddon, *Some Elements of Religion*, p. 54.

But, in reply to this objection, we would ask two questions, which bear directly upon the law of natural selection.

To whom is the existence of the germs of future development in primary forms to be attributed?

By whose power has the development of these germs, through natural selection, been accomplished?

Natural selection can only act upon nature previously prepared. 'Chance variations,' so called, must have been in possibility contained in the first condition of the original matter from which they have proceeded. The completed idea of a glorious cathedral is in the architect's mind before the plans are drawn, or the foundations digged, or the stones quarried, or the trees felled. And is it not, to say the least, reasonable to suppose, that all the variations at present existing in the natural world, were fore-known, planned, and allowed for, by the Great Creator, from the very first, and have been brought to perfection by His Almighty power?

'The belief that all organic beings, including man, have been genetically derived from some simple being,' demands the action of God, as much as the belief that all forms have been separately created by Him. The truth that the development or growth of species is due to the process known as natural selection, in no way dispenses with a divine superintendence of that process; on the contrary it implies such a superintendence. It is no derogation of God's power to say, that He works by law, be it that of natural selection, or gravitation, or any other law.

'For Christians the facts of nature are the acts of God.' The Christian believes that not only the germs of all things now existing were created at the first by Him, but also that they have been developed by Him. He believes that creation is His work from beginning to end, that His creative activity is present everywhere, that nothing is outside His hand. The law of natural selection, 'implies the immanence of God in nature, and the omni-presence of His creative power.' It implies the motion of the Divine Will, informing, impenetrating, and embracing the whole range of nature's operations.

"There is," wrote Mr. Aubrey Moore, "no division of labour between God and nature, or God and law. 'If He thunder by law, the thunder is yet His voice.' The plant which is produced from seed by the 'natural' laws of growth is His creation. The brute which is born by the 'natural' process of generation is His creation. The plant or animal which, by successive variations and adaptations, becomes a new species (if this is true) is His creation. . . . We need hardly stop to remind ourselves how entirely this is in accord with the relation of God and nature, always assumed in the

Bible. What strikes us at once, trained as we are in the language of science, is the *immediateness* with which everything is ascribed to God. He makes the grass to grow upon the mountains. To Him the young ravens look up for food. He holds the winds in the hollow of His hand. Not a sparrow falls without His knowledge. He numbers the hairs of our head. Of bird and beast and flower, no less than of man, it is true that in Him they 'live and move and have their being.' 'O Lord, how glorious are Thy works!' For the Christian theologian *the facts of nature are the acts of God.*"[1]

Thus, it is not unreasonable to believe that the manifold and beautiful order and harmony of the natural world, is the work of a purposeful Mind of unlimited power, wisdom, and intelligence—the work of a personal God.

In concluding this section of our subject, we venture to think that whilst the argument from design, like the argument from general consent, or that derived from the existence of the universe, when taken singly, is not sufficient of itself to demonstrate the existence of God; yet it is at least of such a nature as to command serious attention. 'The strength of a rope is greater than the strength of its separate strands.' The arguments for the existence of God are, it has been said, 'sufficient not

[1] *Science and the Faith*, pp. 225, 226.

resistless, convincing not compelling.' And when the three arguments are considered together, they very greatly tend to strengthen and establish man's instinctive belief in the existence of God, and afford the strongest presumption that HE IS.[1]

[1] "The prophecies, the very miracles and proofs of our religion, are not of such a nature that we can say they are absolutely convincing. But they are also of such a kind, that none can say that it is unreasonable to believe in them. Thus there is both evidence and obscurity to enlighten some and blind others: but the evidence is such that it surpasses or at least equals the evidence to the contrary, so that it is not reason which can determine us not to follow it, and therefore it can only be lust and malice of heart. And by this means there is evidence enough to condemn, and not enough to convince; so it appears in those who follow it, that it is grace and not reason which causes them to follow it; and in those who fly it, it is lust, not reason, which causes them to fly it."—Pascal, *Proofs of the Christian Religion*, p. 206.

Part Third.

The Moral Nature of God.

"God is an Infinite, but Personal Being; existing from eternity in the completeness of His own blessedness, yet willing to become the centre of a realm of personalities. To this end He called into existence a world of personal beings, in a sense independent of Himself, but destined, in communion and intercourse with Himself, to find and fulfil the law of their creaturely perfection. To these free and rational beings, Almighty God deigns to stand in self-imposed relations. . . . He is holy; and appoints that for the entire realm of personality, as for Himself, holiness should be the absolute law. He alone can communicate to His creatures the idea of holiness; of a supreme, eternal, ethical good. The good exists only in Him; is the essential expression of His nature, the reflected light of His personality.

"Christianity lays stress on the principle of personality, with its determining elements, will and self-consciousness. . . . Personality is that element in man which makes him morally akin to God, and capable of holding communion with Him; that which places him in conscious relation to law; gives him a representative character as God's vicegerent on earth, and conveys the right to dominion over physical nature. If religion consists in personal relations between man and God, religious ethics must be concerned with the right culture and development of personality. But in virtue of his creaturely position, man's personality cannot be an end to itself."—R. L. Ottley, in Lux Mundi, *Christian Ethics*, pp. 469, 471.

"The peculiar characteristic of moral actions, moral principles, and moral habits, lies in this, that they always imply some relation to personality. Morality begins with the relation of person to person, and all moral government—preeminently the government of God—is founded upon, and legislates for this relation. We are thus led to the fundamental positions or postulates of moral government—the freedom (personality) of man, and the personality of God." Cocker, in the Princeton Review, Jan. 1879. *Moral Government*, p. 59.

CHAPTER I.

GOD A MORAL BEING.

IN the earlier chapters of this work, we have endeavoured to trace the leading processes through which mankind at large has been led on, from faint surmises of a superhuman and infinite Being, to the higher and nobler conception of a divine Person. In considering the gradual growth of the belief in God, we have seen that man's belief in his own personality gave birth to his belief in a personal God. We are now about to carry the argument a step further in a similar direction, and to trace the way in which man's recognition of his own moral nature and responsibility led on to the perception of God as a Moral Being, a Responsible Agent. We are, in short, about to set forth the moral argument for the existence of a Personal God; basing our conclusions on the question, What does the consideration of man's moral nature lead us to infer concerning the Being and Character of God?

i.

It is impossible to reflect long or seriously upon our personality, without coming face to face with the truth that the possession of personality implies the possession of a moral nature. Morality is 'the very nerve of personality.' What do we mean by a moral nature, what are its characteristics?

We answer the question in the words of Bishop Ellicott—"There is something within us, some power, principle, or faculty of the soul that commands and prohibits, praises and blames, and that is felt to do so with a voice of authority from which there is no appeal, and also (if not tampered with) with a consciously admitted rectitude; in a word, there is in every man a *conscience*, a judge in the forum of the soul whose courts are always open, and whose judgments, unless the whole moral nature has been corrupted, are always prompt, penetrating, and just. Secondly,—There is in each one of us a *sense of duty*, a clearly felt obligation to do that which is recognized to be rightly enjoined, and not to do that which is recognized to be rightly prohibited,—a feeling that we 'ought,' and that we 'must,' if we would be accounted really moral agents in the truest sense of the word. Thirdly,—There is ever present some consciously felt standard, something, however dimly realized, to which our feelings, thoughts, emotions, and acts are always almost instinctively referred; something, at which, at one time, we aim, and to which, at another time, we seek to conform ourselves,—a sort of 'norma vivendi,' to which we give the name of *moral rectitude* or virtue. Fourthly, and by consequence,—There is a *recognition of a rule of right and wrong*,—right and wrong confessedly varying with the circumstances in which men may be placed, but not the less ideally recognized, and, in all simpler cases, decided upon with instinctive correctness by the domestic judge. Such, in simple and plain words, are the principal characteristics of our moral nature."[1]

Thus, under the term 'moral nature,' we are to understand the possession of conscience, the acknowledgment of a sense of duty, the idea of moral rectitude, the recognition of a rule of

---

[1] *The Being of God*, pp. 115, 116.

"Bishop Ellicott puts these truths in a simpler form, thus—"We have clearly engraven, as it were, on our souls, on the fleshly tablets of each individual heart, a few plain broad rules of right and wrong, 'Thou shalt,' and 'Thou shalt not,'—right being conformity with these rules, wrong, disobedience or neglect of them. Further, we have a feeling that we *ought*, and are morally bound to conform to these rules, a judge to decide whenever we may feel in doubt as to their incidence in regard of future action, and to praise or to blame for the past; and lastly, a general recognition, or, at any rate, consciousness, of a standard at which not only we have to aim, but by means of which we can estimate the moral worth of our feelings, motives, and actions."—Ibid. p. 117.

"Two things fill the mind with ever new and growing admiration and awe, the more frequently and the more intensely we ponder on them: the starry firmament above me, and the moral law within me."—Kant, *Works*, Vol. viii. p. 312.

right and wrong. Of each and all of these elements of our moral nature we need say little here; they are the acknowledged possession of every rational being, and of their force and working we have each ample and continuous experience. Obedience to their dictates and rulings ever brings with it the sense of inward satisfaction and peace, disobedience ever brings with it the feeling of remorse and unquiet. Whilst the sense of right and wrong may vary under the influence of surroundings, modes of education, and prevailing custom, yet, speaking broadly, all men "shew the work of the law written in their hearts, their conscience bearing witness therewith, and their thoughts one with another accusing or else excusing them."[1]

"There is," said Cicero, "a true law which is right reason, agreeable to nature, diffused among all men, constant, eternal, which calls us to duty by its injunctions, and by its prohibitions deters us from wrong; which upon the good lays neither injunction nor prohibition in vain; while for the bad, neither its injunctions nor its prohibitions avail at all. This law admits neither of addition, nor subtraction, nor abrogation. The vote of neither senate nor people can discharge us from our obligation to it. We are not to look for some other person to expound or interpret it; nor will there be one law for Rome, and another for

[1] Rom. ii. 15.

Athens, nor one at this date and another later on; but one law shall embrace all races over all time, eternal and immortal; and there shall be hereby one common master and commander of all—God, who originated this law, and proposed it, and arbitrates concerning it; and if any one obeys it not, he shall play false to himself, and shall do despite to the nature of man, and by this very fact shall pay the greatest penalties, even if he should escape all else that is reckoned punishment."[1]

ii.

Now the important question is, What is the origin of the moral law? How are we to account for the authority and precision with which it appeals to our sense of duty? How are we to explain the urgency of its righteous claims? How indeed, unless we refer the moral law to a Moral Lawgiver? "Our inner recognition of a moral law," says Mr. Illingworth, "and our external observation of its inexorable justice, its severe beneficence, its ultimate triumph, are among the strongest arguments of natural religion. But still they are only arguments; they point to a Person, but they are not that Person. Law is universal in its action; it does not individualize; it has no equity, no mercy; it does not behave like a person."[2] Could the moral law appeal to man

[1] *de Republica*, i. 3.   [2] *Bampton Lectures*, v. p. 119.

as strongly as it does, and so often come into violent collision with his will, if there was not behind that law some Other Will? And if the will of man is the centre of his personality, does not that Other Will imply the existence of a Personal God, whose Will the moral law represents? To recognize will working with or against will, can mean nothing else but personality working with or against personality. "I feel within my soul at every moment a righteous voice dealing with me individually; and I conclude that I am in contact with a righteous Person."[1] Obedience or disobedience to law implies obedience or disobedience to the authority which gives such law its force: take away that authority, and the law becomes inoperative. Thus, the force of obligation to the moral law rests ultimately on the source from which it proceeds, the reverence and obedience to the Lawgiver. Disobedience or disregard of the moral law is sin; but sin is a personal offence, not merely against the law which is broken, but primarily against Him who gives the law. "Against Thee, Thee only, have I sinned."[2] The blessedness of obedience, or the misery of disobedience, is only fully realized when the law is viewed as the will of a Personal God. Our consciousness of possessing moral freedom in relation to the moral law suggests the conclusion, that God is not 'a mere tendency which

[1] Wace, *Boyle Lectures*, p. 204.   [2] Psalm li. 4.

God a Moral Being.

makes for righteousness,' but a Righteous Lawgiver, with a power of voluntary self-determination. If man is free, God must be more free. The possession of free will is the evidence that He who gave free will to man has a will also, and that His will, too, is free—in short, that God is a Moral Being, a Personal God.

To sum up this section of our subject, we again quote the words of Bishop Ellicott, "The consideration of the moral elements of our nature has led us to One from whom those elements have come. We have now seen that they point all to the same inference,—the existence of a holy, perfect, and moral Being, who has written a law in our hearts, endowed us with the mysterious sense of duty and responsibility, vouchsafed to us a guide and a judge speaking with the voice of delegated authority, and, lastly, has placed before us a standard to which we are not only inwardly moved, but are actually helped, to attain."[1]

NOTE ON THE TESTIMONY OF CONSCIENCE TO GOD.

"Conscience is an authority. All bow before its power. We may despise its commands, but we must listen to its reproving voice. We may harden ourselves against its reproofs, but we cannot succeed in annihilating them. Conscience is independent of the will. It is not at our disposal. We do not command it, but it commands us. We do not correct and direct it, but it corrects and chastises us. We are not over, but under it. It is not under our power, but

[1] *The Being of God*, p. 132.

has power over us. It follows that it is no descendant of our will or our reason. It is no product of our own mind. It is the product of a moral spirit above and beyond ourselves, whose voice speaks to us through the conscience. Conscience is the supreme and ultimate court of appeal, the highest moral criterion in all cases. Hence it is the product of the supreme mind of the Supreme Lawgiver, of the absolute moral will. The *fact* of its existence proves that of God.

"The office of conscience is also a testimony to God; for it is part of its office to testify of the moral law as the will of God, and to bring our will into union with the will of God. Hence even Cicero says, 'It was always the persuasion of all truly wise men, that the moral law was not devised by men or introduced by nations, but an eternal law, according to which the whole world must be ruled. Its ultimate basis is God, who commands and forbids. And this law is as old as the mind of God Himself. Hence the law upon which all obligation is founded is truly and pre-eminently the mind of the Supreme Divinity.' (*de Leg.* ii. 4)."—Luthardt, *Fundamental Truths*, pp. 59, 60.

"When we put to ourselves the question,—to what or to whom is the duty due? we find the answer which alone appears fully to satisfy. 'I ought' seems really and ultimately to mean, 'I owe it to One who has a claim on my obedience, to whom I stand in a personal relation, whose love I crave, and whose displeasure I dread. Everything tells me that it must be to something more than cold abstract law to which I thus stand bound. It must be some Being to whom my whole inner nature seems to point, and towards whom the set and strain of my soul seems irresistibly to bear me.'"—Ellicott, *The Being of God*, p. 123.

"Conscience, whatever its origin, is *authoritative*, it speaks with power, but it speaks not from itself. Its decision is no mere 'ipse dixit.' It is a derived authority. . . . It speaks from a person to a person. A thing cannot speak with authority to a person."—Aubrey L. Moore, Essays Scientific and Philosophical, *Theology and Law*, p. 239.

iii.

The simple argument which we have above considered, gains increased force in connection with a truth we are now about to discuss.

God a Moral Being.

That truth is that moral likeness to God is needful to the recognition of Him as a Personal and Moral Being. " If we would know God as personal, we must begin with a desire to know Himself, as distinct from His manifestations in nature, or His works in the world. And it is obvious that, in proportion to the awfulness of His personality, this desire must be both intense and sincere. . . . A man cannot understand a character with which his own has no accord."[1] If we would know God, we must become like Him. " Blessed are the pure in heart : for they shall see God."[2] " If any man willeth to do His will, he shall know of the teaching."[3] 'Purity, humility, and gentleness, are notes of the scholars of the truth.'

We have here a point of great importance, upon which it is well to dwell. Bishop Butler has seized upon it, and emphasized its importance; he wrote, "Inattention, among us, to revealed religion, will be found to imply the same dissolute immoral temper of mind, as inattention to natural religion. . . . Revelation claims to be the voice of God : and our obligation to attend to His voice is surely moral in all cases."[4] Bacon, too, in his Essay on *Atheism*, points to the same conclusion in the words, "For none deny there is a God, but those for whom it maketh that there were no God."

---

[1] Illingworth, *Bampton Lectures*, v. p. 120.
[2] St. Matt. v. 8.   [3] St. John vii. 17.
[4] *Analogy*, II. ix. § 3.

Morality is personality at work; it is the recognition of personal responsibility. In each stage of its development personality implies character; and character is the result of attention to, or disregard of the moral law. Personality, morality, and character, are bound up in one bundle of life, whether that life be the life of man or the Life of God. Until we have realized our own personality, we are not in a position to realize the personality of God; and to realize our own personality is to recognize our obligation to fulfil the moral law. Until we have acknowledged the claims of the moral law, and are striving honestly to meet them in obedience, it is idle to expect to rise to the perception of God as a Moral Being, a Responsible Agent. Moral character is ever an indispensable qualification for the personal knowledge of God; and the higher the standard of moral goodness to which a man attains, the clearer will be his conviction of the existence and moral attributes of the Personal God. The good only can recognize The Good. If 'things human must be known to be loved, things divine must be loved to be known.' He who would know God, must first love Him. We venture to think that much of the unbelief in God, which comes to the surface in the religious discussions of our own times, results from the failure to weigh the truth of which we have been speaking.

iv.

If God is a Personal and Moral Being, how is it that it took the world at large so long to grasp the truth? If the revelation of God, as the Supreme Righteous Ruler, was for centuries made to the favoured few, why was it so long delayed to mankind in general?

If moral likeness to God is a needful qualification for knowing Him as He is, on the other hand, it is equally true that a Righteous God cannot reveal Himself in His true character to beings who are unrighteous. 'Holy things for holy persons,' is an axiom in the history of man's search for God. To take an illustration of our meaning, we refer to the words of Professor Drummond, "What delayed the gesture-language of the telegraph was not that electricity was not in nature, but the want of the instrument. When that came, the gesture-language came. . . . What delayed the telephone was not that its principle was not in nature, but that the instrument was not ready. What now delays its absolute victory of space is not that space cannot be bridged, but that it is not ready."[1]

Outside the chosen people, the Hebrew race, God was almost if not altogether unknown as the Supreme Moral Being; because the mind and character of man was not ready to know Him as such.

[1] *The Ascent of Man*, p. 235.

We cannot do better than sum up what we have said in the words of Mr. Illingworth, "The same limitations, which qualify our power of knowing a person, qualify also the possibility of his making himself known to us. This is the case in our human relations, and we should expect it to be still more true of a divine revelation. For a Person who is holy cannot reveal Himself as such to the unholy, since they do not know holiness when they see it; and it appears to them unintelligible, terrible, even hateful; anything, in short, but what it really is. A Person who is loving, in the true sense of the word, cannot reveal Himself as such to those who have no notion that love must involve sacrifice, and has in it, therefore, an awful element of sternness; for to them love would not appear love, but its opposite. An Infinite Person cannot reveal Himself as such to one who, unconscious of his own limitations, persists in measuring all things by the standard of a finite capacity, and denying the existence of what he cannot comprehend. And again, even where there is both desire and aptitude for the revelation, a Person can only reveal Himself partially and gradually, in proportion as these qualifications progressively increase; and we must remember what searchings of heart, and agony of will, that increase must of necessity imply. And if it be objected to all this, that we cannot imagine, *a priori*, what the conditions of a divine com-

God a Moral Being.

munication are likely to be, it is sufficient answer that belief in a Personal God means nothing else, than belief in One who acts towards us as persons act, and therefore to whose action human analogies may be applied."[1]

Bampton Lectures, v. pp. 124, 125.

"I am the Lord, and there is none else ; beside me there is no God. I form the light, and create darkness ; I make peace, and create evil ; I am the Lord, that doeth all these things."—Isaiah xlv. 5, 7.

"The evil principle itself was only created by God in this sense; that He had formed the wills which, in their perverted freedom, gave it birth."—Liddon, *Some Elements of Religion*, p. 145.

"Evil is not any substance ; for were it a substance, it would be good. . . . Thou didst make all things good, nor is there any substance that was not made by Thee. . . . I enquired what iniquity was, and found it not to be a substance, but a perversion of the will, bent aside from Thee, O God."—St. Augustine, *Confessions*, vii. 12. 16.

"There is no substance of evil, no nature of evil, no positive cause of evil. Evil is always a failure, and the cause of evil is always a failure. Whatever is, is good, but good only in its own kind, its own measure, and its own order. For anything, and especially the human will, to be in its right order, it must be in just and due relations with its greater good. Without this due order, it is disorder; and disorder is evil."—Bp. Ullathorne, *The Endowments of Man*, p. 180.

CHAPTER II.

THE PROBLEM OF MORAL EVIL.

FROM the consideration of our moral nature, we arrive at the conclusion that He who fashioned it must be a Moral Being. Man instinctively recognizes and approves that which is true, honest, just, and pure; and this recognition and approval of goodness we believe to be a pale reflection of the moral nature of God. Carlyle founded his belief in "the infinite Good One" on the argument—"All that is good, generous, wise, right—whatever I deliberately and for ever love in others and myself, who or what could by any possibility have given it to me, but One who first had it to give?"

But how about the evil in the world—the moral evil which we call sin, the physical evil which we call pain?

If God is the One Supreme Being, who made all things, He must either have made evil, or have permitted it to enter into His world. If He did not create evil, why did He permit it? In short, if God is the Sovereign Lord of the universe, He must ultimately be held responsible for the existence of evil. If God is good, how are we to reconcile His toleration of evil with His goodness. If God is good, He must hate evil; if He is Almighty, He might have prevented its birth, had He so willed.

These are questions which have perplexed thoughtful minds in all ages. Tertullian's question, asked some seventeen hundred years ago, 'Unde malum et quare'[1]—whence came evil, and why does it exist?—is one which is ever new. Evil is everywhere, we cannot but be conscious of its existence; it is the great black wall, that surrounds the universe of thought. "The whole world lieth in the evil one."[2] Evil is a living, present, and fearful mystery. If human life is on the whole a life of happiness in a world of light and beauty, it is on the other hand a life of sorrow and affliction in a world of sin and pain. And this world is God's world. How, we repeat, is the goodness of God to be reconciled with the existence, the permission, the origination of evil? The answer to this great question must be one which shall, in some measure, satisfy our reason, without calling in question either the unity, the power, or the holiness of God.

The subject before us is one of vast dimensions; and, for the clearer discussion of it, we will address ourselves first to the consideration of moral evil, and then to that of physical evil.

[1] *de Præscr. Hær.* 7.   [2] 1 St. John v. 19.

i.

The earliest attempted solution of the difficulty is that which is known as Dualism.[1] Dualism was originally the belief of the Persians. It consisted in the supposition that there were two Gods—one, the source of light, the other, the fountain of darkness. The Persians "believed in one God, indeed, and thought of Him so nobly that their symbol for Him was a circle with wings,—the circle to denote the completeness, the perfection, the eternity of God; and the wings to denote His all-pervading Presence. But while they believed in one only God, the Maker of all that was good, they also, and out of reverence for One to whom they dared not attribute any wrong, believed in an anti-god, whom they made responsible for all that was evil."[2] It

---

[1] "In ages and civilizations when the idea of God was imperfect or impoverished, men accounted for the existence of evil by ascribing to it a being or principle, coeval with God, independent of Him, and of course opposed to Him. Whether this evil was supposed to be matter out of which the good God had fashioned the world, or whether it was conceived of as something more spiritual, the object and origin of the system was identical. It was an effort to account for the great perplexing mystery—the existence of evil. It is impossible, argued these ancient thinkers, that moral life and death, that good and evil, can flow from a single source. It is impossible that a holy God can have been the author of evil. Evil, then, must be referred to some other origin: it must have had an author of its own."—Liddon, *Some Elements of Religion*, pp. 142, 143.

[2] Cox, *The Genesis of Evil*, pp. 4, 5. The author desires to express his obligation to this able exposition of a great and difficult subject.

was to Cyrus, the Persian king, that the words, "I am the Lord, and there is none else. I form the light, and create darkness; I make peace, and create evil,"[1] were addressed. It is as though God had said, "I am the good creative Spirit in whom you believe; but I have no such rival and antagonist as you suppose. I claim to be the sole Lord and Ruler of the universe. All that *is* is mine. I am responsible for the darkness as well as for the light. Evil is my servant, my creature, no less than good."[2] God then allows us to consider that, in a certain sense, He is responsible for the existence of evil. We are to believe that evil, as well as good, is under His control; and therefore the toleration of evil must be, in some measure, connected with His power and His goodness. Putting aside the undoubted truth that much of the evil within and without is of our own making, that much is also the making of our fellow men, that much which appears to be evil is not really or necessarily altogether evil, there still remains the broad fact of the existence of moral evil to be accounted for.

ii.

What do we mean by moral evil? Moral evil is the evil wrought by responsible and moral agents. The animals are incapable of

[1] Isa. xlv. 5, 7.   [2] *The Genesis of Evil*, p. 6.

moral evil: they are neither responsible nor moral agents, because they possess no personality. At the centre of personality, as we have seen, resides the power of self-determination, or moral freedom. It is this possession of personality which makes man a moral agent. A moral agent is one who is free to act, or not to act, in a given direction. Nothing in the whole universe is so great as man. If "man," as Pascal says, "is but a reed, weakest in nature, he is a reed which thinks. It needs not that the whole universe should arm to crush him. A vapour, a drop of water is enough to kill him. But were the universe to crush him, man would still be nobler than that which has slain him, because he *knows* that he dies, and that the universe has the better of him. The universe knows nothing of this."[1] And what is it, let us ask, which gives man this pre-eminent greatness? It is his possession of personality, with its power of moral freedom.

If we believe that the universe, with man at its summit, owes its existence to God, we may carry thought back to the time when He was pleased to create, and to create in the only way open to Him, as an Intelligent Agent. "Would you have God surround Himself with a merely inanimate world, or tenant that world with mere automata, mere puppets, with no will of their own, capable indeed of reflecting His own glory back on Him, but incapable of a volun-

[1] *The Greatness and Littleness of Man*, p. 47.

tary affection, a spontaneous and unforced obedience? Would it have been worthy of Him, even such as you can conceive Him to be, would it have given scope and verge to His energies and affections to make mere *marionettes*, even though He gave them wings and called them angels? Why, even you yourselves cannot gain full scope for your powers until you are surrounded, or surround yourselves, with beings capable of loving you freely, and obeying you with a cheerful and unforced accord, beings whose wills are their own and who yet make them yours? How much less, then, can you imagine that God should be content with a purely mechanical obedience, with a purely physical and necessary accord with the determinations of His will, with anything short of a voluntary obedience and affection? According to the best conception of Him we can frame, it was inevitable that He should surround Himself with life, thought, affection, with beings resembling Himself and capable of freely becoming one with Him in mind and heart and will." [1]

And if we admit all this, as we must, what is the result? It is this, If man is able to will rightly, must he not, too, be able to will wrongly? If we are free to obey, must we not also be free to disobey? If we are capable of loving, must we not be capable of hating? Creatures who should be free to refuse obedi-

[1] *The Genesis of Evil*, p. 30.

ence, and to withhold love, are the only creatures who can truly obey and love. It is the very essence of obedience and love that they should be voluntary. The idea of involuntary obedience, or mechanical love is inconceivable. There is no place for compulsion in one or the other. A forced obedience or love would have lost all heart, and would be unworthy of the name of obedience and love. If my will is not in my own power, it ceases to be my will: its actions would be involuntary, i.e., lacking in will, and would carry with them no responsibility. If my heart is not in my own gift, I cannot give it; and if it was taken from me by force, it would no longer be my heart. To rob man of his moral freedom—his liberty to love or not to love, to obey or not to obey—would result in his being no longer man, but an irrational, unintelligent animal. And what is all this but to say, that the creation of beings endowed with moral freedom, necessarily carried with it the risk of their abusing that freedom, and so doing evil, and becoming evil?[1]

[1] "God might have created a universe ruled from first to last by physical law, and so incapable of deviation from the true rule of its action. In such a universe, moral evil would have found no place, only because there would have been no creatures properly capable of moral good. Our experience tells us that God has not chosen to stint down His creative activity to these proportions: that we are free agents, is not more a matter of faith than of experience. We know that God has created beings whose high privilege it is to be able freely to choose Him as their King, as the accepted Master of their whole inward life; but if this privilege is to be real, it also carries with it the implied power of rejecting Him. The

iii.

If we carry the argument a step further, we shall find it difficult to avoid the conclusion that, given the freedom to obey or disobey a moral law, sooner or later some at least of the creatures so endowed would risk the experiment, and make the wrong choice. When we reflect upon it, the creation of multitudes of free agents involves not only *the chance*, but also *the extreme probability*, that some at least of that multitude would misuse their liberty. As a Moral Being, God must not only have foreseen this, but also have allowed and provided for it. He must have foreknown that men would avail themselves of their moral freedom, and wrongfully assert it by disobedience. "Man found himself in a vast natural world or order in which all creatures but himself rendered a necessary and involuntary obedience to their Maker and Lord. He was himself part of Nature. He was taken from the dust, and had affinities with the dust; the animal life breathed in his nostrils and pervaded

---

alternative risk is the inevitable condition of the consummate honour: it is actually a substantial part of the honour. A moral being must at least have a capacity for disobedience, if he is to be able freely to obey."—Liddon, *Some Elements of Religion*, p. 154.

"We may regard all moral evil as traceable to selfishness and consequent disobedience, and we may also reverently conceive that without the test of obedience, and the freedom to obey or disobey, moral agency, and the progress to moral perfection, could not have been realized in finite beings such as ourselves."—Ellicott, *The Being of God*, p. 135.

his frame. Was he no more than rocks and streams, plants and trees, birds and beasts? What meant, then, these motions of a higher and less restricted life of which he was conscious, this sense of freedom to do or to forbear from doing? Was he, after all, bound in the same chain of necessity as the creatures around and beneath him; or, if he dared, could he snap that chain, and be as free, though not so strong, as God Himself?"[1]

The question was one which, sooner or later, would be likely to arise in the human mind; and when it did arise, it was only to be expected that man would not long delay making the experiment. "I could sit at ease and quiet in my chamber all day long," said Cowper, "but the moment I knew the door was locked upon me, I should try to get out at all risks." Do we not all as children remember the story of Bluebeard, how the one door in the palace which Fatima was forbidden to open, was just the one which she most particularly desired to open, and which in the end she did open?

The account given in Holy Scripture of the entrance of evil into the universe simply confirms our natural expectations. It tells us that not only on earth, but also in heaven, creatures endowed with moral freedom abused the gift, by taking their own way and following their own will in opposition to God's Will. It tells us that whilst they were free to obey, they

[1] *The Genesis of Evil*, p. 32.

chose to disobey: and that by their evil choice they fell out of harmony with the Divine Will, and only found out the mistake in a consequent misery. Evil, then, is not the creation of God, but the creation of the perverted free will of the creature. And all we can justly ascribe to Him is the responsibility for calling into existence beings capable of evil. We may not attribute more to Him than the permission of the possibility of moral evil, and the willingness to run the risk of its origination and existence.

"The origin of evil, just like that of good, lies in the power of choice. God must have been (if we may so speak) necessitated, by His very goodness, to create beings capable of goodness. And this freedom carries with it an inevitable liability to sin."[1]

iv.

But if God foresaw, as we cannot but believe He must have done, the terrible consequences which would follow the abuse of His gift of moral freedom, how can we reconcile this with a belief in His power and goodness? Even Omnipotence cannot create free will, and then coerce or compel its action. Coercion of the will would be its destruction. The idea of compulsion cannot seriously be entertained in relation to moral

[1] Momerie, *The Origin of Evil*, p. 10.

## The Problem of Moral Evil.	137

freedom. What becomes of the freedom of a fettered prisoner confined to a cell? It does not exist. Thus, to give moral freedom, and then to restrain its action, would be to take it away again and obliterate it. The toleration of evil does not mean that God's power is limited, but that His generosity has been misused. But how about the goodness of God? Surely, if we cannot now see the whole outline of the purpose of moral evil—for we shall find the solution of the mystery only in eternity— we can at least recognize the light which it sheds upon the value, in God's sight, of the willing obedience and generous love of His creatures.

The grandeur of moral goodness, and the beauty of love can only be learnt by considering the awful risk which God was content to run in making both possible. And then, on the other hand, we must not fail to realize how inexpressible must be the blessedness of making the right choice; and, in loving good, to love God, and, in loving Him, to become like Him. For the eternal blessedness of being everlastingly holy could never have been ours without the temptation to moral evil. 'The alternative risk is the inevitable condition of the consummate honour: it is actually a substantial part of the honour.' If we cannot completely solve the dark problem of the divine permission of evil, we can surely see rays of light leading us on to trust that 'all is right that seems most wrong,' and that one day we shall know and confess that "He hath done all things well."[1]

But to the Christian there is much more than all this. He holds that not only did God foresee the origination and the existence of moral evil, but that, in the eternal counsels, He provided for it. In the Incarnation of the Son of God, of which we shall speak later, the Christian finds the recognition of the divine responsibility for the origin of moral evil. He believes that if God foresaw the abuse of His gift of moral freedom, He foresaw much more. The vision arises before the mind, of God, in human form, entering into personal conflict with moral evil, and breaking its power—the vision of the divine remedy, which has proved itself to be far greater than the disease. The Christian believes that, by the Incarnation,

---

[1] "If we must ascribe to God a holy hatred of sin, and if we must also ascribe to God clear prevision of the result of the freedom of sin, how *can* we reconcile the two thoughts, that He should thus hate sin, and yet that He should give a choice which He must have foreseen would introduce it. To this question I must candidly say I do not believe that any *really* satisfying answer ever has been, or ever can be returned. I am persuaded that our finite nature, and still more, our immersion in sin, prevents our properly conceiving the lines within which the answer—for an answer there is—must ultimately lie. But having said this, I thankfully recognize that there are many considerations, such, for example, as the disciplinary nature of the struggle with moral evil, the evolution *per ardua et aspera* of god-like characters, and the almost limitless nature of the holy aspirations which are developed in the conflict, that do really remove all the practical difficulties which the presence of evil may appear to introduce."—Ellicott, *The Being of God*, pp. 135, 136.

The Problem of Moral Evil.   139

God has ordained that "where sin abounded, grace did abound more exceedingly."[1] He believes, with St. Augustine, that "God knew it to be more agreeable to His Almighty goodness even to bring good out of evil, than not to permit evil to exist."[2]

[1] Rom. v. 20.   [2] *de Cor. et Gr.* c. 10.

"The whole creation groaneth and travaileth in pain together until now."—Rom. viii. 22.

"On the whole, the popular idea of the struggle for existence entailing misery and pain on the animal world is the very reverse of the truth. What it really brings about is, the maximum of life and of the enjoyment of life with the minimum of suffering and pain. Given the necessity of death and reproduction—and without these there could have been no progressive development of the organic world—and it is difficult even to imagine a system by which a greater balance of happiness could have beeen secured."—Wallace, *Darwinism*, Ch. ii. p. 40.

"That a price, a price in pain, and assuredly sometimes a very terrible price, has been paid for the evolution of the world, is certain. There may be difference of opinion as to the amount of this price, but on one point there can be no dispute—that even at the highest estimate the thing which was bought with it was none too dear. For that thing was nothing less than the present progress of the world. The struggle for life has been a victorious struggle; it has succeeded in its stupendous task; and there is nothing of order or beauty or perfection in living nature that does not owe something to its having been carried on. The first duty of those who demur to the cost of progress is to make sure that they comprehend in all its richness the infinity of the gift this sacrifice has purchased for humanity."—Drummond, *The Ascent of Man*, p. 262.

CHAPTER III.

THE PROBLEM OF PHYSICAL EVIL.

IN considering the subject of physical evil, as distinguished from moral evil, it is at the outset to be observed, that whilst moral evil forms no part of the original design of the universe, physical evil may have been involved in that design. We need to speak with caution upon this point. The view has been maintained by some theologians that between the first and the second verses of the first chapter of Genesis, the lapse of a great interval of time is to be understood; and that during this interval, the earth, as it left its Maker's hands, fell under the influence or dominion of the fallen angels. If this view be correct, physical evil would be the result of moral evil from the beginning.[1]

---

[1] "There is evidence in the Scriptures, that, before the creation of man, Satan held some high pre-eminence in this world. The state of the earth before the present creation, 'without form and void, and darkness on the face of the deep,' does not read like a work of God, but rather like a ruin of some better work. Probably it was the result of the fall of the angels, the wreck of the storm which, overthrowing them, left its scars even on this solid

It will be our endeavour to show that, as in the case of the divine permission of moral evil, so also in that of physical evil, when thoughtfully and fairly considered, there is nothing inconsistent with belief in the goodness of God.

In the first place, it is well to say that physical evil is to be viewed under two aspects—first, as it affects the lower animals: secondly, as it affects man. It is to the consideration of physical evil in relation to the lower animals, that we will first address ourselves.

globe."—Carter, *The Life of Sacrifice*, p. 4. Whether this was the case or not, can only be a matter for speculation. Some remarks upon this mysterious and awful subject will be found in Hugh Miller's *Testimony of the Rocks*, Lect. iii.

If the opinion above stated is correct, it is not unreasonable to suppose that the angel who led the revolt in heaven, when by his fall he became the evil one, may have poisoned the fountain of life which was under his control, and have brought physical evil and death into the creation. Jesus Christ speaks of him as "the prince of the world" (*St. John* xiv. 30), and declares that "he was a murderer from the beginning" (*Ibid.* viii. 44). St. John states that "the whole world lieth in the evil one" (1 *St. John* v. 19). It is the teaching of the Old Testament that God created everything 'very good'; and it is difficult to understand how death, which, with pain, is an enemy to be abolished at last (Cf. 1 *Cor.* xv. 26 ; *Rev.* xxi. 4), could in the beginning have been good. "God made not death; neither delighteth He when the living perish : for He created all things that they might have their being : and the generative powers of the world are healthsome, and there is no poison of destruction in them" (*Wisdom* i. 13, 14). The New Testament teaches that the removal of 'the curse' follows the casting of the evil one into the lake of fire (Cf. *Rev.* xx. 10 ; xxii. 3).

Physical Evil in relation to the Lower Animals.

i.

Moral evil, as we have said, is a work in which the lower animals can have no share, for the simple reason that they are not endowed with moral freedom. But if they have no part in the experience of moral evil, the same cannot be said concerning physical evil. Physical evil, by which we mean pain and death, is the lot of all living creatures, and, as far as we know, ever has been. Upon this subject we quote the words of Hugh Miller, "We find no trace in nature of that golden age of the world, of which the poets delighted to sing, when all creatures lived together in unbroken peace, and war and bloodshed were unknown. Ever since animal life began upon our planet, there existed, in all the departments of being, carnivorous classes, who could not live but by the death of their neighbours, and who were armed, in consequence, for their destruction, like the butcher with his axe and knife, and the angler with his hook and spear."[1] After a graphic and most interesting description of the natural armour worn, and the weapons used by the creatures, which, in prehistoric ages, lived on our planet, this writer adds, "This early exhibition of tooth, and spine, and sting,—of weapons constructed alike to cut and to pierce,—to unite

[1] *The Testimony of the Rocks*, p. 71.

two of the most indispensable requirements of the modern armourer,—a keen edge to a strong back,—nay, stranger still, the examples furnished in this primeval time, of weapons formed not only to kill, but also to torture,—must be altogether at variance with the preconceived opinions of those who hold that until man appeared in creation, and darkened its sympathetic face with the stain of moral guilt, the reign of violence and outrage did not begin, and that there was no death among the inferior creatures, and no suffering. . . . And it is a truth as certain as the existence of a southern hemisphere, or the motion of the earth round both its own axis and the great solar centre, that, untold ages ere man had sinned or suffered, the animal creation exhibited exactly its present state of war,—that the strong, armed with formidable weapons, exquisitely constructed to kill, preyed upon the weak; and that the weak, sheathed, many of them, in defensive armour equally admirable in its mechanism, and ever increasing and multiplying upon the earth far beyond the requirements of the mere maintenance of their races, were enabled to escape, as species, the assaults of the tyrant tribes, and to exist unthinned for unreckoned ages. It has been weakly and impiously urged that such an economy of warfare and suffering,—of warring and of being warred upon,—would be, in the words of the infant Goethe, unworthy of an all-powerful and all-benevolent Providence, and in effect a libel on His government and character."[1]

It is fully granted that the existence of physical pain amongst creatures who have never sinned is a great mystery. But still we may confidently say that there are considerations connected with animal suffering which go far to reassure us that God's love is over all His works. If, as we shall endeavour to show later, the human race can only be perfected by suffering, may there not be some similar process at work amongst the lower creatures.

ii.

"At first," says a thoughtful writer, "brute force seems to have it all its own way. It is not a survival of the fittest that we behold, but rather of the strongest, the most ruthless, the most cruel. But wait a little, and you shall see that even in the animal kingdom 'the meek,' in spite of all appearances, 'shall inherit the earth.' . . . The animals that rely on violence alone for their existence are disappearing, and the meek and useful are taking their place. Nor is this all. The very qualities which seemed to make the meek easy victims are precisely the qualities which have conduced to their survival—social qualities which have been developed by the discipline of suffering, and have made them more than

[1] *The Testimony of the Rocks*, pp. 74, 75.

a match for their oppressors. Thus we see
that even in the animal world the battle is
not in the long-run to the swift and strong,
but to the gentle and long-suffering. The law
of vicarious sacrifice has thus its place in the
lower creation, which exhibits its martyrs
dying for the amelioration of the race. The
suffering of the animal world may therefore
be less purposeless and arbitrary and cruel
than it seems at first sight." [1]

iii.

There is a further consideration which helps
to reconcile God's permission of animal suffering with the belief in His goodness. Professor
Drummond, in his *Ascent of Man*,[2] has, with
other thinkers, warned us against over-colouring
the picture of pain in the animal kingdom, and
'flooding it with accompaniments of emotion
borrowed from our own sensations,' or 'reading
into it our personal ideas with regard to accompaniments of pain.'[3]

---

[1] Mac Coll, *Christianity in relation to Science and Morals*, 4th ed. pp. 34, 35.

[2] pp. 259, 260.

[3] When dealing with such subjects as that under discussion, we should do well to weigh the words of Mr. Illingworth,—
"When a certain class of facts is urged in objection to our Christian belief, we are entitled to ask how many of those facts are known, and how many are only imagined. There is of course a scientific use of the imagination, but it is only permissible within the bounds of possible, or at least conceivable, verification. Imaginative conjectures which, from the nature of the case, will never admit either of verification

"What then," asks Mr. Illingworth, "do we really know about the suffering of animals? No reasonable man doubts that they suffer. But the degree and intensity of their suffering is almost entirely a matter of conjecture. We speak of, and are affected by the mass of animal suffering; but we must remember that it is felt distributively. No one animal suffers more because a million suffer likewise. And what we have to consider is the amount which an individual animal suffers. We have no knowledge, but we are entitled to meet conjecture by conjecture. We may fairly suppose that the animals do not 'look before and after,' and it is this that gives its sting to human pain. Again, they would seem like children to give strong indications of slight pain. Further, many muscular contortions which simulate extreme suffering are believed on scientific evidence to be due to quite other causes. And then there are the phenomena of fascination, which may well resemble the experience of

or disproof are poetry and not science, and must be treated as such in argument."—Lux Mundi, *The Problem of Pain*, pp. 113, 114.

Bishop Butler emphasizes the same need of caution,— "One cannot but be greatly sensible, how difficult it is to silence imagination enough to make the voice of reason even distinctly heard in this case; as we are accustomed, from our youth up, to indulge that forward delusive faculty, ever obtruding beyond its sphere; of some assistance indeed to apprehension, but the author of all error: as we plainly lose ourselves in gross and crude conceptions of things, taking for granted that we are acquainted with, what indeed we are wholly ignorant of."—*Analogy*, I. i. § 9.

148 *The Problem of Physical Evil.*

Livingstone in the lion's mouth. While many pains are prophylactic (i.e., preservative, or preventive), and directly contribute to the avoidance of danger and maintenance of life. All these considerations may mitigate our view of animal suffering."[1]

iv.

We must remember, too, that the seat of pain is chiefly in the mental and emotional part of our nature. When the mind is otherwise intensely occupied, the nerves, which are the organs of pain, are apparently paralysed. It was not uncommon, Dr. Carpenter assures us, before the introduction of chloroform, for patients to undergo serious operations without giving any sign of pain; and afterwards to declare that they felt none, through intense concentration of mind on some subject which held them engaged during the operation. In the hurry and excitement of battle wounded men often feel no pain from their wounds. As a case in point, we have the well authenticated story of Dr. Livingstone's struggle with the lion.[2] The beast sprang upon him, and seized

---

[1] Lux Mundi, *The Problem of Pain*, pp. 114, 115.

[2] This story is referred to by Mr. Wallace in his work, *Darwinism*, Ch. ii. p. 38. He adds, "The absence of pain is not peculiar to those seized by wild beasts, but is equally produced by any accident which causes a general shock to the system. Mr. Whymper describes an accident to himself during one of his preliminary explorations of the Matterhorn,

The Problem of Physical Evil. 149

his arm with its jaws, shook him violently, then dropped him, and, after watching him for a time, walked away. The arm was lacerated and broken; but Livingstone, who retained consciousness during the whole time, often asserted that he felt no pain, the shock evidently having deprived him of all fear, or power of suffering. In describing the incident, he states that he watched the lion with feelings of curiosity, wondering when the beast would commence eating him. Later, in reflecting upon his marvellous escape, the great explorer arrived at the conclusion that the sensitive nerves of weaker creatures, who become the victims of beasts or birds of prey, are probably similarly paralysed; and, therefore, that they experience neither fear nor pain. There is, perhaps, no spectacle which excites our pity, or stirs our resentment, more than the sight of a cat playing with a mouse. But, putting aside emotion, does not calm reflection suggest that if a human being under the paw of a lion can be insensible to agony, both mental and bodily, a mouse under similar circumstances

when he fell several hundred feet, bounding from rock to rock, till fortunately embedded in a snow-drift near the edge of a tremendous precipice. He declares that while falling and feeling blow after blow, he neither lost consciousness nor suffered pain, merely thinking, calmly, that a few more blows would finish him. We have therefore a right to conclude, that when death follows soon after any great shock it is as easy and painless a death as possible; and this is certainly what happens when an animal is seized by a beast of prey."

is probably equally insensible to misery? It is reasonable to doubt seriously if the sufferings of animals in a wild state are really very great. "When we reflect," wrote Mr. Darwin, "on this struggle, we may console ourselves with the full belief that the war of nature is not incessant, that no fear is felt, that death is generally prompt, and that the vigorous, the healthy, and the happy survive and multiply."[1]

v.

Many of our ideas of pain are associated with its anticipation and remembrance. There are few persons who have undergone any serious operation, who would not freely admit that the anticipation of the operation was far greater than the actual physical suffering. Who is there, for example, who has not left a dentist's operating-room without feeling that anticipation has been a serious part of the trouble. But we may safely say that the lower creatures know nothing of the pain of anticipation or remembrance. They look neither before nor after; and this consideration must be borne in mind, in endeavouring to form a true esti-

---

[1] qu. *Darwinism*, Ch. ii. p. 40.
The author remembers noticing, some years ago, in *The Church Quarterly Review*, an article in which reference was made to the case of a horse, which, after falling down and seriously fracturing a knee, at once dragged itself to the roadside, and commenced eating the grass. It is evident that little, if any, pain was felt by the creature.

mate of the amount of actual suffering endured by the lower animals.

We will conclude our survey of the existence of physical evil in the lower animal world in the weighty words of Professor Drummond—"The probabilities are that the struggle for life in the lower creation is, to say the least, less painful than it looks. Whether we regard the dullness of the states of consciousness among lower animals, or the fact that the condition of danger must become habitual, or that death when it comes is sudden, and unaccompanied by that anticipation which gives it its chief dread to man, we must assume that whatever the struggle for life subjectively means to the lower animals, it can never approach in terror what it means to us. . . . With exceptions, the fight is a fair fight. As a rule there is no hate in it, but only hunger. It is seldom prolonged, and seldom wanton. As to the manner of death, it is generally sudden. As to the fact of death, all animals must die. As to the meaning of an existence prematurely closed, it is better to be to be eaten than not to be at all. And, as to the last result, it is better to be eaten out of the world and, dying, help another to live, than pollute the world by lingering decay. The most, after all, that can be done with life is to give it to others."[1]

[1] *The Ascent of Man*, pp. 260, 261.

Physical Evil in relation to the Human Race.

i.

It now remains to treat of physical evil in relation to the human race. And here we are at once on different ground. At present, no proof exists that the greatest of physical evils—death—formed any part of the original design concerning humanity. Revelation teaches that death followed as a consequence of moral evil. "As through one man sin entered into the world, and death through sin; and so death passed unto all men, for that all sinned."[1] But the same cannot be said of human pain. It is to be carefully noted that it is no doctrine of revealed religion that human pain was introduced into our world by man's participation in moral evil. In saying this, we must not be understood to assert that a great deal of human suffering is not, in the strictest sense, a direct punishment for evil committed. The disease which follows dissolute living, the poverty which results from idleness, are but examples of this law.[2]

---

[1] Rom. v. 12.

[2] "Now, without committing ourselves to the statement that suffering was introduced into the world by sin, which is not a Christian dogma, though it is often thought to be so, a vast amount of the suffering in the world is obviously punishment, and punishment of a very searching kind. For not only are obvious vices punished with remorse, and disease, and shame; but ignorance, impatience, carelessness, even mistakes of judgment are punished too, and that in a

The Problem of Physical Evil. 153

Now, putting aside all thoughts of physical evil as a punishment due to wrong-doing, what explanation are we to give of its visitation upon the innocent.

ii.

Pain is not only to be regarded as punitive, but also as preventive and corrective. It is the natural sentinel which warns and saves. "Pain, we may say, hoists an unmistakable signal, which at one and the same time informs us of the existence of danger, reveals the quarter whence it is to be expected, and suggests to us a means of escape—all, in cases of necessity, with lightning rapidity. . . . Let us take the instance of a workman at a smith's forge unwittingly seizing a piece of apparently cold iron in his fingers. It is, we will suppose, just short of being red-hot. His sense of sight does not suggest to him that it is anything but cold iron, though it is really hot enough to completely destroy the hand that grasps it for any length of time. The workman has no sooner taken it up than he lets it fall again, before he has had time to see any bad result, long before he has had time to reason about it, but in involuntary obedience to the urgent demand of

---

degree which we are apt to consider disproportionate; forgetful that consequences are God's commentaries, and this apparent disproportion may reflect light upon the real magnitude of what we often are too ready to consider trivial things."—Lux Mundi, *The Problem of Pain*, p. 117.

his suffering tissues. Not only has he saved his hand for this time, but he has very probably received a lifelong lesson on the imprudence of handling casual bits of iron near a forge, before he knows whether they are hot or cold. He will avoid making this mistake in future, as he thinks, for fear of giving himself pain; but this is only the aspect of the evil that impresses itself upon him—the real evil which nature wishes to guard against is the possible loss of the hand."[1] The familiar sayings, 'The burnt child dreads the fire,' 'Once bit, twice shy,' are illustrations of the service which pain renders to mankind. Pain is the great preservative of human life, and compels attention; and, by giving heed to its warnings, life is often prolonged or saved. It tells the sufferer of something wrong: it points out the seat of the mischief. Every medical man knows the extreme value of this truth, in the treatment of disease. Bodily pain sounds the alarm-bell of disease in time for its removal. Mental and moral pain arrest the issues of ignorant or evil courses before it is too late.

iii.

Again, if human pain has its uses as a preventive, it has also higher uses. The divine purpose of pain in relation to mankind

[1] Oxford House Papers, Second Series, Dixey, *The Necessity of Pain*, pp. 104, ff.

is also to purify and to elevate the character of those who rightly endure it. God in His love seeks to develop character in man, and He has in His wisdom made pain an instrument in accomplishing this end. The divine purpose of pain is the formation of a holy character in man, in the face of moral evil. To make men good as He is Good, that is the problem. It is a problem which He sees can best be solved by means of suffering. "When we say that men learn wisdom by experience, we mostly mean by experience of something painful. Of course, the most obvious form of this correction is that in which the suffering can be recognized by the sufferer as merited, because due to his own misdeeds. But apart from such causal connection, what we call unmerited suffering exercises the same influence in an even greater measure. Its forces, not being exhausted in the work of neutralising past evil, are able to expand and expend themselves in a positive direction, elevating, refining, dignifying the character to an infinite degree. The men of sorrows are the men of influence in every walk of life. Martyrdom is the certain road to success in any cause. Even more than knowledge, pain is power. And all this because it develops the latent capacities of our being as no other influence can. It requires no mystic insight to see the truth of this. However unable we may be to account for it, it is a fact of everyday experience, visible to ordinary common sense. And this being so, there is nothing of necessity unjust in what we call unmerited suffering, not even in the sad inheritance by children of the results of parental sin. For while the sight of the miserable entail may, if rightly used, become the parent's punishment, its imposition may be the child's call to higher things. True, like all other useful agencies, it often fails of its end; but such failure is of the problem of evil, not of the problem of pain."[1]

Thus, we trust enough has been said to convince those who are willing to look honestly into the matter, that the permission of physical evil, both amongst the lower creation, and amongst mankind, is not inconsistent with a belief in the goodness and the beneficence of Almighty God.

In concluding the previous chapter, we referred to the immense bearing which the doctrine of the Incarnation has upon the existence of moral evil. And the same may be said in reference to physical evil. In the sufferings and death of Christ we see God, clothed in our nature, voluntarily entering into fellowship with all forms of human pain; and thus recognizing His responsibility for its per-

[1] Lux Mundi, *The Problem of Pain*, pp. 117, 118.

mission. And we gain more than this. The Cross and Passion of Jesus Christ were but the prelude to the resurrection, and glorification of the Divine Sufferer; "who for the joy that was set before Him endured the cross, despising shame, and hath sat down at the right hand of the throne of God."[1]

The bearing of the doctrine of a future life, as revealed by Jesus Christ, must not be overlooked in relation to the temporal permission of moral and physical evil. "There can be no doubt," says Mr. Balfour, "that the doctrine of immortality may profoundly modify the whole attitude of mind in which we are able to face the insistent facts of sin, suffering, and misery. . . . The sense of misery unrelieved, of wrongs unredressed, of griefs beyond remedy, of failure without hope, of physical pain so acute that it seems the one over-mastering reality in a world of shadows, of mental depression so deadly that it welcomes physical pain itself as a relief—these, and all the crookednesses and injustices of a crooked and unjust world, may well overload our spirits and shatter the springs of our energies, if to this world only we must restrict our gaze. For thus restricted the problem is hopeless."[2]

Every humble believer in the Incarnate Lord, and the truth of the life to come, which He so fully revealed, who suffers according to the will of God, may say—"I reckon that the

[1] Heb. xii. 2. [2] *The Religion of Humanity*, pp. 9, ff.

sufferings of this present time are not worthy to be compared with the glory which shall be revealed to us-ward. For the earnest expectation of the creation waiteth for the revealing of the sons of God. For the creation was subjected to vanity, not of its own will, but by reason of Him who subjected it, in hope that the creation itself also shall be delivered from the bondage of corruption into the liberty of the glory of the children of God. For we know that the whole creation groaneth and travaileth in pain together until now. And not only so, but ourselves also, which have the firstfruits of the Spirit, even we ourselves groan within ourselves, waiting for our adoption, to wit, the redemption of our body." [1]

[1] Rom. viii. 18–23.

BOOK II.

The Revelation of God.

"Natural theology is based upon principles known by reason with human certainty; supernatural theology has for its foundation principles accepted by faith which rests on the authority of God Himself, who has declared them to us by divine revelation.

"Natural theology draws its arguments from the intuitions of reason and from facts of experience; supernatural theology finds the premisses of its conclusions in the sources of Christian revelation, which are the canonical Scriptures and the documents of divine tradition.

"Natural theology inquires into the existence, the attributes, and works of the one infinite God, without being able to treat of the inscrutable mysteries of the Blessed Trinity and of the Word Incarnate; whereas supernatural theology, although it does not pretend to make these mysteries comprehensible to reason, yet, guided by divine revelation, which has established their reality, analyzes their meaning, shows their consequences, illustrates their harmony with known truths, and thus throws light upon the divine beauty of Christian revelation."—Boedder, *Natural Theology*, pp. 2, 3.

"By nature is meant that vast system of things, taken as a whole, of which we are cognizant by means of our natural powers. By the supernatural world is meant that still more marvellous and awful universe, of which the Creator Himself is the fulness, and which becomes known to us, not through our natural faculties, but by superadded and direct communication from Him. These two great circles of knowledge intersect: first, as far as supernatural knowledge includes truths and facts of the natural world, and secondly, as far as truths and facts of the natural world are on the other hand data for inferences about the supernatural."—Newman, *Idea of a University*, p. 430.

THEOLOGY

NATURAL AND SUPERNATURAL.

IN the first part of this work, we have dwelt upon what may be termed natural theology, i.e., the reasoning about God which rests upon the contemplation of the universe, the study of history, and the facts of human experience. Natural theology is based upon principles discoverable by human reason. Alongside, or following upon, the teachings of natural theology, there is a further and fuller measure of truths concerning God, which rests upon the authority of a divine revelation. These further and fuller truths, though conformable to reason, are accepted by faith, and form what is known as supernatural theology.

We must be careful to notice that the two theologies are but different aspects of one great whole. Supernatural theology is a true development of, or an advance founded upon, natural theology. The process of evolution has its influence not only in the realm of nature, but also in that of truth. The history of the knowledge of God is the history of a gradual growth—the history of the disclosure of truths, as man was able to receive them. The evolution of revelation runs on parallel lines with the intellectual and moral progress of man. The subject-matter of which natural and supernatural theology treat, is one and the same—the knowledge of God, viewed under different aspects.

Whilst natural theology appeals primarily to reason and only secondarily to faith, supernatural theology appeals primarily to faith and secondarily to reason. In apprehending the truth concerning God, whether by reason or by faith, a measure of divine assistance is needed. Neither reason nor faith can of themselves arrive at the truth, without the aid of God. Both are His gift: the light of reason and the light of faith proceed from one and the same source. Christ is "the true light, even the light which lighteth every man, coming into the world."[1] "The spirit of man is the lamp of the Lord."[2] But unless the divine light enters into the heart and mind, neither reason nor faith will lead man aright.

Supernatural theology, as the term teaches, is the science of God which is super-imposed, or built upon, natural theology. Natural theology must precede, and prepare the way for the higher and fuller truths of supernatural

[1] St. John i. 9. [2] Prov. xx. 27.

theology. It is the office of reason both to prepare the heart for the full acceptance of the divine revelation, and to assure men of its truth.

"God, having of old time spoken unto the fathers in the prophets by divers portions and in divers manners, hath at the end of these days spoken unto us in His Son."—Heb. i. 1, 2.

"If God operates on nature only by regular processes, which we call *natural laws*, then He must operate on spirit in a different and a more direct way, and this we call *revelation*. If to the student of nature it is inconceivable that He should operate on nature except by natural laws, then to the student of theology it is equally inconceivable that He should not operate on spirit in some more direct and higher way, i.e., by revelation.

"If, then, the direct influence of the Spirit of God on the spirit of man be what we call revelation, then there is evidently no other kind of revelation possible; and, furthermore, such revelation is given to all men in different degrees. It is given to all men as conscience; in greater measure to all great and good men as clearer perception of righteousness; in pre-eminent measure to Hebrew prophets and Christian apostles; but supremely and perfectly to Jesus alone."—Le Conte, *Evolution*, pp. 332, 333.

CHAPTER I.

THE REVELATION OF GOD.

FROM the thought of God, implanted and suggested by natural religion, there follows 'the implicit hope of something further' —the expectation of His Self-disclosure, or revelation. "Has God answered the great prayer of humanity in all the ages? Has He deigned to grant the prayer that He would on His side give some sign or pledge of real communion with us; that He would not leave us to ourselves, walking after our own ways, feeling after Him if happily we might find Him, but only feeling on, century after century, in the twilight of reason; that He would, in prophetic language, rend the heavens and come down, and bid the skies pour forth righteousness? Is religion only a human instinct or effort upon which no encouragement, no sanction, no corresponding and invigorating acknowledgment has been bestowed from on high? Or has God spoken? Has he unveiled Himself?"[1]

If we really believe in God as a Personal,

[1] Liddon, *Some Elements of Religion*, pp. 201, 202.

Moral Being, we shall be prepared to find that He has not disappointed us. The more truly we realize the personality and the morality of God, the stronger becomes our expectation of His Self-disclosure. The desire for self-communication and mutual intercourse is an essential feature of our personal existence. A person is a being capable of communicating with other persons. And it is difficult to believe that a Personal God would create a race of personal beings, such as mankind, without the intention of holding communication with them when created.[1] And the anticipation of a divine revelation is immensely strengthened by the consideration of the moral nature of God. 'If God has, or rather is, a Heart; if the moral qualities which are discoverable in ourselves have any transcendent and majestic counterpart in Him,' then the expectation of a divine revelation becomes more assured.

It is of this divine revelation that we are now about to treat. Hitherto, we have been occupied in considering man's search after God. By a divine revelation we are to understand God's search after man, His crowning of man's efforts to find Him by the gift of an authenticated and authoritative disclosure of Himself. We are about to view God as 'a rewarder of them that seek after Him.'

[1] See Illingworth, *Bampton Lectures*, vi. p. 138.

i.

In the first place it is to be noted that God's revelation to mankind is no momentary or isolated act, but rather a long series of acts, forming a continuous whole. At no time in the history of the human race has God 'left Himself without witness'; and this testimony to Himself has grown in strength and intensity with the progress of mankind. It is a common though mistaken idea that the divine revelation was given suddenly without preparation, and that it disclosed truths altogether different in *kind* from ideas already held. In this view revelation is regarded in the light of a heavenly vision, utterly unconnected with everything which had gone before. It is erroneously supposed, that between the special revelation claimed by the Jews, and the beliefs of surrounding nations, there was nothing in common; and that the ancient and vast religious systems existing in Jewish times, were entirely void of any measure of the knowledge of God. And further, it has been held that the special or authenticated revelation, gradually made to the patriarchs and the prophets of the chosen race, stamped as altogether false all other forms of belief held outside its sphere. And the same narrow view has been suffered to colour the conception of the Christian revelation. The Christian revelation is sometimes regarded as the only revelation of truth, differing not only in *degree*, but also in *kind*, from every other form of belief. It is held that to be anything but a Christian, is to be in utter ignorance of any kind of knowledge of God.

Such a view is utterly untenable. If the Christian revelation claims to be final, as it certainly does, it throws no discredit upon what was true and right, even in the religions of savage and barbarous tribes. The position claimed for the Christian revelation, in regard to earlier religious beliefs, is similar to that claimed for the human race in reference to the lower animal world. In man is found all the best elements of the simpler and earlier organisms of the animal world. Man is, as far as this world goes, the climax and end of evolution.[1] His present exalted position in creation in no wise throws discredit upon the lower stages of his earlier existence, or merely animal state; it has only been reached by passing through these lower stages, and retaining all that was useful in them. Thus, the Christian revelation in no way depreciates earlier and less perfect forms of religious belief. If such forms of belief are held to be a falling away from a higher and purer revela-

---

[1] "'On the earth there will never be a higher creature than man.' It is a daring prophecy, but every probability of science attests the likelihood of its fulfilment. The goal looked forward to from the beginning of time has been attained. Nature has succeeded in making a man; she can go no further; organic evolution has done its work."— Drummond, *The Ascent of Man*, p. 126.

tion, Christianity claims to have sifted out, and gathered up all that was true and good in them, and to have purged them from what was false. The Christian revelation in no way excludes any germs of truth previously held by man, it rather includes, develops, harmonizes, supplements, and authenticates them.

"Christianity," writes Mr. Gore, "is the one final revelation, the one final religion; but it supersedes all other religions, Jewish and pagan, not by *excluding* but by *including* all the elements of truth which each contained. There was light in Zoroastrianism, light in Buddhism, light among the Greeks; but it is all included in Christianity. A good Christian is a good Buddhist, a good Jew, a good Mahommedan, a good Zoroastrian—that is, he has all the truth and virtue that these can possess, purged and fused in a greater and completer light. Christianity, I say, supersedes all other religions by including their fragments of truth in its own completeness. You cannot show me any element of spiritual light or strength which is in other religions, and is not in Christianity. Nor can you show me any other religion which can compare with Christianity in completeness of light. Christianity is the one complete and final religion, and the elements of truth in other religions are rays of the One Light, which is concentrated and shines full in Jesus Christ our Lord."[1]

[1] *The Creed of the Christian*, p. 29.

ii.

If we would hold true and reasonable ideas as to the position to be assigned to the Christian revelation, we must recognize its connection with what came before. The Christian revelation is not the beginning, but the end of God's Self-disclosure. "The world, throughout its entire historical period, has been constituted the canvas on which the divine revelation (of the Christian religion) has been painted —and painted so gradually that not until the process had been going on for a couple of thousand years was it possible to perceive the subject thereof."[1] The Christian revelation is the latest and most complete of a long series of divine communications to mankind. It is the purification, concentration, enlargement, and conclusion, of all previous ideas about God and man's duty to Him. Revelation has been progressive, not only historically, but also intellectually and morally. It is by this method that it has kept abreast of the progress of our race. It is because men fail to put their minds back far enough in the scale of human progress, that they find it difficult to believe that dim, grotesque, and imperfect conceptions of God, could convey any truth to primitive man. Men will make the mistake of reading modern ideas of the fitness of things into the history of primitive times, and of expecting to find then what

[1] Romanes, *Thoughts on Religion*, p. 173.

The Revelation of God.

is right and proper now. We cannot argue concerning the mind and heart of a savage, living some thousands of years ago, as we do about the mind and heart of a civilized and educated person of our own times. What is reasonable and intelligible in an advanced stage of intellectual and moral progress, is utterly unreasonable and unintelligible in a lower stage. What is now in harmony with the advance of educated thought, would have been completely unadapted to the requirements of man in his infancy. Revelation all along the ages was made as men became capable of receiving it. Thus, the Christian revelation was made in 'the fulness of the time,' that is, at the very moment, not before, when the human race was sufficiently advanced to recognize it.

"God can no more *force* an immediate moral enlightenment upon an existing age, and antedate a high moral standard by two thousand years, than He can instantaneously impart a particular character to an individual. He has endowed man with intellectual faculties of a certain kind, which move in a certain way, and with a gradual progressive motion requiring time. He cannot impart to it a truth in such a way as contradicts the institution of the understanding, and communicate in a moment that which, by the laws of the being's nature, can only be received slowly and by degrees.

The natural motion of the human understanding is by steps and stages."[1]

iii.

The instruments or vehicles of God's revelation to man fall under five heads. His revelation in nature, in man, through prophets, through a chosen people, in Christ. These are 'the many parts and many manners' in which the divine Self-disclosure has been made to mankind.[2]

(1) *God's revelation in nature.* 'Everything which is, is a revelation of God.' All nature is the disclosure of God. "The heavens declare the glory of God; and the firmament sheweth His handywork."[3] "The invisible things of Him since the creation of the world are clearly seen, being perceived through the things that are made, even His everlasting power and divinity."[4] "There is no creature," says the author of *The Imitation of Christ*, "so small and abject, that it representeth not the goodness of God."[5] The natural world testifies to God—to His existence as its Maker, to His wisdom, power, order, and beauty.

"How do you know, a Bedouin was asked, that there is a God? 'In the same way,' he

---

[1] J. B. Mozley, *Ruling Ideas in Early Ages*, p. 244.
[2] See Gore's *Creed of the Christian*, pp. 26, ff., to which the author is largely indebted for the substance of the remainder of this chapter.
[3] Ps. xix. 1.   [4] Rom. i. 20.   [5] Bk. ii. Ch. 4.

The Revelation of God. 173

replied, 'that I know, on looking at the sand, when a man or a beast has crossed the desert—by His footprints in the world around me.'"[1]

> There is a book, who runs may read,
>   Which heavenly truth imparts,
> And all the lore its scholars need,
>   Pure eyes and Christian hearts.
>
> The works of God above, below,
>   Within us and around,
> Are pages in that book, to shew
>   How God Himself is found.
>
> *   *   *   *
>
> Thou, who hast given me eyes to see
>   And love this sight so fair,
> Give me a heart to find out thee,
>   And read thee everywhere.
>
>   Keble, *Christian Year*, Septuagesima.

(2) *God's revelation in man.* The truer and nobler men become, the more clearly they recognize the claims of the moral law on their obedience. The more completely they yield to its claims, the higher they rise in true nobility of character. Thus, man's recognition of the righteous demands of the moral law is a revelation of the righteousness of God. "Ye shall be holy; for I am holy."[2] God is universally revealed to the conscience of mankind. "When Gentiles which have no law (i.e., the Jewish law), do by nature the things of the law, these,

[1] Liddon, *Some Elements of Religion*, p. 55.
[2] 1 St. Pet. i. 16.

having no law, are a law unto themselves; in that they shew the work of the law written in their hearts, their conscience bearing witness therewith, and their thoughts one with another accusing or else excusing them."[1] "Given man such as he is, a belief in divine beings, and, at last, in one Divine Being, is not only a universal, but an *inevitable* fact."[2] Of God's revelation in man, we have already spoken at some length.

(3) *God's revelation through prophets.* By 'prophets,' we understand the flower of mankind in every age,[3] persons possessing greater spiritual insight than their fellows, whose conceptions of God were purer and deeper, whose impressions of His mind and will were more vivid than those of their contemporaries. The prophets proclaimed truths of which they were themselves convinced, and which by their very nature eventually prevailed, and were finally acknowledged. They claimed to be inspired by God, and their claims were recognized by the majority of mankind. In the language of

[1] Rom. ii. 14, 15.
[2] Max Müller, *Anthropological Religion*, p. 93.
[3] "God, while revealing Himself specially and systematically to the people of the election, did not altogether hide Himself from other peoples, but gave them as much light as might suffice to make the darkness of their night tolerable till the dawn should arrive; raising up now and then, here and there, men of comparatively pure, vigorous, moral sentiments, and clear religious intuitions, whose wise thoughts and worthy life should be as starlight amid the gloom of night."—Bruce, *The Chief End of Revelation*, pp. 117, 118.

St. Athanasius, they formed "a sacred school of the knowledge of God, and the conduct of the soul."[1] The prophets in every age are the leaders in science, in art, in moral and social progress, 'the torch-bearers of civilization,' the rulers of kingdoms—"men who feel beyond their fellows some truth of God, and, feeling it, proclaim it, and finding response in the duller consciences of their fellow-men, are recognized as revealers of the light, to be honoured and obeyed."[2] Thus, the mission of the prophets is primarily to their own age, and, in speaking to their own age, they speak also to succeeding ages. It was "by the mouth of His holy prophets, which have been since the world began,"[3] that God spake "by divers portions and in divers manners of old time unto the fathers."[4]

(4) *God's revelation to the Jews.* In pre-Christian history, the Jews stand out as the chosen people of God—the people who enjoyed His special protection. As 'a race eminent in a desire of holiness, they were selected for emin-

---

[1] *de Incarn.* xii. 5
[2] *The Creed of the Christian*, p. 28.
[3] St. Luke i. 70.
[4] Heb. i. 1.

"The whole human race has tended to believe in personal gods, and in the possibility of intercourse with them; and the higher degrees of that intercourse, by the common consent of every nation, have been attributed only to the few; while the few in divers degrees have professed its experience and transmitted its tradition. It is in the company of these few, though eminent above them, that the Hebrew prophets stand."—Illingworth, *Bampton Lectures*, vii. p. 179.

ence in degree of revelation. The Jews claimed to possess a clearer and fuller measure of divine light and truth than any of the surrounding nations. This claim has been generally allowed. All the fragments of truth concerning God possessed by other peoples were held by them in a completer whole. In the Jewish revelation is found gathered together and summed up all the rays of divine light, which had previously fallen upon mankind. The Jewish nation had a more intense consciousness of God than any earlier or contemporary nation. The Jewish idea of God and man's duty to Him, imperfect as it is from a Christian standpoint, was nevertheless well in advance of any such ideas current amongst other nations. Of these higher ideas it is generally admitted that the Hebrew prophets were the best exponents.

(5) *God's revelation in Christ.* This forms the crown and climax of all God's previous Self-disclosures—the end to which everything from the first had been gradually tending. "God, having of old time spoken unto the fathers in the prophets by divers portions and in divers manners, hath at the end of these days spoken unto us in His Son."[1] In Christ, we find the true and perfect revelation of God to mankind: for Christ claimed to be very God in human form. "He that hath seen me hath seen the Father."[2]

"In the beginning was the Word, and the

[1] Heb. i. 1, 2.   [2] St. John xiv. 9.

The Revelation of God.

Word was with God, and the Word was God. The same was in the beginning with God. All things were made by Him; and without Him was not anything made that hath been made. In Him was life; and the life was the light of men. And the light shineth in the darkness; and the darkness apprehended it not. . . . And the Word became flesh, and dwelt among us (and we beheld His glory, glory as of the only begotten from the Father), full of grace and truth."[1]

God's Self-disclosure in the Incarnation was no strange thing, unconnected with His previous disclosures to which we have referred—His revelation in nature, in man, through prophets, to the Jews.[2]

---

[1] St. John i. 1-14.

[2] "God has been everywhere revealing Himself; in nature, in its power, order, beauty; in man, in his individual and social conscience, in his various sciences, in the movements of human progress; in His prophets who have received more vividly than others the impression of His glory and His will. In all ways and places God has been manifesting Himself, and all these various and complex revelations come to a centre where He, the one true God, is personally manifested in a human nature, the human nature of Jesus, very man and very God, in whom is the perfect revelation of the Father's nature and the perfect revelation of the capacity and dignity of man."—*The Creed of the Christian*, p. 34.

"From the Christian point of view, this revelation of God, this unfolding of divine qualities, reaches a climax in Christ. God has expressed in inorganic nature, His immutability, immensity, power, wisdom: in organic nature He has shown also that He is alive: in human nature He has given glimpses of His mind and character. In Christ not one of these earlier revelations is abrogated: nay, they are re-affirmed: but they reach a completion in the fuller exposition of the divine character, the divine personality, the divine love."—Gore, *Bampton Lectures*, ii. pp. 32, 33.

Revelation, from beginning to end, forms one continuous process. At every stage the Word of God, at last manifest in the flesh, was at work in the world. All through the darkness of previous ages the light was dimly shining, though 'the darkness apprehended it not.' The heathen, who were true to such light as they possessed, were unconsciously recognizing the True Light. Even before He was incarnate, 'He was in the world, and the world knew Him not.' He was at all times "the True Light which lighteth every man, coming into the world."[1] His coming into the world was a long and slow process. It had been going on and increasing from the dawn of history. "He had been gradually becoming more and more powerfully present. He was more present in man than in nature: more present in prophets than in common men: most of all present when He personally took a human nature in which to show Himself."[2] He was coming more and more all along the ages, until at last He was no longer coming, but come. Just as from the beginning of creation, God had ever been resident and at work in the natural world, as the Cause of all causation; so the Word had never been absent from the world of human thought and action, though men in their blindness knew Him not.

Surely, this is a doctrine full of comfort when we consider the case of the unnum-

[1] St. John i. 9. [2] *The Creed of the Christian*, p. 36.

bered millions, who lived and passed to their account before the Saviour came. The Christian believes that God made Man is "the Saviour of all men, specially of them that believe," [1] —not only the Saviour of those that believe in Him as revealed in the Incarnation; but of all men who, living before His visible manifestation in the flesh, were true to such light as they possessed, and faithful to the opportunities afforded them.

"Since the Fall, the Spirit of God has assisted from the beginning every man that has come into the world born of Adam; so that there never yet was any soul which had not sufficient grace, if it had sufficient fidelity to correspond with it, to escape eternal death. Keep ever in mind this great truth; for it is the foundation of the whole doctrine of grace. There are men so narrow as to say, that no soul among the heathen can be saved. The perfections of God, the attributes of mercy, love, tenderness, justice, equity—all rise up in array against so dark a theology. The word of God declares, first of all, that the Son of God is 'the true Light which lighteth every man as he cometh into the world.' (St. John i. 9, *marg.*) Every soul created in the likeness of God is illuminated by the light of God, even in his creation. There never yet was a soul born into the world that had not the light of reason, and the light of

[1] 1 Tim. iv. 10.

conscience, that is, the light of God shining in the soul." [1]

NOTE ON THE RELATION OF CHRISTIANITY TO OTHER RELIGIONS.

"We have no interest whatever, as Christians, in pouring any ridicule or contempt upon 'other religions,' or in depreciating the value of any truth or beauty which may be found latent or expressed in any doctrine or myth of the Brahmin, the Buddhist, the Mahommedan, or in the savages' religions, or which can be traced in the exploded mythologies of the defunct religious systems of antiquity. All light is from the Source of Light. We do not look upon our Lord as the founder of a rival religion, but as the Light which lighteth every man that cometh into the world. There, in Him, was and is the light, the true light which lighteth every man; at His coming that light was made manifest, but not created. He was in the world, in the hearts of men, although they knew Him not. We believe He is still working in men now, although they know Him not yet, and have never yet recognized His voice as that of the Word of God. We do not speak thus in spite of our Faith, but because of our Faith, and of our attachment to the fundamental doctrine of the Catholic religion. We do not speak thus because we want to find some excuse for the temporary indulgence of a charitable disposition, or for getting out of the groove of our narrow religious associations. We speak thus because, with the Bible and the Creed in our hands, we must do violence to both if we take narrow views of the Person of Christ and of His work in the universe, or if we look upon Him as having shed no light beyond the pale of Christendom, or as having stirred no yearnings after goodness and glory save in the minds of those who are consciously to themselves under His inspiring illumination, and consciously to themselves the objects of His eternal charity, . . . There must be in the mind of a servant of Christ, a delighted readiness to welcome every good and beautiful thought, every maxim of justice, of purity, or of pity, every effort to bring about a peaceful although costly reconciliation of man to His Maker, and every dream of such a

[1] Manning, *The Internal Mission of the Holy Ghost*, pp. 6, 7.

reconciliation of which he may find any record or traces in any of the religions of the world ; and not only to welcome them, but to own them, as signs that the Word of God has not left Himself without a witness anywhere, and that He is preparing the hearts of men to lay hold on the news, on the Gospel, which they are anxious to hear, and which we believe they all want."—Footman, *Reasonable Apprehensions and Reassuring Hints*, 3rd ed. pp. 104, ff.

"All knowledge of religion," wrote Cardinal Newman, "is from God, and not only that which the Bible has transmitted to us. There never was a time when God had not spoken to man, and told him to a certain extent his duty. . . . We are expressly told in the New Testament, that at no time He left Himself without witness in the world, and that in every nation He accepts those who fear and obey Him. It would seem, then, that there is something true and divinely revealed, in every religion all over the earth, overloaded, as it may be, and at times even stifled by the impieties which the corrupt will and understanding of man have incorporated with it. Such are the doctrines of the power and presence of an invisible God, of His moral law and governance, of the obligation of duty, and the certainty of a just judgment, and of reward and punishment, as eventually dispensed to individuals ; so that revelation, properly speaking, is an universal, not a local gift ; and the distinction between the state of Israelites formerly and Christians now, and that of the heathen, is, not that we can, and they cannot attain to future blessedness, but that the Church of God ever has had, and the rest of mankind never have had, authoritative documents of truth, and appointed channels of communication with Him."—*The Arians of the Fourth Century*, 4th ed. pp. 79, 80.

See also Liddon's *Some Elements of Religion*, pp. 40, 41. "No instructed Christian would deny that certain forms of heathenism embrace incidentally the recognition of considerable districts of fundamental truth," &c.

" I should not be afraid to say before an audience of Brâhmans, Buddhists, Parsis, and Jews, that there is no religion in the whole world which in simplicity, in purity of purpose, in charity and true humanity, comes near to that religion which Christ taught to His disciples."—Max Müller, *Natural Religion*, p. 569.

"Do thou, of whom I see the footprints in natural things, but most of all in human beings, in those who have thoughts, and reasons, and wills—in those who feel that these are not meant to be the servants of their senses, or of the things with which their senses deal,—do thou tell me who thou art, and how I may draw nigh to thee. Tell me what thou hast to do with man, for something thou must have. Tell me if there be a man, and where he is, in whom I may behold thee; one who is not here to-day, and gone to-morrow; but who, amidst all changes of times, the disappearance of generations, lives on. Tell me if there be indeed a King and High Priest of the universe—a man actually divine."— Maurice, *The Religions of the World*, 3rd ed. p. 92.

CHAPTER II.

THE PERSON OF CHRIST

THE EVIDENCE OF THE CHRISTIAN REVELATION.

' IF there is a Deity, it seems to be in some indefinite degree more probable that He should impart a revelation, than that He should not.' That God has imparted a revelation to man, is claimed in greater or less degree, as a fact of experience, by all forms of religion from the very first. It is claimed specially by the Jews, and more completely still by the Christian Church. The *subject* of the Christian revelation is the disclosure of God and of man in Jesus Christ. The *evidence* upon which the Christian revelation mainly relies is the Person and the authority of its revealer, Jesus Christ. The Christian revelation finds its justification in the unique Personality of Christ. It is a revelation which is asserted on the highest historical evidence.

i.

That Jesus of Nazareth, the Son of Mary, lived upon the earth and was put to death nearly two thousand years ago, is an historical fact which admits of no dispute. "Such writers as Strauss and Renan, while deeming themselves free to deal in any manner they please with the Gospel histories, never dream of denying the historical existence of Him whom we describe as Jesus Christ. To them, He is simply Jesus of Nazareth; but at least He is that; and in that character they acknowledge Him to be one of the notable men of history."[1] It is also an unquestioned fact of history that during His life on earth, those who were in closest contact with Him came by degrees to recognize His teaching as authoritative. Even His enemies confessed, "Never man so spake."[2] Through constant association with Him, by hearing His words, by witnessing His acts of love and power, by the influence of His most holy life, by the conviction of His triumph over death,—through experience of all this, those best fitted to judge became gradually convinced that Jesus Christ was more than human, that He was superhuman, divine.

And this belief, which had been so slowly and unconsciously arrived at—the belief that He was the Son of God made Man, His followers proclaimed far and wide. They witnessed to the divine claims of Jesus of Nazareth, and from their testimony has sprung up that vast company of believers in Him in all

[1] Bp. Harvey Goodwin, *The Foundations of the Creed*, p. 75.
[2] St. John vii. 46.

ages, amongst all nations, in all parts of the world. His final charge to His apostles, " Ye shall be my witnesses both in Jerusalem, and in all Judæa and Samaria, and unto the uttermost part of the earth,"[1] they literally and unfalteringly fulfilled, even unto death. All this is hard historical fact, which cannot be gainsaid. The authority of Jesus Christ of Nazareth is the basis of this fact, and this authority He rested on His claim to be divine.

NOTE ON THE APOSTOLIC TESTIMONY.

The apostles "could not be deceivers. By only *not bearing testimony* they might have avoided all these sufferings, and have lived quietly. Would men in such circumstances pretend to have seen what they never saw; assert facts which they had no knowledge of; go about lying to teach virtue; and, though not only convinced of Christ's being an impostor, but having seen the success of His imposture in His crucifixion, yet persist in carrying it on; and so persist as to bring upon themselves for nothing, and with a full knowledge of the consequence, enmity and hatred, danger and death?"—Paley, *Evidences*, Ch. x.

"If ever such a book as the 'History of testimony' is worthily and fairly written, the apostles will take very high rank among the world's witnesses. As represented in the Gospels they were men not of the poorest, but of the most independent trading class; simple, literal-minded men; not superstitious and still less romantic; free from all traces of morbidness; slow of belief through lack of imagination; as individuals strikingly different in character, so as not easily to be led the same way; with the exception of St. John, not well adapted to be theologians, and none of them (like St. Paul) controversial theologians; but singularly well qualified as witnesses. They were qualified as witnesses because, free from all preoccupation with ideas and systems, they were plain men who could receive the impress of facts; who could tell a simple plain tale and show by their lives how

[1] Acts i. 8.

much they believed it. And they were trained to be witnesses. Jesus Christ intended His Gospel to rest on facts; and in correspondence with this intention, the whole stress in the apostolic Church was laid on witness. The first thing the Church had to do, before it developed its theology, was to tell its tale of fact. 'We are witnesses of these things.'"—Gore, *Bampton Lectures*, iii. pp. 74, 75.

"Who among the disciples of Christ, or among their proselytes, was capable of inventing the sayings ascribed to Jesus, or of imagining the life and character revealed in the Gospels? Certainly not the fishermen of Galilee; as certainly not St. Paul, whose character and idiosyncrasies were of a totally different sort; still less the early Christian writers, in whom nothing is more evident than that the good which was in them was all derived, as they always professed that it was derived, from the higher source."—J. S. Mill, *Essays on Religion*, p. 253. See also Bp. Harvey Goodwin's *Foundations of the Creed*, p. 76; and Holland's brilliant sermon, The Gospel Witness, in *on Behalf of Belief*, pp. 50, ff.

ii.

We must remember that the records of the life and work of Christ, which we know as 'the Gospels,' had no share in the first spread of the belief in His Divinity. The life and work came first, the record of that life and work followed later. The eye-witnesses of the life of Christ handed on their faith in His divine claims to others: the record, when it came, corroborated the witness already borne, and preserved that witness to future ages. In our own times the study of the Gospel record of the deeds and words of Jesus Christ, and the permanent experience of His power on believers, makes the original witness of the companions of Jesus Christ more and more credible.

That the record of the life, works, and words of Christ, given in the Gospels, is a true record, is now fully and finally established. The most searching examination to which the Gospels have lately been subjected, has only resulted in establishing more firmly their truthfulness, and trustworthiness, as historical documents. No literature has ever been subjected to more vehement and hostile criticism, to more 'energetic, persevering, inventive, and unsparing attack,' than the Gospels. And in spite of this, or rather as the result of this, their genuineness as historical records stands firmer to-day than ever. "Even within the region of pure reason," wrote Mr. Romanes, "modern science, as directed on the New Testament criticism, has surely done more for Christianity than against it. For, after half a century of battle over the text by the best scholars, the dates of the Gospels have been fixed within the first century, and at least four of St. Paul's epistles have had their authenticity proved beyond doubt. Now this is enough to destroy all eighteenth-century criticism as to the doubtfulness of the historical existence of Christ and His apostles, 'inventions of priests,' &c., which was the most formidable kind of criticism of all. There is no longer any question as to historical facts. . . . The Pauline epistles of proved authenticity are enough for all that is wanted to show the belief of Christ's contemporaries."[1]

[1] *Thoughts on Religion*, pp. 168, 169.

NOTE ON THE GENUINENESS OF THE GOSPELS.

"Since the beginning of the present century the text of the first three, and indeed of all the Evangelists, has been submitted to the minutest investigation. Scholars and critics of every shade of opinion have, with an instinctive sense of the great issues involved in the question of Gospel credibility, bestowed an amount of laborious research upon their task such as no mere forgeries, however skilful, could for a moment have resisted. And although it can hardly be said, even yet, that their assiduity has been crowned with success sufficient to recommend any one theory as to the actual composition of the Gospels as entirely beyond dispute; yet it is hardly too much to say that the historical reliability of the Synoptics (St. Matthew, St. Mark, St. Luke), as genuine and authentic records of actual events, has now been fairly established.

"Turning to *the Fourth Gospel* (St. John), we approach the very central point of modern critical assault. . . . Perhaps the most valuable (as it is certainly not the least laborious and learned) contribution to the study of the Fourth Gospel is Professor Westcott's Introduction, published in 1880, in *The Speaker's Commentary*. After the work of more than twenty-five years, Dr. Westcott has succeeded in producing what may probably be found to be a supreme vindication of the entirely reliable character of the Gospel and its authorship by St. John himself."—H. B. Ottley, *The Great Dilemma*, pp. 10, ff.

The reader, who desires to look into the subject of the genuineness of the Gospels, and certain of St. Paul's epistles, will do well to consult Mr. Ottley's treatise, Lect. i. pp. 10–17, where the matter is fully dealt with, and a long list of authorities given; also Dr. Liddon's *Bampton Lectures*, v. pp. 208–226; and Mr. Gore's *Bampton Lectures*, iii.; v. pp. 58–79, with Appended Notes, pp. 248–250. The subject is also treated by Dr. Sanday, in the Oxford House Papers, First Series, *Free-Thinking*, pp. 22–67: and by Dr. Eagar, in his *Butler's 'Analogy' and Modern Thought*, v. pp. 144–162.

In regard to the alleged discrepancies in the Gospels, it is enough to say, with St. Chrysostom in the fourth century, that they do not touch any main points, but the rather confirm the independent testimony of the witnesses. His words are—"Was not one evangelist sufficient to tell all? One indeed was sufficient, but if there be four that write, not at the same times, nor in the same places, neither after having met together, and conversed one with another, and then they speak all things as it were out of one mouth, this becomes a very great demonstration of the truth.

"But the contrary, it may be said, hath come to pass, for in many places they are convicted of discordance. Nay, this very thing is a very great evidence of their truth. For if they had agreed in all things exactly even to time, and place, and to the very words, none of our enemies would have believed, but that they had met together, and had written what they wrote by some human compact; because such entire agreement as this cometh not of simplicity. But now even that discordance which seems to exist in little matters delivers them from all suspicion, and speaks clearly in behalf of the character of the writers.

"But if there be any thing touching times or places, which they have related differently, this nothing injures the truth of what they have said. And these things too, so far as God shall enable us, we will endeavour, as we proceed, to point out; requiring you, together with what we have mentioned, to observe, that in the chief heads, those which constitute our life and furnish out our doctrine, nowhere is any of them found to have disagreed, no not ever so little.

"But what are these points? Such as follow—That God became Man, that He wrought miracles, that He was crucified, that He was buried, that He rose again, that He ascended, that He will judge, that He hath given commandments tending to salvation, that He hath brought in a law not contrary to the Old Testament, that He is a Son, that He is only begotten, that He is a true Son, that He is of the same substance with the Father, and as many things as are like these; for touching these we shall find that there is in them a full agreement."—*Homily on St. Matt.* I. v, vi.

iii.

Every revelation implies a medium, or mediator, through whom the revelation is made. Every system of supposed revealed religion has rested upon some such mediator—for example, Buddha amongst the Buddhists, Mahommed amongst the Mahommedans. But it is to be observed, that the position claimed for Jesus Christ in regard to the Christian revelation is altogether of a different order. Jesus Christ was not a mere voice, or mouthpiece, declaring truths in which He was interested equally with His hearers. He was not merely a prophet, proclaiming truths of which He was more vividly conscious than His fellows: He was not only the greatest of religious teachers: He was more than all this. He was the subject of His own teaching. He was Himself the revelation. His revelation was the disclosing of Himself. He declared the truth, because He was the Truth. He not only spake the word of God, He was the Word of God.

Thus, all the chief evidences of the truth which Jesus Christ revealed, cluster round His own Person. The truth was not so much revealed *by* Him, as *in* Him. Hence, we believe what Christ revealed, because we believe what He is. "Lord, to whom shall we go? thou hast the words of eternal life. And we have believed and know that thou art the Holy One of God."[1] A true acceptance of the revelation which Jesus Christ made, ever depends upon a true belief in His divine Person. To the innate craving of the human soul for the knowledge of God—"Lord, shew us the Father, and it sufficeth us," Jesus Christ replies, "He that hath seen me hath seen the Father."[2]

Not only did Jesus Christ disclose God to

[1] St. John vi. 68, 69.   [2] Ibid. xiv. 8, 9.

evidence of the Christian revelation. 191

man, but, in the language of St. Irenæus, "He exhibited man to God."[1] As God and Man in One Person, Jesus Christ disclosed perfect God, and perfect man. In Him, we see the true nature and character of God, and the true nature and character of man. We learn in Him to view God, and our own manhood aright. He revealed God as He is, and man as God meant him to be. He revealed God's willingness to receive man into union with Himself, and man's capacity for that union.

iv.

What, then, are the evidences of the truth of the assertion of Jesus Christ to be the revelation of God and man? How are we to be assured of the truth of the Truth? How do we know that Jesus Christ is divine? The evidences of the truth of the claims of Jesus Christ may be considered under five heads, and of these we will now proceed to speak.

i. The characteristics of Christ as the teacher.

ii. The characteristics of His teaching.

iii. The influence of Christ upon the world.

iv. The existence of the Church of Christ.

v. The supernatural elements in His life.

[1] iv. 20. 7.

I. THE CHARACTERISTICS OF JESUS CHRIST AS THE TEACHER.

1. *The unconsciousness in Jesus Christ of any moral defect.* In His character as the revelation of God, it was necessary for Christ often to speak of Himself; but He never once spoke of Himself, or seemed to conceive of Himself, as liable to sin. He claimed to have power on earth to forgive sins,[1] and to be the final judge of all men.[2] Such a tremendous claim at least implied His own freedom from sin. In the whole range of His lofty moral teaching, there is a complete absence of any sense of unworthiness, such as One so transparently sincere must have acknowledged, had there been in His life the slightest deviation from the moral law which He proclaimed. The messengers of the Lord, in declaring His righteous law, have ever felt their personal unfitness to deliver His message to man. "Woe is me! for I am undone; because I am a man of unclean lips,"[3] has ever been the cry of those commissioned by God to proclaim His law to their fellow-men. And this sense of personal unworthiness has been always felt in exact proportion to the holiness of the speaker. "Conscious of many shortcomings, a human teacher must at some time relieve his natural sense of honesty, his fundamental instinct of justice, by noting the discrepancy between his

[1] St. Mark ii. 10.   [2] St. Matt. xxv. 31, ff.   [3] Is. vi. 5.

weak, imperfect, perhaps miserable self, and his sublime and awful message."[1] They who live nearest to God, are ever those who most feel their unfitness for such nearness. "Blemishes which might have passed unobserved in a spiritual twilight, are lighted up with torturing clearness by those searching, scorching rays of moral truth, that stream from the bright sanctity of God upon the soul that beholds it."[2]

But Jesus Christ lived in the closest communion with God, without betraying the slightest consciousness of fault. No confession of sin, no cry for mercy, no expression of remorse, ever escaped His lips. One who approached Him with the salutation, "Good Master," without realizing the full import of his words, was met by the rebuke, "Why callest thou me good?"[3] when all the time He was encouraging those who knew what they meant, to use 'language far higher' in addressing Him, and to pay Him 'more deliberate honours.' In the midst of His unparalleled sufferings, He made no admission of any sinfulness for which they might be the just desert. He fearlessly challenged His enemies to convict Him of sin, "Which of you convicteth me of sin?"[4] and the challenge was unanswered. He enforced the highest possible morality, "Ye therefore shall be perfect, as your heavenly

[1] Liddon, *Bampton Lectures*, iv. p. 163.   [2] Ibid. p. 164.
[3] St. Mark x. 17, 18.   [4] St. John viii. 46.

Father is perfect,"[1] without giving the least expression of any imperfection in Himself. He bade men be like God, whilst giving not even the slightest hint of any consciousness of unlikeness to God in Himself. He declared unhesitatingly, "I do always the things that are pleasing to the Father."[2] When we consider all this in connection with His absolute truthfulness and genuine humility, "it is," as Dr. Liddon points out, "at the very least, suggestive of a relation to the Perfect Moral Being altogether unique in human history."[3]

2. *The conscious authority of Jesus Christ.* "He taught them as one having authority, and not as their scribes."[4] The scribes, like all other merely human teachers, argued, explained, strove to prove what they taught; but Jesus Christ simply declared tremendous truths without argument or justification, and often without explanation. As a teacher, He ever assumed a lofty attitude towards those whom He taught. He spoke as one from whose authority there was no appeal. He contrasted His teaching with that of the teachers of the Law of Moses, "It was said to them of old time. . . . But I say unto you."[5] As a teacher, He set Himself up as higher than Moses, the great law-giver, and the law written

---

[1] St. Matt. v. 48.   [2] St. John viii. 29.
[3] *Bampton Lectures*, iv. p. 166.
[4] St. Matt. vii. 29.   [5] Ibid. v. 21, 22.

by the finger of God on the tables of stone. His common preface to His higher doctrines was, "Verily, verily, I say unto you." He taught mankind with the consciousness that He not only spoke the truth, but that He was the Truth.[1]

And this authoritativeness of Jesus Christ goes far beyond His teaching, it enfolds Him and His actions as a robe. "With authority He announces beforehand His passion and resurrection after three days, and the worldwide spread of His Gospel, and the glory of the saints with Himself when He shall come at the last day to exercise divine judgment. With authority He controls the devils. With authority He governs physical nature. He heals men's bodies, and commands their allegiance."[2]

As we listen to His authoritative declaration of sublime truths, do we not instinctively feel that we are listening no longer to a human, but to a divine teacher? The whole attitude of Jesus Christ as a teacher of truth is that of One who is more than man, of One who is divine.

3. *The self-assertion of Jesus Christ.* The most striking characteristic of Jesus Christ as a

---

[1] "Jesus Christ said great things so simply that He seems not to have considered them, and yet so tersely that it is clear He had considered them. This clearness joined with simplicity is wonderful."—Pascal, *Proofs of the Divinity of Jesus Christ*, p. 221.

[2] Gore, *Bampton Lectures*, iii. p. 65.

teacher is His self-assertion. As we study the records of His words in the Gospels, we cannot fail to be struck again and again by the absolute self-confidence with which He speaks. He declared Himself to be "greater than the most venerable names in Jewish antiquity; greater than the men whose greatness had been felt most widely and deeply beyond the boundaries of Israel. He is greater than Jonah, whose preaching brought Nineveh to penitence;[1] greater than Solomon, in whom not Israel only, but the whole East, recognized the wisest of men.[2] Not merely is He David's descendant; He is David's Lord.[3] When Abraham was yet unborn, He was already in existence.[4] Thus He could refer to 'the glory which He had with the Father before the world was,'[5] and to the fall of the rebel-spirit, which He had witnessed.[6] God is, in an entirely unique sense, His Father;[7] the Jews feel[8] that He uses the word in a manner which implies a tremendous claim."[9] He asserts pre-existence before His human birth, again and again.[10] He claims the king-

---

[1] St. Matt. xii. 41.   [2] Ibid. xii. 42.
[3] Ibid. xxii. 41-46; Ps. cx. i.
[4] St. John viii. 56-58; cf. i. 15, 27, 30.
[5] Ibid. xvii. 5; cf. verse 24.   [6] St Luke x. 18.
[7] St. Matt. x. 32; xv. 13; xvi. 17; xviii. 19; xxvi. 39, 42; St. Luke xxiii. 46; xxiv. 49; St. John v. 36; x. 29; xiv. 2, 6.
[8] St. John v. 17, 18.
[9] Liddon, *Some Elements of Religion*, p. 216.
[10] St. John vi. 38, 51; viii. 23, 42; xvi. 28.

dom of God as His own.[1] The angelic host is His.[2] He possesses power over all mankind, and gives eternal life to the redeemed.[3] All power is His in heaven and earth.[4] All nations are to be baptized into His Name, equally with that of the Father and the Holy Ghost,[5] and to be taught all things which He had commanded.[6] He asserts that unless men eat His Flesh and drink His Blood, they have no life in them.[7] He claims dominion over the dead,[8] and declares that the hour is coming when they shall hear His voice, and shall come forth.[9] He promises to appear in the last day clothed with the glory of the Eternal Father.[10] To Him the Father hath committed all judgment, and at the last all nations shall be gathered before Him, to receive at His hands the sentence of their everlasting destiny.[11]

If these are true words, are they the words of man, or of God? If the speaker is not God, what can we say but that he is guilty of blasphemous arrogance, and intolerable presumption. *Christus, si non Deus, non bonus*—Christ, if He is not God, is not a good man. If men will not worship Jesus Christ, then they must despise Him. This is the terrible

---

[1] St. Matt. xiii. 41; St. John xviii. 36.
[2] St. Matt. xiii. 41; xvi. 27; xxiv. 31.
[3] St. John xvii. 2.   [4] St. Matt. xxviii. 18.
[5] Ibid. xxviii. 19.   [6] Ibid. 20.   [7] St. John vi. 53.
[8] Ibid. v. 21.   [9] Ibid. 28, 29.   [10] St. Matt. xvi. 27.
[11] Ibid. xxv. 31, ff.

alternative to which the rejecters of His divine claims are committed. This is the dilemma in which unbelievers in the Godhead of Jesus Christ find themselves. It is a dilemma from which there is but one mode of escape. Is our Lord's language, then, that of an impostor, or is it the language of One who speaks the truth?

The question is one which can best be answered from a consideration of the moral character of Jesus Christ, as depicted in the Gospels. In every single particular of the life of Christ, in which the Gospels are a record of ascertained fact or experience, the moral character of Christ is set forth as one which absolutely forbids our doubting either His sincerity, truthfulness, or humility. To disbelieve in His moral integrity, is simply to disbelieve in Him altogether. Putting aside, for the moment, the large class of sayings to which we have referred, and studying what remains in the Gospel record of the life of Christ, there can be no possible doubt but that He lived a life of highest morality, of simple and faultless beauty. And this being so in that of which we have experience, what grounds are there for supposing that, when He speaks of things beyond human experience or verification, He becomes another man? What reason is there for assuming that the grandest and noblest of men was guilty of habitually asserting that which He knew to be false?

What possibility is there of any man living a life of the highest and most stainless moral beauty, and yet being an inveterate blasphemer and impostor? How could any height of moral goodness exist in a heart steeped in such deceit and arrogant self-assertion? The continuance in such iniquity would prove fatal to the moral excellence of any man.

Thus, there is but one way of escape from the dilemma which we have stated. It is to regard the unquestioned holiness of Jesus Christ, as the guarantee of the truthfulness of His divine claims.[1] It is to read His claims in the light of His life—in the light of what we positively know to be true of His character; and to confess that when He claimed the attributes of God, He only spoke the truth —to confess that, in very deed, Jesus Christ is God.

II. THE CHARACTERISTICS OF THE TEACHING OF JESUS CHRIST.

1. *The morality of the teaching of Jesus Christ.* The teaching of Jesus Christ is universally admitted to be that of the highest morality ever proposed to mankind. This is an ad-

[1] "It is easier to believe that God has consummated His works of wonder and of mercy by a crowning Self-revelation in which mercy and beauty reach their climax, than to close the moral eye to the brightest spot that meets it in human history."—Liddon, *Bampton Lectures*, iv. p. 204.

mission which is freely made by those who reject the truth of His Godhead. In the doctrine of Christ is found the concentration of every ray of moral light and excellence previously perceived by man. He pointed out the clear distinction between right and wrong, as it had never before been pointed out. He urged the obligation to inward righteousness, and convinced men of sin, in a degree never before realized. Whilst previous systems exposed the moral defects of man, they failed to suggest the remedy for such defects. In the teaching of Jesus Christ, whilst men are warned of the danger of the least departure from righteousness, they are taught how to avoid it. By His life, He gave the world an example of perfect conformity to the will of God. By His death, He exposed the deadly malice of sin, and provided the means of pardon. By His resurrection, He gave men the power of rising to newness of life.

The study of the Sermon on the Mount, in which Jesus Christ reiterated, enlarged, and spiritualized the teaching of the Mosaic Law, is in itself sufficient to convince any candid mind of the unapproached purity and perfection of His doctrine. "It is," wrote Dr. Liddon, "in the equal balance of all excellence, in the absence of any warping, disturbing, exaggerating influence, that modern writers have been forward to recognize a moral sublimity, which they can discover nowhere else in history."[1]

Man's conviction of the righteousness of the moral law has been rightly considered a conviction of the existence of a righteous Lawgiver. When Jesus Christ proclaimed the moral law, He proclaimed it as only the Author of that law could have proclaimed it. Of this we have already spoken.

2. *The adaptability of the teaching of Jesus Christ to human needs.* Whilst other codes of morality are local, national, or confined to certain stages of human progress, the doctrine of Christ is of universal and permanent application. "The Christian religion," writes Mr. S. Laing, ". . . is an existing fact. It is a fact which for nineteen centuries has proved, on the whole, in accordance with other facts, and with the deepest feelings and highest aspirations of the noblest men and women of the foremost races in the progressive march of civilization."[2] The adaptation of the teaching of Christ to all human needs has been tested by experience through long centuries; and it has stood the test. It is as fresh, and as suitable to human needs to-day, as it was when He first proclaimed it. 'It has passed into the lives of men of all shades of thought and character: it has met human nature in all its varieties.' Its precepts

[1] *Some Elements of Religion*, p. 212.
[2] *Modern Science and Modern Thought*, p. 294.

form the highest rule of life for the prince, and for the peasant. In the words of Principal Tulloch, "beneath all differences of intellect, race, and culture, there is a common soul which the Gospel reaches, and which nothing else in like manner reaches."[1]

"We hear a great deal of progress, intellectual advances, men of culture, and the like. Now, I will ask, Has all the advancement of civilization, in ethics, in politics, and in social culture, refuted, or superseded, or changed the bounds of one revealed truth? Does not Christianity remain at this moment imperishable and immutable? It is constituted of these three aboriginal elements; namely, the purest and most perfect conception of God that man ever knew; the purest and most perfect conception of man, revealed in the Incarnation, that the world ever saw; the purest and most perfect morality—that is, the relations between God and man, and between man and man. I ask whether Christianity, which contains these three great and constructive elements, has in any sense been set aside or shaken by the intellectual, or moral, or political, or social progress of mankind? Has it elevated or corrected the Christian conception of God, or of man, or of morals? Now, I will affirm that it has done no such thing. Like as the ark floated on the waters; the deeper they became, the higher it rose, so does Christianity at this

[1] qu. *Butler's 'Analogy' and Modern Thought*, p. 166.

moment repose in all calmness and majesty on the great flood of human science in its highest cultivation."[1]

The adaptability of the teaching of Jesus Christ to the moral needs of all sorts and conditions of men, in every age, of every nationality, under all possible circumstances, is a most impressive fact. This adaptedness of His teaching to the common and universal needs of mankind, when fairly considered, is a strong testimony to its divine origin.[2] And when we add to this the universal appeal of His death and resurrection to men in all ages, the human heart, which accepts these facts, is prepared to recognize in Jesus Christ One who is more than man.

III. THE INFLUENCE OF JESUS CHRIST.

1. *The influence of Jesus Christ in the progress of the world.* The moral and social progress of

---

[1] Manning, *The Internal Mission of the Holy Ghost*, p. 373.

[2] Mr. Romanes considered the permanent adaptation of the teaching of Christ to be 'one of the strongest pieces of objective evidence in favour of Christianity.' "It is," he wrote, "the absence from the biography of Christ of any doctrines which the subsequent growth of human knowledge —whether in natural science, ethics, political economy, or elsewhere—has had to discount. This negative argument is really almost as strong as is the positive one from what Christ did teach. For when we consider what a large number of sayings are recorded of—or at least attributed to—Him, it becomes most remarkable that in literal truth there is no reason why any of His words should ever pass away in the sense of becoming obsolete."—*Thoughts on Religion*, p. 157.

the world is chiefly due to the influence of Jesus Christ. "It is the example and teaching of Jesus of Nazareth," says Mr. S. Laing, "which have been mainly instrumental in diffusing ideas of divine love, charity, and purity throughout the world."[1] The Incarnation has moulded the history of the human race, for its progress and for its good, ever since it took place. The influence of Christ has proved a solid and actual contribution to the advance of human progress. "Is it not," asks Dr. Liddon, "a simple matter of fact that at this moment the progress of the human race is entirely identified with the spread of the influence of the nations of Christendom?"[2]

"The religion of Christ," writes Mr. Gladstone, "has assumed more visibly than ever a commanding position in the world. It is for mankind the greatest of all phenomena, the greatest of all facts. It is the dominant religion of the inhabitants of this planet at least in two important respects. It commands the largest number of professing adherents. If we estimate the population of the globe at fourteen hundred millions (and some would state a higher figure), between four and five hundred millions of these, or one-third of the whole, are professing Christians; and at every point of the circuit the question is not one of losing ground, but of gaining it. The fallacy which accepted the

[1] *Modern Science and Modern Thought*, p. 289.
[2] *Bampton Lectures*, iii. p. 120.

vast population of China as Buddhists in the mass has been exploded, and it is plain that no other religion approaches the numerical strength of Christianity; doubtful, indeed, whether there be any that reaches to one-half of it. The second of the particulars now under view is perhaps even more important. Christianity is the religion in the command of whose professors is lodged a proportion of power far exceeding its superiority of numbers; and this power is both moral and material. In the area of controversy it can hardly be said to have a serious antagonist. Force, secular or physical, is accumulated in the hands of Christians in a proportion absolutely overwhelming, and the accumulation of influence is not less remarkable than that of force. This is not surprising, for all the elements of influence have their home within the Christian precinct. The art, the literature, the systematised industry, invention, and commerce—in one word, the power — of the world are almost wholly Christian. In Christendom alone there seems to lie an inexhaustible energy of world-wide expansion. The nations of Christendom are everywhere arbiters of the fate of non-Christian nations."[1]

2. *The influence of Jesus Christ upon individuals.* The influence of Christ, which has been the

[1] *The People's Bible History*, General Introduction, p. 6; quoted by permission of Messrs. Sampson Low, Marston and Co.

ground of moral and social progress amongst the nations, has been ever exerting its force upon individuals. As the 'leaven hid in three measures of meal,' the influence of Jesus Christ has permeated the whole mass of believers in His Name, and attracted and energized the inner personal life of countless individual members of our race. When Napoleon I. on a certain occasion was "conversing, as was his habit, about the great men of the ancient world, and comparing himself with them, he turned, it is said, to Count Montholon with the enquiry, 'Can you tell me who Jesus Christ was?' The question was declined, and Napoleon proceeded, 'Well, then, I will tell you. Alexander, Cæsar, Charlemagne, and I myself have founded great empires; but upon what did these creations of our genius depend? Upon force. Jesus alone founded His empire upon love, and to this very day millions would die for Him. . . . I think I understand something of human nature; and I tell you, all these were men, and I am a man: none else is like Him; Jesus Christ was more than man. . . . I have inspired multitudes with such an enthusiastic devotion that they would have died for me, . . . but to do this it was necessary that I should be *visibly* present with the electric influence of my looks, of my words, of my voice. When I saw men and spoke to them, I lighted up the flame of self-devotion in their hearts. . . . Christ alone has succeeded in so raising the mind of man towards the Unseen, that it becomes insensible to the barriers of time and space. Across a chasm of eighteen hundred years, Jesus Christ makes a demand which is beyond all others difficult to satisfy; He asks for that which a philosopher may often seek in vain at the hands of his friends, or a father of his children, or a bride of her spouse, or a man of his brother. He asks for the human heart; He will have it entirely to Himself, He demands it unconditionally; and forthwith His demand is granted. Wonderful! In defiance of time and space, the soul of man, with all its powers and faculties, becomes an annexation to the empire of Christ. All who sincerely believe in Him, experience that remarkable supernatural love towards Him. This phenomenon is unaccountable; it is altogether beyond the scope of man's creative powers. Time, the great destroyer, is powerless to extinguish this sacred flame; time can neither exhaust its strength nor put a limit to its range. This is it which strikes me most; I have often thought of it. This it is which proves to me quite convincingly the Divinity of Jesus Christ.'"[1]

It is this universal range, and permanent character of the influence of Jesus Christ, which is so unique and impressive. The teaching of Christ, as set forth in the Sermon on the Mount, and the Parables of the Kingdom, has been marvellously realized in human history.

[1] qu. Liddon, *Bampton Lectures*, iii. pp. 147, 148.

At this moment, in all parts of the globe where Christianity has come, there is a vast company of souls, living lives of unselfishness, purity, and humility, who, but for Jesus Christ, would be selfish, sensual, and proud. At this moment, there are numbers of men and women living, who have given up all for Christ, and are ready to lay down their lives for His sake. Jesus Christ has produced a new type of humanity, and it is moreover a permanent type.

3. *The influence of Christ beyond the circle of the Christian world.* 'The era of *humanity* is the era of the Incarnation.' The influence of Jesus Christ has radiated from His own Person into the outer world. It is to Christianity that slavery owes its suppression. It is through Christianity that the rights of the poor are more and more recognized and respected. It is to Christianity that the sick and suffering owe the blessings of loving care in our hospitals.[1] It is by Christianity that woman has

[1] "When, in the terrible pestilences with which Carthage and Alexandria were visited in the third and fourth centuries of the Christian era, the sick and dying were abandoned by their heathen relatives, it was by Christians that they were received and cared for."—qu. Stewart, *Handbook of Christian Evidences,* p. 75.

"Although in ancient times there may have been places for the reception of strangers and travellers, it seems at least doubtful if there was anything of the nature of a charitable institution for the reception of the sick, such as existed after the introduction of Christianity."—*Encycl. Brit.* 9th ed. vol. xii. p. 301.

See also Lecky, *History of European Morals,* vol. ii. pp. 84, 85.

been raised from degradation to honour. It is through Christianity that the nations are being taught to regard each other as brethren.[1]

What is the secret of this wonderful, lasting, and living influence of Jesus Christ? Is it His miracles of love and mercy, His character, His teaching, His death, His resurrection? Is it all these put together? Assuredly not. Combined together they are inadequate to account for the secret of His mighty influence. But one fact can possibly explain the marvel—the fact that He is divine. If Jesus Christ is not God, then all the striking phenomena of His influence are based on misrepresentation and fraud. Such a supposition has only to be entertained to be rejected. There is but one solution which adequately explains the problem. The influence of Jesus Christ is the divine influence—Jesus Christ is God.

IV. THE EXISTENCE OF THE CHURCH OF JESUS CHRIST.

The story is related of a certain prince, who doubted, requesting his chaplain to produce some clear evidence of the truth of the Christian religion; and to do this briefly, since his time to attend to the matter was limited. The chaplain answered the demand in the concise words, 'The Jews, your majesty.' The chaplain

[1] See Liddon, *Bampton Lectures*, iii. p. 130.

seems to have meant that the whole history of the Jewish people was a testimony to Christ. Had the request been made for some clear evidence of the truth of the claim of Christ to be divine, the answer might well have been, 'The Christian Church.'

Jesus Christ claimed to be the founder of a world-wide and imperishable society, the Kingdom of Heaven, the Church. When we consider the circumstances and prospects of the infant Church, the fewness of its adherents, their social insignificance, their lack of political influence, the unveiled opposition of the ruling powers of the time, His claim was surely amazing. But the event has fully justified the claim He then made. The Church of Jesus Christ is still here, as an existing fact, a thing of experience and of power. It is here, in spite of frequent relentless persecutions, chilling unbelief, faithless treachery, deadly heresies, and grievous schisms. His prediction that "the gates of Hades shall not prevail against it,"[1] has been fulfilled. Its rapid progress from an apparently insignificant and humble origin, its expansion in the face of difficulties and hindrances of every kind—all this is worthy of serious attention, on the ground of high evidential value. 'The Church is a great fact, which every man ought to measure.'

In the words of Dr. Liddon, "It is now scarcely less than a thousand years since

[1] St. Matt. xvi. 18.

Jesus Christ received at least the outward submission of the whole of Europe; and from that time to this His empire has been continually expanding. The newly-discovered continents of Australia and America have successively acknowledged His sway. He is shedding the light of His doctrine first upon one and then upon another of the islands of the Pacific. He has beleagured the vast African continent on either side with various forms of missionary enterprise. And although in Asia there are vast, ancient, and highly organized religions which are still permitted to bid Him defiance, yet India, China, Tartary, and Kamschatka have within the last few years witnessed heroic labours and sacrifices for the spread of His kingdom, which would not have been unworthy of the purest and noblest enthusiasms of the Primitive Church. . . . The society founded by Jesus Christ is here, still animated by its original idea, still carried forward by the moral impulse which sustained it in its infancy." [1]

What is the secret of the Church's continued existence, vitality, and expansion? The answer which will best meet all the circumstances of the case is, that the Church is no merely human society, but a divine society. And, by a divine society, we mean a society whose founder and sustainer is God.

[1] *Bampton Lectures*, iii. pp. 120, 131.

V. THE SUPERNATURAL ELEMENTS IN THE LIFE OF JESUS CHRIST.

1. *The expectation of the miraculous in Jesus Christ.* If we believe that Jesus Christ is more than man, it is reasonable to expect a manifestation of the superhuman in His life. 'Claiming more than a man's authority,' it was to be expected that 'He should display more than a man's power.' The Incarnation of God was no common event, and the life and actions of the Incarnate must consequently be extraordinary. It has been said, with much force, that the absence of the superhuman from the life of Jesus Christ would of itself be the greatest of all miracles. Thus, the expectation of the miraculous in the history of our Lord is simply a natural expectation.

But in saying this, we must be careful to give the miraculous events recorded in the Gospels their true place in relation to our argument. We are right in regarding them as a class of events antecedently probable, and as a corroboration of the previous conviction that Jesus Christ is divine. 'Evidence is never absolute, but always relative to our antecedent sense of whether the event is credible or probable. The miraculous can never create conviction or faith—it can only support them.' As Mr. Illingworth observes, "We who believe the miracles of Christ, as rooted in our records and congruous with our creeds, do

evidence of the Christian revelation. 213

not rest our faith upon them, or feel serious concern when they are attacked. For, once brought home to the minds of men, the Incarnation is its own evidence."[1] We are not now concerned in showing the credibility of miracles in general; we hope to do this later. We are simply concerned in studying some of the miraculous events with which Jesus Christ was personally associated, in relation to the truth of His Divinity.

In the story of the evolution of the world, we are taught to see in nature the unfolding of a progressive order. As newer and higher levels in creation are reached, new phenomena present themselves. Each advance, when it came, was a new thing; and each new thing presented features, and put forth powers, previously unknown. Thus, that which at one time was regarded as supernatural, later came to be regarded as only natural. New types or kinds of life necessarily exhibited new and strange

---

[1] *Bampton Lectures*, viii. p. 203.

The place to be assigned to miracles as evidence for the Christian revelation, is admirably stated by Archbishop Trench, *The Miracles of our Lord*, 12th ed. pp. 95, ff. At the close of his argument, the Archbishop says, "When we find fault with the use often made of these works (miracles), it is only because they have been forcibly severed from the whole complex of Christ's life and doctrine, and presented to the contemplation of men apart from these; because, while on His head are 'many crowns,' one only has been singled out in proof that He is King of kings and Lord of lords. . . . It may be more truly said that we believe the miracles for Christ's sake, than Christ for the miracles' sake."—p. 104.

phenomena. But when such new states were reached, or such new types and kinds of life became established, the new phenomena no longer excited wonder. Man's view of the supernatural is ever changing, as his view of nature changes.[1]

By the Incarnation a new type of being appeared, and consequently a new order of things. The coming of God in the flesh was distinctly a new thing, the entrance into the world of a new nature, a new kind of nature. And the advent of this new kind of nature gives the expectation of the appearance of new phenomena. Thus, we may regard the miracles of Jesus Christ as laws of His divine nature. The Gospel according to St. John describes the miracles of our Lord as His 'works.'[2] As viewed from the standpoint of His divine Person, miracles are no longer extraordinary, but ordinary. The more fully we realize the Incarnation, the easier it becomes to believe in the miracles of Christ, as the natural and 'proper phenomena of His Person.' A true belief in Jesus Christ as a divine Person, prepares the mind to believe His miracles.[3]

---

[1] "The term supernatural is purely relative to what at any particular stage of thought we mean by nature. Nature is a progressive development of life, and each new stage of life appears supernatural from the point of view of what lies below it."—Gore, *Bampton Lectures*, ii. p. 35.

[2] vii. 3; x. 38; xiv. 11.

[3] "Depend upon it, the more you contemplate the personality of Jesus Christ and His moral authority and purpose, the more you will find that His miracles are according to the law

evidence of the Christian revelation. 215

2. *The consideration of the miracles of which Jesus Christ was the subject.* The two chief miracles of which Jesus Christ was the subject, are connected with the opening and the close of His earthly life—His Incarnation by the Virgin-birth, and His Resurrection from the dead. It will be sufficient for our purpose to devote our attention to these only.

THE VIRGIN-BIRTH OF JESUS CHRIST. Two of the Gospels are explicit in teaching that Jesus Christ was conceived by the Holy Ghost, and born of the Virgin Mary—in other words, that His human nature was miraculously conceived without the agency of a human father.[1]

of His being, 'in rational sequence,' to use an expression of St. Athanasius (*de Incarn.* 31.), with the character of His Person and mission. It is not that the miracles prove the doctrine, or that the doctrine makes credible the miracles. It is rather that as parts of one whole they cohere as soul and body."—Gore, *Bampton Lectures,* ii. p. 49. The author has followed Mr. Gore's line of thought in the above argument.

[1] The miraculous conception of Jesus Christ was no violation of natural law, as some have supposed. According to the teaching of Evolution, life first started on its various paths from single germs, and for a long time was propagated and multiplied through single stems. "But if that is so, what is there against reason or natural law in the belief that, at another critical period in the evolution of the Divine will, life should be transmitted through a single parent; that a new head of humanity should be produced in a new way; that the moral entail of descent from Adam should in Him be broken, while the connection should remain intact through the female line in all that appertained to the essentials of humanity; the fecundating element being supplied direct by 'the Lord, and Giver of Life'? . . . We have, even at the

The Scriptures further imply that, by the virgin-birth, He was fitted to be the Second Adam, the new head of the redeemed race.

It is evident that the miraculous conception of Jesus is a truth which cannot rest primarily upon the witness of the apostles. There were but two sources from whom the knowledge of the circumstances of the birth of Christ could be derived, Joseph, and Mary the mother of Jesus. The story of the miraculous birth is recorded in the opening chapters of St. Matthew and St. Luke. The first chapter of St. Matthew clearly gives Joseph's account of the mysterious transaction—'his perplexities, the intimations which he received, his resolutions, his actions.' St. Luke's account bears evident traces of having been derived originally from Mary herself. "It is so intensely coloured by Jewish national hopes that it is hardly possible to think of it as embodying feelings subsequent to the rejection of the Christ. It appears to be in special view of this opening narrative, that St. Luke in his preface emphasizes the fact that his accurate information reaches back to the beginning."[1] The two narratives, whilst

---

present day, in the lower forms of life, instances of virgin-births—both in the vegetable kingdom and in the animal. . . . If God then deviates occasionally even now from the ordinary process of propagating life, why should it be thought a thing incredible that He did so on so momentous an occasion as the Incarnation of the Eternal Word?"—MacColl, *Christianity in relation to Science and Morals*, pp. 119, 120.

[1] Gore, *Bampton Lectures*, iii. p. 78.

possessing an independence of statement, are agreed in the assertion of the main fact, the virgin-birth of Jesus Christ. There is an air of simplicity and truthfulness surrounding the two records, which goes far to assure us of their trustworthiness as statements of historical fact. " Further," as Mr. Gore remarks, "the virgin-birth holds a firm place in the earliest traditions of East and West. 'The virginity of Mary, her child-bearing, and the death of the Lord,' constitute to Ignatius at the beginning of the second century, 'three mysteries of shouting (that is, of loud proclamation) which God wrought in silence' (Ign. *ad Eph.* 19)."[1] It is an impressive fact that, in the history of the Church, no believers in the truth of the Incarnation are to be found, who are not also believers in the miraculous conception of Jesus Christ.

Is the belief that Jesus Christ was miraculously conceived a reasonable belief? We think it is eminently reasonable, when considered in relation to the work which He came to fulfil. It is the teaching of Christ and His

[1] *Bampton Lectures*, iii. p. 78.
"In the creed-like formulas of the churches, the statement of the virgin-birth had its place from so early a date, and along so many different lines of ascent as to force upon us the conclusion that already before the death of the last apostles the virgin-birth of Christ must have been among the rudiments of the faith in which every Christian was initiated."
—Gore, Dissertations, *The Virgin Birth of our Lord*, p. 42. Readers, who desire a fuller discussion of the subject, are referred to Mr. Gore's most valuable defence.

apostles, as recorded in the New Testament, that He came to be the Deliverer of mankind. He came to " save His people from their sins." [1] He came not only to save men from the consequences of sin, but from sin itself. Man's universal proneness to moral evil can only be attributed to heredity. As a matter of fact, the tendency to wrong-doing passes on from father to son, as 'a baneful inheritance.' And it is only reasonable to suppose, that this tendency to evil is due in the long run to our natural connection with our first father in his fallen state. The river of human life is poisoned at its very source. There is no experience of any descendant of the originator of our race coming into the world free from bias towards evil. Man's only chance of escape from the universal taint lay in a radical change, a renewal of the very roots of his nature. The fundamental evil of humanity required a fundamental remedy. Mankind needed before all things a fresh start.[2] And the Christian revelation asserts that this new start was given by the entrance of a new type of man into the ranks of humanity, with whom that humanity might be brought into a

---

[1] St. Matt. i. 21.

[2] "No natural ability, no power of human mind, can make us other men. God alone can do this. For who can change his own heart? A higher power must come upon us, if our heart is to be made new. We are utterly incapable of such an act. That moral power which is to liberate and renew us can come from God alone."—Luthardt, *Fundamental Truths*, p. 190.

new and supernatural relation.[1] Mankind needs a new birth—a new and restored relation to God. And this new birth, this restored relationship to God, implies the need of a new head of humanity.

The new head of the new race must of necessity be of the old stock, yet untainted by its inherent defects: otherwise he himself would stand in need of the very help he came to give to his brethren. The deliverer must be human, yet sinless, 'true man, yet new man.' He must be capable, too, of bringing the whole race into union with himself. Moreover, to accomplish so stupendous a task of restoration, he must be more than man. The virgin-birth, accomplished by the sanctifying power of the Spirit of God, is the pledge and guarantee of the fulfilment of these conditions.[2]

Given the real state of things, the real situation of mankind in his fallen state, what could be more reasonable than that God should intervene, by a miraculous birth, to accomplish man's deliverance from within?

---

[1] "Amid the universal ruin of the whole human race, there was but one remedy which, under the mysterious law of the divine procedure, could come to the aid of the prostrate; and that was, if some son of Adam could be born, unconnected with original transgression, and innocent, who could benefit the rest, both by his example and by his merit."—St. Leo, *Serm.* iv. Bright's translation.

[2] This subject is more fully treated in the author's *Expositions of Catholic Doctrine*, Pt. II. Ch. i, ii.

The moral end in view was surely worthy of a miraculous display of divine power.

THE RESURRECTION OF JESUS CHRIST. In considering the apostolic testimony, no thoughtful person can fail to be impressed by the great stress laid upon the fact of the resurrection of Jesus Christ. The chief work of the apostles, after Christ's departure, was to bear witness to His resurrection from the dead. Let us study the record of the matter. One of the first actions of the apostles, after they became convinced of the reality of the resurrection of their Master, was to fill the vacancy in their number, caused by the suicide of the traitor Judas. In doing this, they had in their minds the selection of one, who should be a competent witness to the fact of the resurrection. "Of the men therefore which have companied with us all the time that the Lord Jesus went in and went out among us, beginning from the baptism of John, unto the day that He was received up from us, of these must one become a witness with us of His resurrection."[1] On the day of Pentecost, St. Peter, as spokesman of the apostolic college, declared, "This Jesus did God raise up, whereof we all are witnesses."[2] Later, it is recorded that "with great power gave the apostles their witness of the resurrection of

[1] Acts i. 21, 22.   [2] Ibid. ii. 32.

the Lord Jesus."[1] This witness was based upon experience. Each apostle was, in the strictest sense, an eye-witness of the fact of the resurrection. "To the apostles whom He had chosen, Jesus shewed Himself alive after His passion by many proofs, appearing unto them by the space of forty days."[2] St. Paul writes, "For I delivered unto you first of all that which also I received, how that Christ died for our sins according to the scriptures; and that He was buried; and that He hath been raised on the third day according to the scriptures; and that He appeared to Cephas; then to the twelve; then He appeared to above five hundred brethren at once, of whom the greater part remain until now, but some are fallen asleep; then He appeared to James; then to all the apostles; and last of all, as unto one born out of due time, He appeared to me also."[3]

It is specially to be noted that Jesus tarried

[1] Acts iv. 33.   [2] Ibid. i. 2, 3.
[3] 1. Cor. xv. 3-9.

It is well here to state that St. Paul's epistles to the Corinthians, along with those to the Galatians and the Romans, are documents which bear 'the most unmistakable evidence of authenticity.' His group of epistles are admitted by M. Renan as 'undisputed and indisputable.' "In these four epistles," says Dr. Sanday, "we have at once documents that are extremely early, dating in all probability from the years 57 and 58, or less than thirty years, at the longest reckoning, from the Ascension, and which are also, beyond all reasonable doubt, the actual work of the author whose name they bear, the Christian apostle St. Paul." Oxford House Papers, First Series, *What the First Christians thought about Christ*, p. 70.

upon the earth for forty days after His resurrection, in order that He might give to His followers a thorough conviction that His rising again was a real event. He made the fact quite plain by many appearances to them. In this way a number of reliable witnesses were trained to go forth into the world, who could say, We know that He rose from the grave, for we saw Him alive as certainly as we see you. And this testimony was borne unflinchingly, in the face of hostility and incredulous opposition, even unto death. The testimony was grounded on the facts which had been witnessed, " We cannot but speak the things which we saw and heard." [1]

It is no exaggeration to say that the resurrection of Jesus Christ is better attested than any other fact in history. And this evidence is so strong that, in order to refute it, refuge has been taken in the baseless assertion that the witnesses were the victims of delusion. It is hardly necessary to say that such a feeble argu-

---

[1] Acts iv. 20.

"The apostles were men whose later lives can only be accounted for by a certain fact, the fact of the resurrection. This fact transferred them from one level of character to another; it transferred men first confounded and desperate after their Lord's death, then slow of heart to believe what seemed too good to be true, into men confident, quiet, strong, invincible in the might of a fact experienced on certain definite occasions, and not again. . . . The apostles' lives were rapidly driven round a sharp turning with a force which only objective facts can exercise. The resurrection moulded them, they did not create the resurrection."—Gore, *Bampton Lectures*, iii. p. 76.

evidence of the Christian revelation. 223

ment but attempts to overthrow one miracle by the supposition of a greater, namely, that the existence of a powerful and world-wide society, the Christian Church, is founded on fraud and myth. The continued existence of the Church is in itself evidence of the very highest order for the truth of the resurrection of Jesus Christ.

In the words of Dr. Arnold, "The evidence of our Lord's life and death and resurrection may be, and often has been, shewn to be satisfactory; it is good according to the common rules for distinguishing good evidence from bad. Thousands and thousands of persons have gone through it piece by piece, as carefully as ever judge summed up upon a most important cause. I have myself done it many times over, not to persuade others, but to satisfy myself. I have been used for many years to study the history of other times, and to examine and weigh the evidence of those who have written about them; and I know of no one fact in the history of mankind which is proved by better and fuller evidence of every sort to the understanding of a fair inquirer, than the great sign which God has given us, that Christ died and rose again from the dead."[1]

And is not the belief in the resurrection of Jesus Christ a reasonable belief? Granting that He is God, must He not be superior to death; and was it not fitting that He should triumph over it by rising again to life? Grant-

[1] *Rugby Sermons on Christian Life*, p. 14.

ing too the unjust charges and the false witness, by means of which His death was accomplished, was it not reasonable that God should vindicate the righteousness of Jesus Christ, by intervening to work a mighty miracle for great moral ends? Had He not risen, then the most perfect life would have ended in failure and darkness, and evil would have remained unreproved, and in undisputed possession of the world. A miracle is 'an event in physical nature which makes unmistakably plain the presence and direct action of God working for a moral end.' The murder of Jesus Christ, the Righteous, was the most outrageous violation of the true divine order of the world. And, this being so, what more reasonable and fitting, than that God should interfere, and vindicate the true order of things, by a startling display of His almighty power. The crucifixion of Jesus Christ was the most unjustifiable and basest of crimes, the climax of all conceivable iniquity, and what more proper than that God should bare His arm, expose and set His mark upon the wrong, by a great and astonishing sign, the resurrection of His Son. "Jesus of Nazareth, a man approved of God . . . Him, ye by the hand of lawless men did crucify and slay: whom God raised up, having loosed the pangs of death: because it was not possible that He should be holden of it."[1]

[1] Acts ii. 22-24.

evidence of the Christian revelation. 225

The miraculous birth and resurrection of Jesus Christ do not stand alone, they have a close relation to His divine Person. And to those who accept His claim to be more than man, to be the divine redeemer and restorer of mankind, they assume the aspect of events probable, reasonable, and credible, no more contrary to experience than His absolute holiness and claim to moral authority.

We have thus stated the many grounds upon which belief in the trustworthiness of Jesus Christ as the revealer of the truth rests. And we trust that enough has been said to convince every candid mind of the reasonableness and validity of His claims to be regarded as the Incarnate God—as One who teaches the way of God in truth.

NOTE ON THE CUMULATIVE CHARACTER OF THE EVIDENCE FOR THE DIVINE CLAIMS OF CHRIST.

"The evidence for the authority of Jesus Christ is essentially of a cumulative character . . . we decline to consider any portion of it in entire isolation from the rest. It is true that when He entered on His work, and made His first appeal to one nation, He based that appeal very largely on the Scriptures of the earlier dispensation. But even then His fulfilling of the Scriptures, His concentration in His Person, and His teaching of every ray which had enlightened His Jewish ancestors, did not constitute more than a small portion of the evidence which convinced His first followers; the appeal of those first followers to the Gentile world of their day travelled far beyond the narrower region of His fulfilment of the earlier dispensation; the Roman world submitted itself to Him on the ground of the correspondence of His work, of the appeal of His death and resurrection, of the exact adaptation of His teaching to primary needs of human nature, independent altogether of the Jewish Scriptures; and our own belief in Him and His religion appeals, again, to what I would call with all reverence, His actual, historical contribution to the advance of human progress, to the permanence of all that He has done for human life under aspects the most varied, individual, national, world-wide; to His ability tested through the centuries, to supply every need of humanity—whether those of individual souls in the spiritual wants of their inmost being, or those of society at large, on the highest scale of its organization. It is by taking all these things into account that we arrive at our belief in His Person."—Bp. Mylne, *Churchmen and the Higher Criticism*.

"The apostles lived in a vivid sense of experienced intercourse, first with the Son, then with the Father through the Son, later with the Holy Ghost, and with the Father and the Son through the Holy Ghost. This vivid experience, outward and inward, made logical formulas unnecessary. When the formula of the Trinity—three Persons in one Substance—was developed in the Church later on, through the cross-questioning of heresies, it was with many apologies for the inadequacy of human language, and with a deep sense of the inscrutableness of God. The formula was simply intended to express and guard the realities disclosed in the Person of Jesus Christ, and great stress was laid on the divine unity."—Gore, *Bampton Lectures*, v. pp. 132, 133.

CHAPTER III.

BELIEF IN THE HOLY TRINITY

THE RESULT OF THE CHRISTIAN REVELATION.

HAVING established the authority and trustworthiness of Jesus Christ, as the divine discloser of the truth, we now pass on to consider that which He revealed. In other words, from the Person of Christ as the *evidence* of the Christian revelation, we proceed to consider the *result* of His revelation. What are the main truths which He disclosed?

i.

First, and foremost: from a belief in His own Person, Jesus Christ led the apostles to a belief in the doctrine of the Holy Trinity. This belief grew out of the experience of the apostles. Trained as Jews to believe in the unity of God, without losing their sense of the divine unity, they came, through their realization of Christ as a divine Person, to recognize a plurality in the Godhead. And this belief was further enlarged, as they learned about and received the Holy Spirit. It is important to notice that the apostles' belief in the doctrine of the Holy Trinity was a matter of experience, the outcome of their intercourse with Jesus Christ. And when they received the Holy Spirit on the day of Pentecost, their faith in the Father, the Son, and the Holy Ghost, as included in the being of God, received its full and satisfactory confirmation. "When the Comforter is come, whom I will send unto you from the Father, even the Spirit of truth, which proceedeth from the Father, He shall bear witness of me."[1]

Whilst clearly proclaiming the unity of God,[2] Jesus Christ revealed Himself as God's equal,[3] and spoke of the Spirit, whom He was about to send from the Father, as a divine Person.[4] He declared that it was expedient, or advantageous, that He should depart, in order that the Spirit might come;[5] and thus implied that the Spirit was His equal. Christ's departure could not have been expedient, unless the Spirit was divine as He was. He commanded His apostles, and their successors, to baptize all nations "into the name of the Father and of the Son and of the Holy Ghost."[6] In this command, He

---

[1] St. John xv. 26.
[2] St. Matt. xix. 17; St. Mark xii. 29; St. John v. 18; xvii. 3.
[3] St. John v. 17-24; x. 30-34; xvii. 11, 22.
[4] St Matt. xii. 31, 32.   [5] St. John xvi. 7.
[6] St. Matt. xxviii. 19.

summed up the doctrine of the unity of God in a trinity of Persons.[1] Thus, Christ's language about Himself, the Father, and the Spirit, is the basis of the Christian belief that there is one God in three Persons. The Father is God, the Son is God, and the Holy Ghost is God: and yet they are not three Gods, but one God—this is the Church's interpretation of the teaching of Jesus Christ.

ii.

The doctrine of the Holy Trinity is essentially a Christian doctrine. Whatever hints of a plurality of Persons in the Godhead are to be found in the Old Testament,[2] the doctrine was only fully made known by Jesus Christ. By the Incarnation, God came nearer to man, and man was brought nearer to God, than had been the case before. And this nearness gave man an enlarged and more detailed view of

[1] The following prayer, which forms the conclusion of St. Augustine's treatise on the Trinity, proves that, in the mind of that great father, the doctrine of the Trinity took its theological form from the baptismal formula.

"O LORD our God, we believe in thee, the Father and the Son and the Holy Ghost. For the Truth would not say, Go, baptize all nations in the name of the Father and of the Son and of the Holy Spirit, unless thou wast a Trinity. Nor wouldest thou, O Lord God, bid us be baptized in the name of Him who is not the Lord God."

[2] See Gen. i. 1, where the Hebrew noun 'God' is plural, whilst the verb 'created' is singular; i. 26; iii. 22; xi. 7; xviii.; Num. vi. 22, ff.; Isa. vi. 1-4.

God. In Christ, man came to see in God that which he had not seen before; he came to see distinctions in the Godhead, before unperceived.[1]

In the first part of this work we have seen that God's Self-disclosure has been a slow and gradual process. To the Jews was given the revelation of God as one personal being. "Hear, O Israel: the Lord our God is one Lord."[2] The Jews were surrounded by nations who multiplied gods, and worshipped gods many and lords many: it was therefore necessary to guard them from the perils of polytheism, or the worship of more gods than one. Thus, a premature revelation of the threefold personality of God would have been fraught with danger, and hence the revelation of the Trinity was delayed. The Jews beheld God at a distance, and at such a distance they saw but one single Being. By means of the Incarnation man began to see more of the nature of God. He began to see that though God is one in being, He is threefold in personality. Jesus Christ revealed the Father sending the Son, and the Spirit proceeding from the Father and the Son. And, as time went on, the Church recorded the result of Christ's revelation in the New Testament and in the Creeds, thereby expressing and protecting the disclosure of the Godhead made by Jesus Christ.

[1] See Gore, *The Creed of the Christian*, p. 20.
[2] Deut. vi. 4.

iii.

But, it may be asked, Is not the doctrine of the Trinity in Unity an unreasonable doctrine? Would it not be much more reasonable to believe that there is but one God, without distinction of Persons? We reply, Certainly not: the belief in the threefold being of God is much more conformable to reason than the belief in one single Deity. And this we will now endeavour to show.

The most natural, and therefore the truest conception of God, is that of a being, who is both eternally living and loving. Reason teaches that the eternal God had life in Himself for unreckoned ages before created life began to be. But life implies productiveness: and eternal life implies eternal productiveness. The difference between a living and a dead man is, that the living man manifests and expresses his life in thinking, speaking, and acting: the dead man does none of these things. The difference between a living and a dead tree is that one is fruitful in putting forth shoots and leaves, the other is barren. If God then is ever living, He must have been ever fruitful. And the eternal fruitfulness or productiveness of God implies the eternal existence of more than one Person in the Godhead. The Christian doctrine of the eternal generation of the Son, and the eternal procession of the Spirit from the Father and the Son, is consistent with the belief in God as the supreme eternal being. In other words, the eternal co-existence of the Son and the Spirit with the Father, is but the reasonable result of the belief in the everliving God.

And a similar argument is to be derived from the consideration of God as love. Love is 'the intensest, mightiest, holiest thing we know.' It is therefore quite natural to believe that God is love. God did not begin to love, or become love, when He created the universe and man. Creation produced no change in the divine character. God is eternally love. But love implies a subject to give, and an object to receive and return, love. Love without an adequate object upon which to expend itself, would exist as an unsatisfied desire. If God ever existed alone, in solitude, He cannot have been eternal love. The idea of God ever loving, implies an eternal object upon which to pour forth His love. If God is infinite and eternal love, such love can only have been satisfied by an infinite and eternal return of love. Thus, the belief that God is love carries with it, of necessity, the belief in a plurality of Persons in the Godhead. Love, even on earth, implies a trinity in unity. We are indebted to St. Augustine for bringing out this teaching. He says, " Love is of some one that loves, and with love something is loved. Behold, then, there are three things—he that loves, and that which is loved, and love. What, then, is love except a certain life which couples or seeks to couple together some two things, namely, him that loves, and that which is loved?" And St. Augustine adds, "When I love anything there are three things concerned—myself, and that which I love, and love itself. For I do not love love, except I love a lover; for there is no love where nothing is loved. Therefore there are three things—he who loves, and that which is loved, and love."[1] Thus, the Christian doctrine that the Father ever loved the Son, and that both ever loved the Spirit, who in turn is the eternal bond of love between the Father and the Son, however mysterious, is a reasonable doctrine.

We trust that enough has been said to prove that the Christian belief in One God in Three Persons, is much more intelligible than the Unitarian belief in God as a simple Unity. And, if we cannot understand the doctrine, we can at least confess that it is a doctrine most agreeable to reason.

NOTE ON THE REASONABLENESS OF THE DOCTRINE OF THE TRINITY.

"The doctrine of the Trinity is not discoverable by reason, but agreeable to reason. It corresponds to upward-soaring trains of thought which reason itself originates, but is not able to bring to a conclusion. For the reasons which lead us to believe in God at all, lead us to think of Him as an eternal and spiritual being. Now the life of spirit, the

[1] *de Trin.* viii. 10; ix. 2.

highest life we know, is made up of the action of will and reason and love. In God then, we imagine, is a perfect and eternal life, of will and reason and love. But must not this be a life of relationships? Most surely love is only conceivable as a personal relationship of a lover and a loved. If God is eternal love, there must be an eternal object for His love. Again, the life of reason is a relationship of the subject which thinks to the object thought, and an eternally perfect mind postulates an eternal object for its contemplation. Once more, the life of will means the passage of will into effect: there is no satisfaction to will except in production; an eternally living and satisfied will postulates an eternally adequate product. Thus it is that our upward-soaring trains of thought lead us to postulate over against God in His eternal being, also an eternal expression of that being, which shall be both an object to His thought and a satisfaction to His will and a repose to His love."—Gore, *Bampton Lectures*, v. p. 134.

Mr. Illingworth, in his *Bampton Lectures*, iii. pp. 69, ff., similarly, and at greater length, illustrates the reasonableness of belief in the doctrine of the Trinity, from the triune constitution of human personality as involving a subject, an object, and their relation.

"As in the human spirit, so, too, in the outward world of nature, there are certain indications and reflections of the Trinity. This truth is not only revealed in Scripture, . . . but it is, so to speak, omnipresent throughout the world. We constantly see one *life* in various members; in each one it acts in a special manner, yet in all it is one and the same. In one *sun* we see light and warmth as different, and yet intermingling and co-operating forces. We have the one *space* divided into three dimensions of length, breadth, and height; *time*, similarly, into past, present, and future; all *bodies* into solid, liquid, and gaseous. In analogy with the three parts required to form a *sentence*, we find that the kingdom of sound is governed by the *triad*, as the basis of all chords; nor does this destroy the original unity of the key note, but, on the contrary, makes it an organized unity embracing multiplicity. What remarkable analogies are shown by the laws of *colour* and of *light!* The three fundamental colours, red, yellow, and blue, dissolve into the unity of white light, so that an English naturalist (C. Woodward) might well call this white light, a trinity in unity. But they coalesce in such a manner, that 'each of the three rays preserves its distinctive attribute. Red is the caloric, yellow the luminous, blue the chemical (activic) ray.' God is Light; and, verily, natural light, the first of His creatures, bears the immediate impress of His triune being. No less does the number three govern the arrangement of *nature's forces;* whether we adopt the classification of Ohm, who divides the fundamental forces into those of 'attraction, tension, and polarity,' or the more general enumeration, attraction, repulsion, equilibrium. The whole of nature is ruled by the law of polarity, with its two magnetic poles and their equipoise. Positive and negative electricity are balanced by the electric spark. The entire development of the *vegetable world* takes place in a process of three degrees. First, the self-enclosed potential unity (seed, germinal cell, root), then the self-development into multiplicity (inward dilation and ramification of the germ, stem), and, finally, conclusion of the multiplicity in organized unity (leaf, fruit, return to the seed and germinal cell). Is not the Eternal Origin of life visible in all these things in a thousand pictures? Were we not right in saying that the idea of the Trinity was omnipresent?"—Christlieb, *Modern Doubt and Christian Belief,* p. 277.

NOTE ON THE TERM 'PERSON' AS APPLIED TO GOD.

The inadequacy of human language is nowhere more apparent than in its application to the being of God. In applying the term 'Person' to the Father, the Son, and the Holy Spirit, we do not mean that the three sacred Persons are three distinct individuals, three Gods, "so that it could be argued that what one of the sacred three does another does not do, as we commonly argue about persons amongst ourselves, regarding each person as separate and exclusive of others. God in three is inseparably one. Thus if He creates, it is the Father through the Son by the Holy Ghost; if He redeems, it is the Father who is the fount of redemption through the Son by the Holy Ghost; if the Spirit comes, He brings with Him in His coming the Son and the Father, for in eternal subordination and order the three are one inseparable God."—Gore, *Bampton Lectures,* v. p. 133.

"With regard to God, it was only with an expressed apology for the imperfection of human language that the Church spoke of the Divine Three, as Three *Persons* at all. But 'we have no celestial language,' and the word is the only one which will express what Christ's language implies about Himself, the Father, and the Spirit."—Gore, in Lux Mundi, *The Holy Spirit and Inspiration,* p. 337.

"Call no man your father on the earth: for one is your Father, which is in heaven."- -St. Matt. xxiii. 9.

"Christ was the first who distinctly and clearly taught men to look upon God as a Father, as one in whom is united the whole fulness of what is called love. In the Old Testament, indeed, God was represented as a Father, but chiefly in relation to the people He had chosen out and educated; and the contemporaries of Jesus, if they declared themselves to be the children of God, had before their eyes simply the fact of their belonging to the chosen people. But He taught men to acknowledge God as a Father, and themselves as His children, because they were designed to attain a moral and spiritual likeness to this Father of theirs through love, and thereby to inherit His kingdom; because the love which God has from eternity for His Son is also extended to those who believe in Him."—Döllinger, *The First Age of the Church*, vol. i. p. 26.

"The Fatherhood of God is a truth accepted by Christians, without question, as a starting-point for their life and work. People who are not Christians may borrow it and hold it, for it finds an echo in every heart—'the testimony of the soul naturally Christian'—yet, in historical fact, it came into the world as a part of Christianity."—Gore, *The Creed of the Christian*, p. 14.

CHAPTER IV.

THE REVELATION OF THE FATHER.

"IN many, if not in most religions," says Max Müller, "man has addressed God as his Father, and has looked upon himself as His son."[1] He has done this from the conviction that he owes the origination and the continuance of his life to God. "Have we not all one Father? hath not one God created us?"[2] If I am the offspring of God, then I am a son of God,—this is a truth of natural religion, 'the testimony of the soul naturally Christian.' We find St. Paul appealing to this truth of natural religion in his address to the Athenians on Mars' Hill. Quoting the words of the Greek poet, he declared, "We are the offspring of God."[3] When St. Chrysostom was being driven into exile, he is reported to have said, 'All the world is my home, for the world belongs to God, and God is my Father.' These words find an echo in every human heart.

But the Christian belief in the Fatherhood

[1] *Anthropological Religion*, p. 381. [2] Mal. ii. 10.
[3] Acts xvii. 28, 29.

of God goes far beyond this natural belief in God as the creator of all men. Jesus Christ declared that "no one knoweth who the Father is, save the Son, and he to whomsoever the Son willeth to reveal Him."[1] Thus, the knowledge of the Fatherhood of God is part of Christ's revelation of God, and consequently a Christian doctrine. His revelation of the Father concerns the relation of God to man, the relation of man to God, and the relation of man to his fellows.

I. THE RELATION OF GOD TO MAN.

i.

Jesus Christ disclosed the true character of God as a Father. Hitherto, the Jewish conception of God had chiefly emphasized His *righteousness*, His demand of a righteous life in His children, His just severity towards all who failed to fulfil His demand. Christ's revelation of God is summed up in the disclosure of the *love* of God. "A God of righteousness is certainly a great advance on a God of mere power; yet it is only a step upwards towards a higher idea of God, in which the divine Being becomes Self-communicating redeeming Love. God cannot be said to have been fully revealed till He has been revealed in this aspect. And as God has

[1] St. Luke x. 22.

The Revelation of the Father. 241

manifested Himself in nature as Power controlled by intelligence, and in the moral order of the world as a righteous Ruler, so we should expect to find Him revealing Himself as a loving Father." [1]

Christ's own presence in human form, His sacrifice for human sin, His reconciliation of sinful man to God,—this is the evidence of the Father's love. "God so loved the world, that He gave His only begotten Son." [2] This was Christ's proclamation of the love of God. "Herein was the love of God manifested in us, that God hath sent His only begotten Son into the world, that we might live through Him. Herein is love, not that we loved God, but that He loved us, and sent His Son to be the propitiation for our sins." [3] Jesus Christ declared, "He that hath seen me hath seen the Father." [4] He thus taught men to view the love of God in the light of His own measureless love for man.

ii.

Jesus Christ inspired His followers to believe that behind all that is so cruel, unjust, wrong, and perplexing in the world, there beats the Father's heart. And He made

[1] Bruce, *The Chief End of Revelation*, p. 59.
[2] St. John iii. 16.   [3] 1 St. John iv. 9, 10.
[4] St. John xiv. 9.

this belief credible by Himself voluntarily submitting to cruelty, injustice, and wrong, by becoming "a man of sorrows, and acquainted with grief," [1] by disclosing the love of God in pain and through pain. "Himself took our infirmities, and bare our diseases." [2] "Out of the very heart of pain and failure He manifested that self-sacrificing love which is nothing else than God's love; and by His resurrection on the third day from the dead, finally proved the divine love triumphant through pain and over pain." [3]

iii.

Jesus Christ revealed the love of God as an individual love for every human being. The death of Christ was the climax of the divine love. "Greater love hath no man than this, that a man lay down his life for his friends." [4]

---

[1] Isa. liii. 3.   [2] St. Matt. viii. 17.
[3] *The Creed of the Christian*, p. 15.
"With all the evil and misery in the world, men would not have been able to believe in the Fatherhood of God, meaning His love, without the revelation of it given by Jesus Christ. . . . 'You know how my Mary has been trying to comfort our poor neighbour whose wife has just died with her first child. She has been trying to persuade the poor, heart-broken, despairing fellow of the love of God. But she said, truly enough, that one could not have the face to mention divine love in the neighbourhood of such agony as his, if it were not the Man of Sorrows who assured us of it.'"—Ibid. p. 19.
[4] St. John xv. 13.

The Revelation of the Father. 243

His death was not only for all men in general, but for every man in particular. There is no one but can say, " The Son of God loved me, and gave Himself up for me."[1]

This individual love of God for every human being contains the true idea of His wrath against sin. Sin is an outrage against the love of God, and by the law of His being He is bound to hate it. As a Father, He demands the loving obedience of His children. "If then I be a Father, where is mine honour?"[2] Thus, whilst declaring God's infinite love for man, Jesus Christ was necessarily stern, to an awful degree, in denouncing sin as an unfilial act. The love of the human father shows itself in the desire to keep his child from harm. It is not true love, but only unregulated affection, which makes light of a child's faults, and forbears to punish them. Hence, our Lord's terrible denunciations of evil, His awful revelation of the consequences of sin, are in truest keeping with His manifestation of the divine love. If God is a Father, He must be full of righteous indignation against unfilial impiety; and whilst He freely forgives upon penitence, He is nevertheless bound in truest love to mark and punish such impiety. " For whom the Lord loveth He chasteneth, and scourgeth every son whom He receiveth."[3]

[1] Gal. ii. 20.   [2] Mal. i. 6.
[3] Heb. xii. 6.

Providence.

iv.

Connected with Christ's disclosure of the Fatherhood of God, is that of His providence. Jesus Christ revealed not only God's general providence over all His works, but also His special providence over mankind and over individuals in particular. His words are, "Therefore I say unto you, Be not anxious for your life, what ye shall eat, or what ye shall drink; nor yet for your body, what ye shall put on. Is not the life more than the food, and the body than the raiment? Behold the birds of the heaven, that they sow not, neither do they reap, nor gather into barns; and your heavenly Father feedeth them. Are not ye of much more value than they? And which of you by being anxious can add one cubit unto his stature? And why are ye anxious concerning raiment? Consider the lilies of the field, how they grow; they toil not, neither do they spin: yet I say unto you, that even Solomon in all his glory was not arrayed like one of these. But if God doth so clothe the grass of the field, which to-day is, and to-morrow is cast into the oven, shall He not much more clothe you, O ye of little faith? Be not therefore anxious, saying, What shall we eat? or, What shall we drink? or, Wherewithal shall we be clothed? For after all these things do the Gentiles seek; for your heavenly Father knoweth that ye have need of all these things. But seek ye first His kingdom, and His righteousness; and all these things shall be added unto you."[1] And again, "Are not two sparrows sold for a farthing? and not one of them shall fall on the ground without your Father: but the very hairs of your head are all numbered. Fear not therefore; ye are of more value than many sparrows."[2] Thus, Jesus Christ declared that all things created by God are not left to themselves, but are under His fatherly care and protection.

Providence is defined by St. Thomas Aquinas, following Boethius, to be "the all-regulating and stable plan of God, the supreme Ruler of the universe."[3] Thus, a belief in a divine providence is a belief in God's purpose, plan, and intention, in regard to all His creatures.

[1] St. Matt. vi. 25, ff. [2] St. Matt. x. 29, ff.
[3] *Sum. Theol.* 1a. q. 22. art. 1.
"Providence as well as prudence (which is its doublet), considered in its etymological meaning, is equivalent to *foresight*. This etymological signification of the word coincides pretty well with the real import of what we call *prudence* in a man, and *providence* in God. We say that a man is prudent, when the whole tenor of his life justifies the supposition that, in his undertakings, he has a definite object in view, and uses constantly the means fit for the attainment of his purpose. In a similar sense, we attribute providence to God; for this predicate is given to Him in order to imply that He has settled from eternity the final goal toward which the whole of His creation and each particular creature is to be directed, that He has ordained the means by which the end shall be reached, and that He rules in the course of ages all events so perfectly, as that nothing shall occur to bar His final and absolute intention."—Boedder, *Natural Theology*, pp. 381, 382.

V.

It is held by some, who do not accept the teaching of Christ, that God, after creating a few original forms and giving them their primary impulse, retired from any further care or supervision of them—that He is 'well out of the way of active human interests,' and has left things to self-development. And it is further asserted by such persons, that this self-development has proceeded according to natural law and order, by evolution, natural selection, the survival of the fittest, without any divine aid whatsoever. In short, it is held that the recognition of the working of natural law is inconsistent with belief in a divine providence.

We have already dealt with this objection to the idea of God's providence in an earlier part of this work.[1] It will be sufficient to say here, that the Christian doctrine of a divine providence, whilst fully recognizing such natural processes as those above named, attributes their activity, force, and continuance, to God's immanence in nature.[2] Christ declared, "My Father worketh even until now, and I work,"[3] and taught men that the constant efficacy of God's power, resident in the natural world,

[1] See pp. 102, ff.
[2] By the expression 'God's immanence in nature,' is meant His abiding and sustaining presence in the natural world, not as a soul in a body, but as a cause in its effect.
[3] St. John v. 17.

is the secret of its life and progress. It is the Christian doctrine that the world does not go on merely because of the original impulse given to it by its Creator, but because of His constant, vivifying, and sustaining presence; and that, were He to withdraw that presence, the instant annihilation of the world would ensue. In other words, the Christian believes that evolution or development implies an evolver or developer, selection a selector, law a lawgiver. In short, he believes that law, order, and progress, in nature are but departments of the divine providence, whereby God 'directs all things to an end fixed by Him in harmony with His eternal plan.' The Christian thinker recognizes in nature the continual presence of the mind, will, and power of God. He believes that "there is nothing useless, nothing meaningless in nature, nothing due to caprice or chance, nothing irrational or without a cause, nothing outside the reign of law. This belief in the universality of law and order is the scientific analogue of the Christian's belief in providence."[1]

[1] Aubrey L. Moore, *Science and the Faith*, p. 197.
"One who believes in the God of Christianity is bound to believe that creation is His work from end to end, that it is a rational work, and the work of a Being who is wholly good. He is bound to believe that 'God's mercy is over all His works,' that 'not a sparrow falls to the ground' without His knowledge, that there is design and purpose everywhere. But he is not bound to know, or to say that he knows, what that purpose is, or to show that marks of beneficence are everywhere apparent."—Ibid. p. 199.

vi.

The Christian belief in providence does not necessarily mean that God approves all that He permits or tolerates. Christianity does not oblige men to say that God wills whatever happens. If this were true, it would imply that God willed the commission of sin, which would be inconsistent with His moral nature and attributes. But we may say that, in His wisdom, He tolerates what He cannot approve. Of this we have already spoken in regard to the permission of moral evil. When we say that God permits moral evil we do not mean that He 'gives permission to sin, but only that for good reasons He does not hinder those sins, which rational creatures commit through the abuse of their free will.'[1] If, in His providence, He has allowed sin to enter the world, He has emphasized His providence by providing for its remedy and removal, in the Incarnation and Passion of His Son. The existence of moral evil, which at first sight appears to contradict the doctrine of the divine providence, has only served to throw that doctrine into stronger relief.

vii.

"Intelligent observation of the course of events strongly suggests that there is 'a provi-

---

[1] "Sin, in the strict sense of the word, is not committed without disobedience to the voice of conscience, which re-echoes the will of the Supreme Lawgiver. But it is one thing to disapprove of sin, and quite another thing not to impede it."—Boedder, *Natural Theology*, p. 400.

dence that shapes our ends, rough-hew them how we will.' . . . We have in the world-process the working of an intelligence which not only guides the actions of the unconscious material existences, but overrules those of the conscious intelligences. The only possible inference from the fact of the constant and definite tendency of the world-process is, that it is purposed by the intelligence of a real being, of a God, who, though not seen, is yet known by His action on the phenomenal world."[1]

The effect upon human life of the belief in the providence of God is a matter both of experience and observation. There are not wanting those, in every age and place, who can testify to the fact 'how beautiful and free and joyous life may be, which commits itself and all its cares wholly into the Father's hands.'

II. THE RELATION OF MAN TO GOD.

Not only did Jesus Christ reveal God's true relation to man, but He also made known man's true relation to God. He did this in His own Person, as God and Man. In Jesus Christ man is enabled not only to *know*, but also to *realize*, his true relation to God. This relation is that of a son to a father.

[1] *Riddles of the Sphinx*, p. 371.

i.

By the Incarnation the whole human race has been in possibility elevated, enriched, and rendered capable of fellowship with God. "The alliance of the elder brother ennobled the whole household from which His kindred was derived."[1] 'The Son of God became Son of Man, in order that the sons of men might become sons of God.'[2] The Incarnation is the ground upon which man's true filial relation to God rests. It is by union with Jesus Christ, through grace, that a man is raised from a natural relationship to God as His creature, to a supernatural relationship as His adopted son. By nature all men are 'the offspring of God,' but the full realization of the idea of sonship is beyond this creaturely relationship. In Jesus Christ, the only begotten Son of God, we may be adopted out of a merely creaturely relation to God as our Maker, into a special nearness to Him as our Father. It is the doctrine of Christ that this adoption is accomplished by the agency of His Spirit in a new birth—that this new birth makes men members of Christ, the only begotten Son of God, and hence, in Him, sons of God. The fact of birth ever implies the idea of fatherhood; and a new birth, such as Jesus Christ

[1] Wilberforce, *The Doctrine of the Incarnation*, vi. p. 196.
[2] See St. Leo, *Serm.* xxv. 2. So also Bishop Andrewes, "Since sure it is that the Son of God is made the Son of Man, it is not incredible but that the sons of men may be made the sons of God."—*Sixth Sermon on the Nativity*.

asserted to be a necessity,[1] implies a new fatherhood. "When the fulness of the time came, God sent forth His Son, born of a woman, born under the law, that He might redeem them which were under the law, that we might receive the adoption of sons. And because ye are sons, God sent forth the Spirit of His Son into our hearts, crying, Abba, Father. So that thou art no longer a bondservant, but a son; and if a son, then an heir through God."[2] "The God and Father of our Lord Jesus Christ . . . foreordained us unto adoption as sons through Jesus Christ unto Himself."[3]

The disclosure of man as the son of God is the disclosure of man's true dignity, and his capacity for fellowship with God as his Father. And it is a fact of experience in the history of our race, that the men who have reached the summit of moral excellence, have ever been those who have recognized and realized their supernatural relationship to God in Jesus Christ.

Prayer.

ii.

In disclosing man's dignity as the son of God, Jesus Christ also revealed man's capacity

---

[1] St. John iii. 3–8.   [2] Gal. iv. 4–8.   [3] Eph. i. 3, 5.

A king may have natural sons, adopted sons, and servants. God has an only begotten Son by nature, adopted sons by grace, and servants by creation. Natural sons have rights, adopted sons have privileges, servants have duties only.

for fellowship and communion with God as his Father. This fellowship and communion is realized in prayer. Prayer is man's intercourse with God. It is significant that when the disciples urged the request, "Lord, teach us to pray," Jesus Christ replied by instructing them to address God as a Father. "When ye pray, say, Our Father which art in heaven."[1] Moreover, it is an impressive fact that, in alluding to the subject of prayer, Christ always spoke of Him to whom men should address their prayers by the title 'Father.'[2] Thus, it is strictly true to say that, in bidding man to pray, Jesus Christ at once disclosed the Fatherhood of God, and the sonship of man. If prayer is the privilege of God's children, it is also the bond whereby the filial relationship is both realized and strengthened.

iii.

Some objections to the practice of prayer have been made, which we will proceed to state, and endeavour to meet.

First, it is urged that as the world is governed according to fixed laws, and so in a sense under the reign of law, prayer cannot avail to disturb or alter the course of law. Hence, it is objected that to pray is a useless waste of time and strength We reply that any

[1] St. Matt. vi. 9; St. Luke xi. 1, 2.
[2] See St. Matt. vi. 6, 8, 32; vii. 11; St. Luke xii. 30; St. John xv. 16; xvi. 23.

prayer which is an attempt to interfere with God's working is both unwise and irreverent, and will, by the very nature of things, fail of its purpose. But it must be remembered that God's law is not a blind unreasoning force, which works in a groove as a mere unthinking piece of machinery. His law is the free action of the intelligent will of a Moral Agent. Almighty God is not bound by rules, and surely He can, if He wills, for moral ends supersede a lower rule of action by a higher. It is true that 'the help that is done upon earth, He doeth it Himself,' yet, cannot He do it as He wills, unfettered by the bondage of any rules whatever? Prayer really exalts God, by acknowledging that He is not the slave of His own rules of action, where moral ends are in view; and that with Him "all things are possible." [1]

And, again, if it is true that the world is ruled by law, it by no means follows that no room is left for the play of human action. The laws of the natural world in many cases depend for their fulfilment on man's co-operation. Some of the greatest blessings which come to mankind in the natural order, are blessings which would never be his without his own active co-operation. The bread we eat would not be ours, unless we worked with nature in sowing the seed and reaping the harvest; and it is so in many other things. The true idea of prayer,

[1] St. Matt. xix. 26.

as disclosed by Christ, is not that of an attempt to change or resist natural law, but to realize and co-operate with the divine Will. God's dealings with man are doubtless affected by man's conduct, and why not equally so by the prayers we address to Him? His providence is ordered by our conduct, and why should not our prayers enter into His calculations as factors and causes, working out those final results, which all along He has foreseen and allowed for? God works out His plans not only *in* us, but also *by* us.

The second objection to the theory of prayer has been based on the consideration of God's greatness, and man's littleness. The objector takes on his lips the cavil of the man reproved by the son of Sirach, "Who shall remember me from on high? I shall not be known among so many people: for what is my soul in a boundless creation?"[1] Is it reasonable that the Maker and Ruler of this vast universe should be expected to attend to the prayers of so insignificant a being as man? Is not God too much occupied in the ordering of His great creation, to pay attention to the desires of one of His creatures? Is not the prayer of man too trifling to be heeded by One so infinitely great as God? The reply to such questions as these is, that to our knowledge nothing is greater in creation than man; and that such is God's marvellous love for every-

[1] Ecclus. xvi. 17.

thing that He has made, that the welfare of the least of His children is a matter of deep concern to Him. The Christian, instructed by Jesus Christ, believes that God's providence, which is over all creation, is over every life in detail. If He clothes the grass of the field and protects the sparrows, surely, the needs of His children are not beneath His fatherly attention.

iv.

The influence for good, which the habit of prayer has upon the characters of those who pray, is a matter of both observation and experience. "The moral effects of devotion," wrote Dr. Liddon, "are striking and abundant. Habitual prayer constantly confers decision on the wavering, and energy on the listless, and calmness on the excitable, and disinterestedness on the selfish. It braces the moral nature by transporting it into a clear, invigorating, unearthly atmosphere: it builds up the moral life, insensibly but surely remedying its deficiencies, and strengthening its weak points, till there emerges a comparatively symmetrical and consistent whole, the excellence of which all must admit, though its secret is known only to those who know it by experience. Akin to the moral are the social effects of prayer. Prayer makes men, as members of society, different in their whole bearing from those who do not pray. It gilds social intercourse and conduct with a tenderness, an unobtrusiveness, a sincerity, a frankness, an evenness of temper, a cheerfulness, a collectedness, a constant consideration for others, united to a simple loyalty to truth and duty, which leavens and strengthens society." [1]

> "More things are wrought by prayer
> Than this world dreams of. Wherefore, let thy voice
> Rise like a fountain for me night and day.
> For what are men better than sheep or goats
> That nourish a blind life within the brain,
> If, knowing God, they lift not hands of prayer
> Both for themselves and those who call them friend?
> For so the whole round earth is every way
> Bound by gold chains about the feet of God."
>
> Tennyson, *Morte d'Arthur*.

"Prayer diffuses a spirit of peace over our life. In prayer the soul gains repose. Then are the storms and passions of the heart silenced; the disturbances of its cares and anxieties, of its sufferings, and even of its joys, cease. And thus fresh vigour and cheerfulness break forth upon us. As the bracing air of the mountains fills us with a sense of renewed power, so do we in prayer breathe an atmosphere of divine encouragement, and come

---

[1] *Some Elements of Religion*, pp. 176, 177.
The whole subject of Prayer is treated with an admirable fulness in Lecture v. of Dr. Liddon's work. See also Mr. Gore's contribution to the Oxford House Papers, Second Series, *Prayer and the Reign of Law;* and his articles on Prayer, in *The Commonwealth*, 1896.

The Revelation of the Father. 257

forth from the inner sanctuary of communion with God to enter with new alacrity into external life."[1]

III. THE RELATION OF MAN TO HIS FELLOWS.

Jesus Christ's revelation of the Fatherhood of God contains the disclosure of man's true relation to his fellows. In manifesting God as the universal Father, He taught men their common relation as brethren. The doctrine of Christ is, 'God is your Father, therefore, as children of your Father, ye are brethren.' Jesus Christ introduced a new spirit amongst mankind, the spirit of humanity. Of this we have already spoken in a previous chapter.[2] Every time the Christian uses the 'Our

[1] Luthardt, *Fundamental Truths*, pp. 160, 161.

The following story is worthy of record, as an example of the experience of prayer. In the course of a sermon preached at the Lichfield Diocesan Choral Festival, July 4, 1895, Dean Forrest said: "Long years have passed since, in conversation with one of the greatest, if not the very greatest singer of this century, I happened incidentally to mention that a young man in his very last hours told me that his first religious impressions, his first thoughts of his Saviour, were derived from hearing that person (Jenny Lind, to whom I was speaking) sing 'I know that my Redeemer liveth,' from Handel's *Messiah*. She looked at me with that searching expression that belonged characteristically to herself, and then slowly there gathered two large tears in her eyes, and with white and trembling lips she said, 'I don't remember ever to have sung that air without prayer beforehand, and this is by no means the first time that I have had a similar answer to my prayers.'"

[2] See p. 208.

Father,' he acknowledges the brotherhood of mankind.

The revelation of the Fatherhood of God is the disclosure that "there is no respect of persons with God."[1] In the light of the Christian revelation, all men are equal and of equal value in the sight of God. "For ye are all sons of God, through faith, in Christ Jesus. For as many of you as were baptized into Christ did put on Christ. There can be neither Jew nor Greek, there can be neither bond nor free, there can be no male and female: for ye all are one man in Christ Jesus."[2]

It is the belief in the dignity of man as revealed in the Incarnation, and the brotherhood of mankind as disclosed in the Fatherhood of God, which will best help men to respect the rights of others, and to recognize their mutual duties. And the teaching of Christ, concerning man's true relation and responsibility to his fellows, as implied in the doctrine of the Fatherhood of God, is a thing which has been verified in history and in experience.

[1] Rom. ii. 11.
[2] Gal. iii. 26, ff.; see also Col. iii. 11.

"Through Him we have our access in one Spirit unto the Father."—Eph. ii. 18.

"Christ came as Mediator, Reconciler, and Redeemer. He is Mediator, from the fact of being Man, for in Him human nature in its sinless purity was exalted to the closest personal fellowship with the Godhead, and He, as the Second Adam, has the office and the power and means to cleanse men from sin, and unite them to Himself. For, in His full union, on one side with God, on the other with humanity, He, and He alone, is in a position to put away the enmity of man against God, by the real removal of the sin which divides them. Therefore did He not only devote His whole earthly life, without any personal reserves, to that great mission, by a continuous self-oblation, but crowned and closed it by the sacrifice of a voluntary death for the sins of men. Thus, His whole life was an atonement; all its moral acts were a chain of propitiatory acts for the sins of men. Through the atonement, the Mediator also wrought the reconciliation of man with God, and became the author of a new covenant between man and God, based on His sacrificial death."—Döllinger, *The First Age of the Church*, vol. i. pp. 287, 288.

"In Jesus Christ, then, we have the guarantee or bond of religion; He is the means of an actual communication between the soul of man and the Eternal God. 'There is one Mediator between God and men, the man Christ Jesus.' He is the Mediator in virtue of the very terms of His being: His office of mediation is based upon the two natures which are united in His single Person. On the one hand, as the Eternal Son, He is one with the All-Holy and Infinite God; on the other, as the child of Mary, He shares all the finiteness and weakness of our manhood; He shares with it everything except its sin. Thus he impersonates and maintains, by the very fact of being what He is, a true vital bond between earth and heaven."—Liddon, *Some Elements of Religion*, p. 228.

CHAPTER V.

THE REVELATION OF THE SON.

IN disclosing the Fatherhood of God, Jesus Christ revealed man's filial relation to God. And more than this, He came to enable man to realize this relationship, by entering into fellowship with God as his Father.

By nature man is estranged from God, and every one who thinks seriously is conscious of this estrangement. Whilst man craves for intercourse with God, he feels unworthy of such intercourse, and shrinks from it. We naturally dread God, rather than love Him. This estrangement is due to moral evil, or sin. Sin not only provokes the divine displeasure, it breaks up the bond between man and God. Sin is the fatal obstacle to the mutual communion of God and man. It is sin which mars and destroys the filial relationship between man and God. " Depart from me; for I am a sinful man, O Lord,"[1] is the natural utterance of the human heart conscious of its sin. " Your iniquities have separated between you and your

[1] St. Luke v. 8.

God, and your sins have hid His face from you."[1] As Theophylact says, "Sin is a great ditch and wall, dividing us from God."[2] This is a truth of natural religion, and of its force every thoughtful man has experience.

When we say that Jesus Christ came to enable man to realize his filial relation to God, we mean that He came to break down the barrier which separates man from God. Jesus Christ "was manifested to take away sins."[3] He came to abolish the alienation caused by sin, and to restore man to fellowship with God, as his Father.

In order to accomplish this great reconciliation and restoration, two things are necessary—

i. The removal of the penal consequences of sin.

ii. The destruction of the power and habit of sin.

I. THE REMOVAL OF THE PENAL CONSEQUENCES OF SIN.

i.

"The wages of sin is death,"[4] i.e., death of the soul. Sin separates the soul from God, who is the source of its life. Finally separated from God, the soul must die eternally. "Sin, when

---

[1] Isaiah lix. 2.
[2] *in Luc.* xiv.
[3] 1 St. John iii. 5.
[4] Rom. vi. 23.

it is fullgrown, bringeth forth death."[1] It was to save man from the eternal consequences of sin, that God in Christ interposed. The wrath of the Righteous God rose up in awful grandeur against human sin, and, in strictest justice, demanded a satisfaction.[2] Jesus Christ made this satisfaction by offering up Himself in man's stead. As the sin-bearer, "Him who knew no sin He made to be sin on our behalf."[3] Jesus Christ was "holy, guileless, undefiled, separated from sinners,"[4] but as the representative of our race, He allowed Himself to be treated as though He were guilty of our sins. In surrendering His life in unspeakable agonies, He endured the penalty due to man's sin. As Man, He suffered death for us: as God, He gave an infinite value to His sufferings and death. It is not so much the *painfulness* of the sufferings of Jesus Christ which gave them their power with God, as the *obedience* of which they were the evidence. "It was not His death," says St. Bernard, "but His freely dying, which was pleasing to God." The Passion and Cruci-

---

[1] St. James i. 15.

[2] "The legal sense of the word 'satisfaction' is the appeasing a creditor on the subject of his debt, not necessarily by the payment of it, but by any means that he will accept. The word implies a debt which we have not the means of paying, a debt of punishment in consequence of our sins, or of obedience to compensate former disobedience."—Archbp. Thomson, in Aids to Faith, *The Death of Christ*, p. 350.

[3] 2 Cor. v. 21. [4] Heb. vii. 26.

fixion of Christ were the witness to His perfect conformity to the will of God. In dying, He satisfied to the full the righteous claims of God on the obedience of man. His obedience knew no bounds or limits, for He became "obedient even unto death, yea, the death of the cross."[1] Thus, in bearing "our sins in His body upon the tree,"[2] Jesus Christ reconciled sinful man to God. This is the Christian doctrine of the Atonement, the making of God and man to be 'at one' in Christ.

ii.

There is an objection raised against the reasonableness of the doctrine of the Atonement. It is urged that God is not just in freeing the guilty by the punishment of the innocent. "This would be a very real difficulty if we looked upon our Lord as an unwilling victim punished by God for our sins. But we have assumed the great and original Christian doctrine, that He is not only Man but God, and that, as God, He and the Father are one in will. When it is said that 'God gave His only begotten Son,' that 'He spared not His own Son, but delivered Him up for us all,' we have to remember that what God the Father wills the Son wills also, and that the victim who suffered was also the priest who offered, and the God who accepted the sacrifice. The

[1] Phil. ii. 8.   [2] 1 St. Pet. ii. 24.

death of Christ is never described in the Bible as a punishment, but it is very often called a sacrifice. To punish an innocent and unwilling victim instead of the guilty is unjust; but there is no question of injustice when one willingly sacrifices himself for the sake of others. . . . If the death of Christ was necessary to propitiate the wrath of God, it was necessary to propitiate His own wrath also; if it was the manifestation of His love, it was the manifestation of the Father's love also."[1] The Atonement is not only the Son's offering of Himself, it is also the Father's offering of the Son. "They went both of them together."[2]

If it is unjust to forgive the guilty without demanding the full penalty of the offence, then all human forgiveness must be unjust. In human forgiveness, strict justice is seldom enforced. If a man robs his neighbour, he is, by the law of the land, liable to a penalty; but if the thief is forgiven by the man he has wronged and no compensation demanded, we cannot say that such forgiveness is unjust. In like

---

[1] A. T. Lyttelton, in Oxford House Papers, Second Series, *The Justice of the Atonement*, pp. 42, 43.

[2] Gen. xxii. 6, 8.

The doctrine of the Atonement "is not unjust, because the Father's will to punish never outstripped the Son's to suffer, and because His death was a solemn offering of Himself in love, for man's redemption. Nor can there be any tendency to transfer from the severe Father to the loving Son, the love we owe to both; for the mode of our redemption was designed by both, and the Son adopts the Father's and the Father sanctions the Son's loving self-sacrifice."— *Aids to Faith*, p. 365.

manner God, in pardoning sin for Christ's sake, does not necessarily prove Himself to be unjust.

Hitherto, we have been speaking of God's remission of the eternal consequences or penalty of sin. In saying that Christ suffered for man, we are not to suppose that no part of the punishment of sin falls upon the pardoned sinner. In a variety of ways temporal punishment is visited even upon those who repent and are forgiven. This is a matter of common experience. "Thou wast a God that forgavest them, though thou tookest vengeance of their doings."[1] As Mr. Gore has pointed out, "There is no passage in the New Testament which naturally suggests that there is any sort of suffering which Christ suffered, which we are not also called to suffer in our degree."[2]

iii.

But it must be remembered that if Jesus Christ offered Himself as man's *substitute*, He offered Himself also as man's *representative*. The human race, though composed of countless individuals, nevertheless forms one organic whole, one vast family—mankind. The Incarnation is the taking up of the whole of our race into union with God, in the Person of Jesus Christ. He is set forth as "The first-

---

[1] Ps. xcix. 8. [2] *The Creed of the Christian*, p. 53.

born of all creation,"[1] "The beginning of the creation of God."[2] In taking our nature, He assumed a real relationship to every member of our race.[3] In the language of St. Irenæus, He 'recapitulated,' or summed up, humanity in Himself.[4] It was in this capacity, as the new head of the redeemed race, that Jesus Christ offered Himself to the Eternal Father, and wrought the great Atonement. And He did this, as we have said, by a life and death of perfect obedience.

It is because of the organic unity of our race, that the separate sins of all sinners in all ages are described in the New Testament as forming but one huge sin—the sin of the world. Jesus Christ was proclaimed to be "the Lamb of God, which taketh away the sin of the world."[5] He did this in His representative character, as the Son of Man. Sin is, in its essence, strictly a defective moral act, an act of the will in a wrong direction: the Atonement was essentially a perfect moral act, an act of the will of the Son of Man in harmony with the divine will. "Lo, I am

---

[1] Col. i. 15.   [2] Rev. iii. 14.
[3] "There is such a thing as that common nature of man which is handed down through an innumerable series of personal inheritors; and He who was personally God, took His place in this series by Incarnation, and thus assumed a common relation to all its possessors."—Wilberforce, *The Doctrine of the Incarnation*, Ch. iii. p. 56.
[4] See the author's *Expositions of Catholic Doctrine*, Pt. ii. Ch. i.
[5] St. John i. 29.

come to do Thy will, O God."[1] The sin of man forms one vast act of disobedience; and to make amends for this disobedience, Jesus Christ, in man's nature, and as his representative, yielded a perfect obedience as a great central act of reparation to God. This obedience He offered by His life and sacrifice, in the name and in the person of all mankind.[2]

[1] Heb. x. 7.

[2] "Suppose that the members of a tribe have revolted against their foreign rulers, that the revolt is foolish and wicked, and that the head of the tribe has done all in his power to restrain them, but in vain. The revolt goes on, though he will not join it, and it fails hopelessly. Then suppose that the head of the tribe should come forward and say, 'Though I am personally innocent of their offence, yet I am theirs and they are mine; I cannot separate myself from them, I take the responsibility for their sin; put me to death, and let these go free.' This is no impossible supposition: history records deeds as grand in their generosity, as deep in their sympathy."—*The Justice of the Atonement*, p. 46.

"All nations have delighted in and treasured up instances, whether mythical or historic, of self-sacrifice and voluntary surrender of life for the benefit of others, or for the preservation of country. The valour of the three hundred Greeks, who perished in the Pass, nobly fighting against the hosts of the enemy for their country; the story of the Roman patriot, who is said to have spurred his horse and plunged into the chasm in the market-place, at the instance of the oracle, that the earthquake might cease and the city of Rome be preserved, are cases in point. Or to take an instance from history near our own time; we read, how in the Reign of Terror, when thirty victims were summoned every morning to the place of execution, a father and son, by name Loizerelles, were in the prison of S. Lazare; and that on the morning when the son's name was called amongst those condemned to die, the father came out from his cell and took the place of the son. Amid the excitement of the scene, the act of substitution was not discovered till the guillotine had done its work, and the father had died in the son's stead."— Hutchings, *Some Aspects of the Cross*, Serm. ii. p. 60. The whole of this grand sermon will repay perusal.

iv.

The following summary of the doctrine of the Atonement, from the pen of Archbishop Thomson, may be useful here.

"1. God sent His Son into the world to redeem lost and ruined man from sin and death, and the Son willingly took upon Him the form of a servant for this purpose; and thus the Father and the Son manifested their love for us.

"2. God the Father laid upon His Son the weight of the sins of the whole world, so that He bare in His own body the wrath which men must else have borne, because there was no other way of escape for them; and thus the Atonement was a manifestation of divine justice.

"3. The effect of the Atonement thus wrought is, that man is placed in a new position, freed from the dominion of sin, and able to follow holiness; and thus the doctrine of the Atonement ought to work in all the hearers a sense of love, of obedience, and of self-sacrifice.

"In shorter words, the sacrifice of the death of Christ is a proof of divine *love*, and of divine *justice*, and is for us a document of *obedience*."[1]

v.

Let us pause to ask, Is not the revelation of the Son in the Atonement, however mysterious, a reasonable doctrine?

[1] *Aids to Faith*, p. 337.

Does not the Atonement disclose God's love for man, as nothing else could do? If God dies to save sinners from the eternal consequences of sin, how great must His love for sinners be! The Cross and Passion of Jesus Christ is the revelation of God's measureless love for man.

Does not the Atonement mark the enormity, and exhibit the awful malignity of sin, as nothing else could do? Man could never have fully realized the deadly nature of moral evil, if it had not touched God. If evil leads to everlasting shame, was not God merciful in showing evil in its true colours, and, by the death of His Son, giving man a startling object-lesson, which should arrest and compel attention? Is not the Atonement the truest remedy for carelessness about sin?

Does not the Atonement persuade men to repent and forsake sin, as nothing else could do? If God Himself so hates sin as to die to save men from it and from its everlasting consequences, does not all this form an irresistible appeal to every right-minded man to hate sin too?

Does not the Atonement teach us, as nothing else could do, that, if God has permitted evil to enter His world, He has recognized His responsibility for its permission by coming into personal conflict with it, and by suffering it to touch His own Person? Does not the Cross and Passion of Jesus Christ reveal the divine

The Revelation of the Son.

sympathy with the victims of moral and physical evil?

Does not the Atonement disclose God's almighty power over sin, just when it reached its supreme height and greatest climax, as nothing else could do? "In the death of Jesus sin stood revealed to itself. In that deed it first reached its full height; it brought forth into act all the potential consequences of ages of lust and malice. The devil was a liar and a murderer from the beginning, and men obeyed him in all falsehood and wrong. But he never showed what he was capable of till he murdered the sinless Redeemer in the name of God. And with that crowning act his power was scattered and overthrown. . . . Satan, as lightning, fell from heaven, just as he stood upon the highest heap of ruin. And out of the discord and the darkness of that hour, the most terrible in human history, was heard a voice proclaiming peace to man, just when Satan's foot was planted most firmly on His neck."[1]

Surely, when rightly considered, the doctrine of the Atonement, if exceeding mysterious, is a reasonable doctrine.

vi.

Again, the doctrine of the Atonement finds its verification in human experience. The

[1] *Aids to Faith,* p. 356.

Redeemer declared, "I, if I be lifted up from the earth, will draw all men unto myself."[1] Here, as on other occasions, Jesus Christ clearly foretold His Passion,[2] and His prediction was literally fulfilled. He *was* lifted up on the cross on Calvary. And, beyond this, His promise to "draw all men unto Himself," through the cross, has been universally realized. In all ages the cross of Christ has possessed an irresistible attraction for mankind. The sinful contemplate Christ crucified, and forthwith hearts are melted in true penitence, and the hope of pardon and reconciliation becomes assured. The tempted find in Christ crucified a source of strength to resist and to conquer. The sorrowful and afflicted obtain sympathy, comfort, resignation, and peace.

> "Is it not strange, the darkest hour
>   That ever dawned on sinful earth
> Should touch the heart with softer power
>   For comfort, than an angel's mirth?
> That to the cross the mourner's eye should turn
> Sooner than where the stars of Christmas burn?"
>
> Keble, *The Christian Year*, Good Friday.

---

[1] St. John xii. 32; see also Ibid. iii. 14; viii. 28.

[2] See St. Matt. xvi. 21; xvii. 12, 22, 23; xxvi. 2; St. Mark viii. 31; ix. 12; x. 33, 34; St. Luke ix. 22; xii. 50; xvii. 25; xxiv. 7. The precise fulfilment of these prophecies is a striking proof of the truth of our Lord's claim to be divine.

II. The Destruction of the Power and Habit of Sin.

Hitherto, we have considered the revelation of the Son in the Atonement, in what He did *for* us, in our stead. Now, we pass on to consider the revelation of the Son in the renewal and restoration of mankind, in what He does *in* us, with our co-operation. The redemption of man is inseparably connected with his reformation.

Man needs more than pardon for sin; he needs freedom from the power and habit of sin. By birth man comes into the world under the dominion of moral evil. By actual sin he contracts the habit of sin. Jesus Christ is revealed as the deliverer from all sin, both original and actual.

i.

Christ's deliverance of mankind from Original Sin.

It is a matter of observation that every new-born life comes into the world with a mysterious, innate, and inevitable bias towards moral evil. Man's inborn proneness to evil is a fact of sad experience, which unbelievers in the Christian revelation have in vain attempted to explain. Whilst the general law of the natural world is one of progress from lower to higher levels, in man this law has been interrupted by the presence of moral evil. If science teaches that man's career has been one of progress in the physical sphere, the same cannot be said in reference to the moral sphere. The tendency to moral evil is a disease or defect, which has fastened upon the root of human nature; and it is an unmistakable sign or mark, not of progress, but of deterioration. "To me who would do good, evil is present."[1] "The imagination of man's heart is evil from his youth."[2] "Behold, I was shapen in iniquity; and in sin did my mother conceive me."[3] "The evil leaven," says Rabbi Moses Haddarschan, "is placed in man from the time that he is formed."[4] We instinctively feel that the bias towards evil is both an unnatural and a degrading thing. Whence came it? It is impossible to believe that it is any part of our original nature, as planned by God.

The divine revelation alone gives an adequate, satisfactory, and reasonable answer to the question. It teaches that God made man at the first "very good,"[5] and that the sinful inclination, which is the common experience of all men, was no part of man's original outfit. Even if it be true that man was at the first barbarous, such a supposition does not necessarily imply that he was prone to sin. The Christian account is, that "at

---

[1] Rom. vii. 21.
[2] Gen. viii. 21.
[3] Ps. li. 5.
[4] qu. Pascal, *of Original Sin*, p. 193.
[5] Gen. i. 31.

the beginning of human life, properly so called, when first a being truly called a man woke up to consciousness of his relation to God, to nature, to himself, he did not find sin part of his being; he might have obeyed the movement of the Spirit of God, and realized his true sonship by keeping his animal nature under the control of the spirit: so he would have fulfilled the law of his destined manhood."[1] It is the Christian belief that the first man, placed on his trial, fell into actual sin, and thereby lost his fellowship with God; and that he transmitted his nature, thus disordered, to all his descendants. Every leaf of a tree suffers from the decay of its roots.

"The objection has been made, that the Bible, while describing the first sin as an external sensuous occurrence, and almost as a childish act, yet makes it an event entailing the most tremendous consequences upon the whole human race. But instead of dwelling on the outward circumstances, we should penetrate this external covering, and observe the moral transactions going on within the heart. And these are of the deepest significance. When we contemplate man in the original, happy harmony of his mind and will with God, and then behold him misconceiving God's love, suspecting that He was arbitrarily and enviously denying him a good in which

[1] Gore, in Lux Mundi, *The Christian Doctrine of Sin*, p. 533.

his future happiness was involved; then rejecting God's commandment, and taking his future into his own hand, to fashion it for himself in the way of disobedience to God,— we shall be constrained to admit that the whole disposition of his heart towards God, his Father, was perverted; that he had departed from his childlike relationship to God— had separated himself from God—had, like the prodigal son, in heart forsaken his Father's house, and gone into the far country of alienation from Him. What wonder, then, was it that he met with misery? We must not stop merely at externals; these were indifferent, and caused by the infant-like condition of the first man; but must strive to appreciate the true moral significance of the occurrence. We shall then perceive and confess it to have been an event of momentous importance, and the more so from its position at the very commencement of history, and while the race was still in its youth, and its nature not yet settled. It is this which gives this event the importance of a catastrophe, involving in its consequences all mankind.

"This deed at the beginning was, by its very nature, fatal to the whole race; for it was the deed of their head, in whom the whole race was represented and comprised. We cannot but feel that it concerns us all, that it is no indifferent or accidental matter, but that we are personally concerned therein, as is ever

The Revelation of the Son.

and everywhere the case in the transactions of one who represents a community."[1]

It is the Christian doctrine that man's proneness to sin is an evil inheritance, derived from his natural connection with 'the first parent and historic representative of the race,' in his fallen state. Having lost the robe of grace and original righteousness, the first man was unable to bequeath it to his offspring.

But Jesus Christ came to restore this loss in a supernatural manner. He came to remedy the defect by bringing man into a new and supernatural relationship to Himself as the New Man, the Second Man. "As in Adam all die, so also in Christ shall all be made alive."[2] Of this we have already spoken in connection with the virgin-birth of Jesus Christ.[3]

NOTE ON ORIGINAL SIN.

"The moral objections supposed to lie against the doctrine of the transmission of original sin lose sight of the fact, that in nature, as in Scripture, men are regarded under two aspects, (1) as forming an organic whole, (2) as separate personalities. The transmitted loss of supernatural grace, which is the essence of the Fall, is analogous to the providential 'visiting the sins of the fathers upon the children unto the third and fourth generation' in the entail of loss of property or reputation, or of constitutions impaired by self-indulgence. The objections from the point of view of natural justice assume man to be only a person, not a member of an organism, viz., humanity, in the collective destinies of which, for good and evil, the individual man inevitably shares."—Liddon, *Explanatory Analysis of St. Paul's Epistle to the Romans*, p. 104.

[1] Luthardt, *Fundamental Truths*, pp 186, ff.
[2] 1 Cor. xv. 22.
[3] See pp. 217, ff.

Archbishop Thomson's remarks in Aids to Faith are well worthy of attention. "Alike in the good and evil qualities of men, the effect of hereditary transmission comes under daily notice. . . . Absolute freedom is more than rare, it is impossible. Men enter this world the heirs of passions, perhaps cultivated in the last generation to an unnatural height; they are nurtured on bad examples and a low morality, so that they cannot do the things that they would. And it is the rule, and not the exception, that men's moral actions are tinctured with the colour of the actions of others before and around them, which they could not possibly have caused. Now, if these facts are admitted,—if, instead of that perfect isolation of responsibility which some insist on, a joint responsibility is the universal rule,—with what show of reason can they pretend, that it is on this ground that the Christian scheme is untenable? Look into the black London alleys teeming with ignorance, improvidence, and vice; do you not see written in those faces eloquent in wretchedness, 'We did not place ourselves here: were the choice given us freely, we would not be as we are'? Then what do we think of the consistency of those, who see guilt brought on by others, but think it revolting that another should take it off? Living comments upon the words 'In Adam all die' abound, and cannot be blotted out: it ought not then to revolt our moral sense that those other words are added, 'In Christ shall all be made alive.' The latter words, in fact, go far to solve the mystery of the former. For the constant transmission of sinfulness, the heritage of sins bequeathed from the fathers to their children, is revolting to the moral sense when severed from the thought of a Deliverer."—*The Death of Christ*, pp. 353, ff. The whole essay deserves careful perusal, as a thoughtful and masterly exposition of the mysterious doctrine of the Atonement.

ii.

Christ's deliverance of mankind from Actual Sin.

Just as God in Christ is revealed as interposing to remedy man's inherited defect of birth sin, so also is He manifested as the liberator of man from the chain and habit of actual sin.

The Incarnation and Passion of the Son of God is the breaking of the power of sin. By the Incarnation there appeared One who lived without fault—One over whom, from the moment of His conception to that of His death, sin had no dominion. The life of Jesus Christ was a new thing. "The Lord looked down from heaven upon the children of men, to see if there were any that did understand, that did seek after God. They are all gone aside; they are together become filthy; there is none that doeth good, no, not one."[1] But in Jesus Christ was found the great exception to the universal rule. To the moral excellence of Christ we have already referred.[2]

By His sacrifice on the cross, Jesus Christ consummated a life of perfect obedience. He became "obedient even unto death, yea, the death of the cross."[3] His obedience in death was but the last and crowning act of a long line of faultless conduct. Thus in Jesus Christ, we see the example of what human life should be; and this example is a source of hope, encouragement, and power, to all who keep it before their eyes. "Christ also suffered for you, leaving you an example, that ye should follow His steps: who did no sin, neither was guile found in His mouth."[4]

But far beyond the moral support to be derived from the example of Jesus Christ, is

[1] Ps. xiv. 2, 3.   [2] See pp. 192, ff.
[3] Phil. ii. 8.   [4] 1 St. Pet. ii. 21, 22.

the actual communication of His divine grace to His brethren. Through the Incarnation the fulness of grace is bestowed upon mankind. "The Word became flesh, and dwelt among us, full of grace and truth.... Grace and truth came by Jesus Christ."[1] The effect of sin is to defile the heart, to darken the understanding, and to weaken the will. Sin injures man at the centre of his moral being. The work of grace is to cleanse the heart, to enlighten the understanding, and to strengthen the will—to make men like Christ, by uniting them to Himself. It is the Christian doctrine that this divine grace is merited for mankind by the obedience and sacrifice of the Son of God. Thus, Jesus Christ is revealed as the source of the recreative power for all mankind.

"Christian holiness," says a recent writer, "is the reproduction in the individual of the life of the Incarnate Son of God. That this might be possible, there took place that series of events which St. John describes as the glorification of Jesus Christ. The life, perfectly well-pleasing to God, and therefore the supreme standard of holiness, passes through the stage of death. The sacrifice on Calvary removes the barrier raised between the Creator and His creatures by sin. The resurrection is, on the one hand, the seal of God's acceptance stamped upon His Son's

[1] St. John i. 14, 17.

atoning work; on the other, marks the final stage in that process by which Christ's human nature is 'perfected.' For by the resurrection that nature is spiritualized, is released from earthly limitations, and becomes available as a recreative force. The ascension is the condition of Christ's manifestation as 'a quickening Spirit,' as the 'power of God.' By sacramental channels He communicates to our entire nature His life-giving humanity, as the means of our recreation after the image of God. Thus the life of the Incarnate is extended in the life of the redeemed, and by a natural and orderly growth, the character of Christ is reproduced in His members through the continuous operation of the Spirit, whose office it is to 'take of the things of Christ and shew them unto' men. He who is outwardly our example thus becomes an inward principle of life." [1]

[1] R. L. Ottley, in Lux Mundi, *Christian Ethics*, pp. 505, 506.

"The Spirit of the Lord shall rest upon Him, the Spirit of wisdom and understanding, the Spirit of counsel and might, the Spirit of knowledge and of the fear of the Lord."—Isaiah xi. 2, 3.

"I will pray the Father, and He shall give you another Comforter, that He may be with you for ever, even the Spirit of truth: whom the world cannot receive; for it beholdeth Him not, neither knoweth Him: ye know Him; for He abideth with you, and shall be in you."—St. John xiv. 16, 17.

CHAPTER VI.

THE REVELATION OF THE SPIRIT.

THE manifestation of the Spirit was a gradual process, and thus in great measure parallel with the manifestation of Jesus Christ. As Jesus Christ was present in nature, in man, in prophets, before His open manifestation in the Incarnation, so it was with the Spirit.

i.

Mr. Alfred Russel Wallace, in his work on *Darwinism*, says, "There are at least three stages in the development of the organic world, when some new cause or power must necessarily have come into action.

"The first stage is the change from inorganic to organic; when the earliest vegetable cell, or the living protoplasm out of which it arose, first appeared. This is often imputed to a mere increase of complexity of chemical compounds; but increase of complexity, with consequent instability, even if we admit that it may have produced protoplasm as a chemical compound, could certainly not have produced *living* protoplasm—protoplasm which has the power of growth and of reproduction, and of that continuous process of development which has resulted in the marvellous variety and complex organisation of the whole vegetable kingdom. . . .

"The next stage is still more marvellous, still more completely beyond all possibility of explanation by matter, its laws and forces. It is the introduction of sensation or consciousness, constituting the fundamental distinction between the animal and vegetable kingdoms. Here all idea of mere complication of structure producing the result, is out of the question. We feel it to be altogether preposterous to assume, that at a certain stage of complexity of atomic constitution, and as a necessary result of that complexity alone, an *ego* should start into existence, a thing that *feels*, that is *conscious* of its own existence. Here we have the certainty that something new has arisen, a being whose nascent consciousness has gone on increasing in power and definiteness, till it has culminated in the higher animals. No verbal explanation or attempt at explanation—such as the statement that life is the result of the molecular forces of the protoplasm, or that the whole existing organic universe, from the amœba up to man, was latent in the fire-mist from which the solar system was developed—can afford any mental satisfaction, or help us in any way to a solution of the mystery.

"The third stage is the existence in man of a number of his most characteristic and noblest faculties; those which raise him furthest above the brutes, and open up possibilities of almost indefinite advancement. These faculties could not possibly have been developed by means of the same laws, which have determined the progressive development of the organic world in general, and also of man's physical organism.

"These three distinct stages of progress, from the inorganic world of matter and motion up to man, point clearly to an unseen universe—to a world of spirit, to which the world of matter is altogether subordinate."[1]

It is reasonable to believe that the 'new cause or power, which came into action' at each of these three stages, was the presence and operation of the Spirit of God, the Lifegiver.

All life in nature is the gift of the Spirit, and manifests His hidden presence. It is the Spirit who has 'beautified and garnished' all the works of nature. He has ever been at work in the material world, evolving, by His presence, form, beauty, order, life.[2] "The

---

[1] Ch. xv. pp. 474, ff.

[2] The theory "of evolution, if verified, would only enlarge the work of the Spirit in the material world, for it leaves the primary act of creation untouched. . . . The presence of the Spirit seems only grander in nature, if instead of special creations and monotonous reproduction, we may view Him

Spirit of God," says Ruskin, "is around you, in the air that you breathe, His glory in the light that you see; and in the fruitfulness of the earth, and the joy of its creatures, He has written for you, day by day, His revelation, as He has granted you, day by day, your daily bread."[1]

But the operation of the Holy Spirit, previous to the Incarnation, was not confined to the bestowal of life in the material sphere; He had ever been at work in the moral sphere also. All man's early efforts after truth and righteousness, all moral excellence attained by man from the dawn of history, is to be attributed to His inspiration. From the time of Abraham, the father of the chosen race, the Spirit's presence became more intense. As Mr. Hutchings, following St. Augustine, has pointed out, "the workings of the Spirit began to be linked with a chosen family, which was, henceforth, to be the recipient of a series of blessings and manifestations. Hitherto, the Spirit had been striving with individuals separately, but now there was to be an order, and locality, for His communications. His work would be, so to speak, condensed."[2] The prophets, who pro-

who is 'the Lord, and Giver of life,' as producing by means of environment and natural selection, within certain limits, fresh forms of beauty and elaborateness, thus leading on to a perfection of endless variety that which was at first a shapeless mass."—Hutchings, *The Person and Work of the Holy Ghost*, ii. pp. 48, 49.

[1] *Deucalion*, i. xii. 40.
[2] *The Person and Work of the Holy Ghost*, ii. p. 57.

claimed the moral law, owed their inspiration to the Spirit's enlightening gift. The prophet was a spiritual man, "a man that hath the Spirit,"[1] who was more vividly conscious than his fellows of the mind and will of God. He owed this deeper insight to the operation of the Holy Spirit.

"The action of the Spirit upon man after the Fall was chiefly in three ways. First, by direct striving with his conscience, to convince him of sin by its penalties; secondly, by revealing to man an external law of righteousness; and, thirdly, by successive communications through the prophets, of instruction, promise, and judgment. All the operations of the Holy Spirit before the coming of Christ, may be arranged under this division:—striving with the conscience, revealing an outward law, inspiring the prophets."[2]

ii.

But all these manifestations of the Spirit's presence in the natural and moral spheres, reached their climax in the Person and work of Jesus Christ. The Incarnation itself was, according to the Gospel record, brought about through the agency of the Holy Spirit. To Mary's question as to how the Incarnation

[1] Hos. ix. 7.
[2] *The Person and Work of the Holy Ghost*, ii. p. 54.

should be accomplished, the reply came, "The Holy Ghost shall come upon thee, and the power of the Most High shall overshadow thee: wherefore also that which is to be born shall be called holy, the Son of God."[1] In his natural perplexity Joseph was admonished, "Fear not to take unto thee Mary thy wife: for that which is conceived in her is of the Holy Ghost."[2] In His baptism in the river Jordan, "Jesus saw the Spirit of God descending as a dove, and coming upon Him."[3] This event was witnessed by St. John the Baptist, who testified to it.[4] "Jesus was led up of the Spirit into the wilderness to be tempted of the devil."[5] "Jesus returned in the power of the Spirit into Galilee."[6] He received the Spirit without measure.[7] He declared, "The Spirit of the Lord is upon me, because He anointed me to preach good tidings to the poor: He hath sent me to proclaim release to the captives, and recovering of sight to the blind, to set at liberty them that are bruised, to proclaim the acceptable year of the Lord."[8] It was "through the eternal Spirit" that Christ "offered Himself without blemish unto God."[9] It was through the Spirit that Christ was raised from the dead.[10]

[1] St. Luke i. 35.
[2] St. Matt. i. 20.
[3] Ibid. iii. 16.
[4] St. John i. 32-35.
[5] St. Matt. iv. 1.
[6] St. Luke iv. 14.
[7] St. John iii. 34.
[8] St. Luke iv. 18, 19.
[9] Heb. ix. 14.
[10] Rom. viii. 11.

iii.

Jesus Christ's manifestation of God was completed in His revelation of the Spirit. He promised that He would send forth the Spirit from the Father upon men. "It is expedient for you that I go away: for if I go not away, the Comforter will not come unto you; but if I go, I will send Him unto you."[1] As a fact of history, and as a matter of experience, the promise of Jesus Christ has been fulfilled. As a fact of history, it was fulfilled ten days after He left the world in visible presence, in the descent of the Holy Spirit on the Day of Pentecost. "When the day of Pentecost was now come, they were all together in one place. And suddenly there came from heaven a sound as of the rushing of a mighty wind, and it filled all the house where they were sitting. And there appeared unto them tongues parting asunder, like as of fire; and it sat upon each one of them. And they were all filled with the Holy Spirit."[2] That the advent of the Spirit was an actual fact, is attested by the marvellous change which passed over the characters of the apostles. Previously timid and fainthearted, they suddenly exhibited signs of supernatural courage, bearing their witness to Jesus Christ far and wide in the face of ridicule, persecution, and death. "The boldness of Peter and John" was a matter for marvel to

[1] St. John xvi. 7.   [2] Acts ii. 1-4.

the Jews. The apostles "spake the word of God with boldness."[1] Twelve unlearned and ignorant men went forth to found the Christian Church, and to convert the world. History certifies to their success. The Christian thinker attributes the marvel to the coming of the Holy Spirit, which Jesus Christ promised. "Ye shall receive power, when the Holy Ghost is come upon you: and ye shall be my witnesses both in Jerusalem, and in all Judæa and Samaria, and unto the uttermost part of the earth."[2]

iv.

Jesus Christ declared that the Spirit should come upon men as an abiding possession for all time. "I will pray the Father, and He shall give you another Comforter, that He may be with you for ever, even the Spirit of truth."[3] The presence of the Holy Spirit in the hearts of men is a matter of experience. The Christian religion has produced a new development of humanity, a new type of character, a higher level of life, wholly unlike anything to be discovered before Christ came and sent the Spirit into the world. This new type of character has to be accounted for. It cannot fairly be attributed to Christ's example alone, great as its power is. A good and great example may

---
[1] Acts iv. 13, 31. [2] Ibid. i. 8.
[3] St. John xiv. 16, 17.

persuade to imitation, but it is powerless to *secure* imitation without a corresponding inward movement in the heart and will.[1] This new type of character is best and most reasonably accounted for, by allowing that a new influence has asserted itself in mankind. This higher level of life, this height of moral excellence, appeared suddenly in the world. And its appearance dates from, and coincides with, the time of Christ's gift of the Holy Spirit. Thus, belief in the Holy Ghost is consistent with the rise of this new spiritual force amongst men.

V.

Whilst Jesus Christ proclaimed Himself to be "the Life,"[2] He declared that "it is the Spirit that quickeneth."[3] It is thus the Christian belief that as Jesus Christ is the Life, the Holy Spirit is the Life-giver—that it is the

---

[1] "If we look higher still, we do indeed behold our Lord setting an example: but we observe also that there is something which He appraises higher than this function of example. Had this been His highest work, it would, beyond a doubt, have been expedient for us, if possible, that He should not have gone away. As it was, it was 'expedient' that His disciples should lose His visible example, that they might gain a greater gift—the gift of the Spirit. 'If I go not away, the Paraclete will not come unto you; but if I go, I will send Him unto you.' In fact the Paraclete did come at Pentecost, and in virtue of His coming the Church became a body instinct with a new life, and Christianity a thing 'not in word, but in power.'"—Gore, *Bampton Lectures*, viii. p. 217.

[2] St. John xiv. 6.   [3] Ibid. vi. 63.

office of the Spirit to convey to man the life of Christ, by rooting, grafting, and embodying man in Him. 'As the Son by Incarnation bound human nature to Himself, the Spirit by indwelling carries on and completes His work.' The Spirit "effects an influx into the regenerate man of the blessed virtues of the nature of the Second Adam, an infusion of the exalted life of Jesus Christ, through an open duct, living, and divine, into the man who is born again into Him, the incarnate and glorified Son of God."[1]

If we would know the secret of heavenly-mindedness, of Christ-like uprightness, purity, gentleness, truthfulness, self-sacrifice, and charity, we must confess the sanctifying agency of the Holy Spirit, uniting the souls of men to Jesus Christ, and enabling them to follow His perfect example. It is only when men yield to, and co-operate with, the blessed influences of the Spirit of God, that others will " take knowledge of them, that they have been with Jesus." [2]

[1] Moule, *Veni Creator*, pp. 39 ff.   [2] Acts iv. 13.

"Our Lord has actually founded upon the earth His holy city, the new Jerusalem, His sheep-fold, His spiritual house, and has stored it with the treasures of His truth and grace; a spiritual sphere, the scene of His especial presence, of the clearest expressions of His mind and will, and love, and of all-sufficient help to be as He is and to do as He commands."
—E. F. Russell, in *Misericordia*, Vol. iv. p. 83.

"Our Redeemer founded upon earth a visible and permanent society, cohering, and intended always to cohere, by means not only of a common profession of belief, but also of common and public ordinances, which by their outward form constituted and sealed the visible union of believers; while by the inward spiritual grace attached to them, they were also destined to regenerate men in Christ, and to build them up in Him. . . . If a society were founded by Christ, does not this imply the foundation of a government? If ordinances of grace were established, did they not require to be entrusted to the hands of the persons constituting that government, for their permanent conservation?"—W. E. Gladstone, *Church Principles considered in their Results*, p. 191.

CHAPTER VII.

THE REVELATION OF THE CHURCH.

OF the Church of Jesus Christ as an objective fact, we have already spoken. We have urged the permanence and expansion of the Christian Church as evidence of the truth of the divine claim of its Founder. It is not of these aspects of the Church that we are now about to treat, but rather of the mission of the Church to the world, of its purpose and work, as disclosed by Jesus Christ and His Spirit.

The best Christian thought on the subject of the Church is as follows:—

As the second Adam, the new head of the human race, Jesus Christ came to restore mankind to fellowship with God. For this end He organized a world-wide society in which to accomplish His gracious purpose. He willed that the redemptive and restorative virtue, residing in His own Person as the Incarnate God, should be extended to His brethren throughout the ages. In order to secure this extension of His Incarnate Life, He constituted the Christian Church to be the sphere in which the process of redemption and restoration might be most effectually carried out for all time. He ordained that in the Church, by the agency of His Spirit, mankind should enter into an assured union with Himself as the redeemer and restorer of humanity; and thus regain that true fellowship with God, which had been interrupted and forfeited by sin.

By the Incarnation God came into the world bearing in His Person the two great necessities for man's restoration to fellowship with God —grace and truth. "The Word became flesh, and dwelt among us, full of grace and truth."[1] "Grace and truth came by Jesus Christ."[2] That these two great necessities might be preserved and continued in the world, He organized His Church to be the divine society in which He enshrined the treasures of grace and truth for the benefit of mankind.

It was by the agency of the Spirit that this disclosure of the Church, as the sphere of grace and the organ of truth, was made. Jesus Christ declared that He would build His Church,[3] and that He had come to found the kingdom of God amongst men.[4] But it was reserved to the Spirit to reveal and to carry into effect the full intention of Christ in regard to His Church. To the apostles the promise was made by

[1] St. John i. 14.
[2] Ibid. v. 17.
[3] St. Matt. xvi. 18.
[4] Ibid. xiii., etc.

Christ, " The Comforter, even the Holy Spirit, whom the Father will send in my name, He shall teach you all things, and bring to your remembrance all that I said unto you."[1] " Howbeit when He, the Spirit of truth, is come, He shall guide you into all the truth."[2] Whilst Jesus Christ drew the outlines of the picture of the Church, it was left to the agency and abiding presence of His Spirit to fill in and to complete the design, and to make the Church the effectual instrument for applying the redemptive and restorative work of Christ to mankind.

i. THE CHURCH, THE SPHERE OF GRACE.

Man is a creature gifted with intelligence, affection, and will. By a right use of these endowments he is able by *nature* in some measure to know, to love, and to serve God. That he may be able to do these things more perfectly, it is the Christian belief that God adds to man's natural endowments a supernatural gift, a gift above nature. This supernatural gift is termed *grace*. By grace man is lifted out of his fallen state into fellowship with God. By cleansing the heart, illuminating the mind, and invigorating the will, grace fits man for union with God. The state of grace is the state of restored intercourse or communion with God.

[1] St. John xiv. 26   [2] Ibid. xvi. 13.

It is the Christian tradition that God has organized His Church as the sphere in which mankind may, in this life, be received into a state of grace. It is held that in the Church Jesus Christ, through the agency of His Spirit, raises men out of their fallen state, and places them in the state of grace, and thus fits them for the life of glory hereafter. The Church on earth is thus set forth as the highway of grace, the sure and certain road along which mankind may pass to glory. It is held that in the Church the work of redemption and restoration is carried on by the Holy Spirit uniting men to Jesus Christ, the redeemer and the restorer of humanity.

Jesus Christ came to restore man to fellowship with God as a race. By the Incarnation Christ entered into the ranks of human nature, and assumed a real relationship to the whole of humanity. As a race, mankind had, in the fall of the first Adam, lost fellowship with God. As a race, mankind in Jesus Christ, the second Adam, may be restored to fellowship with God. "For as in Adam all die, so also in Christ shall all be made alive."[1] Christ died to take away 'the sin of the world,' the sin of humanity; and He rose to life, and sent down His Spirit, to renew humanity as a whole.[2]

[1] 1 Cor. xv. 22.
[2] "The name *humanity* expresses just this, that individual human creatures are not mere examples of an universal, but

Thus, there comes home to the Christian consciousness the idea of the Church as a world-wide and enduring society, in which reside the spiritual forces of redemption and restoration which flow from Jesus Christ. These spiritual forces we know as grace, 'the power that worketh in us.' Grace is the power whereby Jesus Christ works upon the hearts, the minds, and the wills of mankind.

It is the teaching of Christ that His grace should be assured to mankind in the Church, as the sphere of grace, by means of outward and visible signs, or sacraments. He declared that He would bestow a new birth upon the soul by the sacrament of water and the Spirit.[1] It is the teaching of Christ that by the Spirit's operation the new life of Christ is planted in the soul in Baptism, and that this new life is supported and increased by a real though spiritual feeding upon Himself in the Communion of His Body and Blood.[2]

---

are preordained parts of a whole."—Lotze, *Microcosmus*, Vol. ii. Bk. vii. Ch. iv. p. 211.

"It is in correspondence with a fundamental law of man's social nature that the religion of the Son of Man should not deal with us first as isolated individuals; that it should present itself as a society incorporating individuals and developing the individual life by first absorbing it. It is because man is social that 'the perfect man' (Eph. iv. 13) is to be realized, not by the single Christian, but by the whole Church."—Gore, *The Mission of the Church*, p. 13.

[1] St John iii. 3, ff.   [2] Ibid. vi. 53, ff.

"The individual soul as it turns to God requires to be assured of the personal right of approach to Him, and then of the power of continuous fellowship with Him. This assur-

For the valid or secure administration of these two great ordinances, Jesus Christ appointed an order of men to be the stewards of His grace for all mankind. It has been the constant belief of the Christian Church that the apostolic succession [1] in the ministry is the guarantee of the bestowal of grace, by means of the sacraments.

Is it not reasonable to believe that, if God wills to impart His saving and sanctifying grace to mankind, He would give man the pledge and assurance of its bestowal by the appointment of visible channels for its communication; and that if He established ordinances of grace, He should have entrusted their administration to duly authorized persons? The Christian

---

ance is given to us, in a form suited to the circumstances of our life, in the two Sacraments of the Gospel—the Sacrament of Incorporation, and the Sacrament of Support. In these we have, according to our need, the revelation of our union with Christ and the revelation of His impartment of Himself to us."—Bp. Westcott, *Christus Consummator*, p. 69.

[1] "The principle of apostolic succession is that no man in the Church can validly exercise any ministry, except such as he has received from a source running back ultimately to the apostles, so that any ministry which a person takes upon himself to exercise, which is not covered by an apostolically received commission, is invalid."—*The Mission of the Church*, p. 31. See the author's *Plain Words on the Holy Catholic Church*, 5th ed. Pt. iii. Lect. vi; also *The Catholic Religion*, 7th ed. Pt. i. Ch. iii.

"There has been in practice the closest connexion between the doctrines of a visible Church, and that of a spiritual grace in the sacraments, and that of an apostolical succession in the ministry; so that in general they have been received or rejected together."—W. E. Gladstone, *Church Principles*, p. 192.

The Revelation of the Church.   301

doctrine of the Church as the sphere of grace, of the sacraments as the means of grace, of the apostolic ministry as the dispenser of grace, is surely eminently reasonable.

ii. THE CHURCH, THE ORGAN OF TRUTH.

The Church is to be regarded as the society to which Jesus Christ has committed the custody and proclamation of the truth which He came to reveal. The truth, which had been slowly and gradually disclosed to man, was completed and made known in its fulness by Christ. Our Incarnate Lord was "full of truth."[1] He expressly declared, "To this end have I been born, and to this end am I come into the world, that I should bear witness unto the truth."[2] And this sum of truth, which resided in Jesus Christ, was brought home to the apostles in its completeness by the coming of the Holy Spirit. "But the Comforter, even the Holy Spirit, whom the Father will send in my name, He shall teach you all things, and bring to your remembrance all that I said unto you."[3] It was the mission of the apostles, first to bear witness to the truth of which they were conscious, and then to hand it on to their successors in the ministry. Thus, the doctrine of Christ is ours to day. "If we believe," wrote Dean Church, "that God cares at all,

[1] St. John i. 14.   [2] Ibid. xviii. 37.
[3] Ibid. xiv. 26.

that what He sent among men by Jesus Christ should survive and should affect mankind, it is reasonable to think that Christian ideas would not be merely thrown broadcast on men, to take their chance in the throng and crush of all the rival interests, which come across and occupy men's minds. . . . If Christianity had been a philosophy, or a literature, or an aristocratic religion, a religion for a select few raised above their fellows by power of intellect and thought, its great ideas might have been left to wander about the world, seeking and finding their homes in individual minds. But Christianity was neither a philosophy, nor an aristocratic religion. It was a kingdom, and a system of discipline and life for mankind. God provided a home for great religious ideas in an organized society, the Church, as He provided a home for great moral and political ideas in an organized society, the State."[1]

In all departments of scientific truth, we are thankful to enter into the labours of others, and to accept as true the results of their study and experience. And it is in accordance with this spirit, that the Church calls upon men to accept the truth of which she has become possessed. Man is the heir of the ages, as much in the sphere of divine truth as in any other sphere of knowledge. It is not wisdom, but folly, to ignore the knowledge and experi-

[1] Oxford House Papers, Second Series, *The Christian Church*, pp. 65, 67.

ence of the past. As members of a corporate body, the Christian Church, we do not come into her ranks to discover the truth afresh. The truth, which has ever been coming to mankind from the dawn of history, and which reached its final disclosure in the Incarnation and the advent of the Spirit, is the inheritance of the Church of Jesus Christ for all time.

It is the belief of the Church that the apostolic ministry is of divine appointment, not only for the due communication of grace, but also for the due preservation and imparting of truth. And the Church regards the apostolic succession in the ministry as the guarantee of the unimpaired transmission of the doctrine of Christ. It is in the apostolic succession of the Christian ministry that men will best recognize the authentication of divine truth, and its application to the needs of mankind.

Is it not reasonable to believe that, if God has revealed His truth to man, He has made provision for its due preservation and transmission in the world? Is it not reasonable to believe that He has constituted a visible organization in which men may be assured of the possession of divine truth?

Is not the revelation of the Church of Jesus Christ eminently satisfactory? Does not the Church, with its scriptures and creeds, its ministry and sacraments, its code of discipline, answer an instinctive desire for some divine pledge that we are within the circle of the saving and renewing influences of Jesus Christ and His Spirit? The disclosure of the Catholic Church as the divinely appointed channel of grace, and the organ of truth, is a thing which commends itself to practical reason. As men come to accept the Church's claims, they find their act of faith justified by experience—the experience of belief supported, of grace received.

x

"When the Son of Man shall come in His glory, and all the angels with Him, then shall He sit on the throne of His glory: and before Him shall be gathered all the nations: and He shall separate them one from another, as the shepherd separateth the sheep from the goats: and He shall set the sheep on His right hand, but the goats on the left. Then shall the King say unto them on his right hand, Come, ye blessed of my Father, inherit the kingdom prepared for you from the foundation of the world. . . . Then shall He say also unto them on the left hand, Depart from me, ye cursed, into the eternal fire which is prepared for the devil and his angels."—St. Matt. xxv. 31, ff.

"All which can positively be asserted to be matter of mere revelation seems to be, that the great distinction between the righteous and the wicked, shall be made at the end of this world; that each shall *then* receive according to his deserts. Reason did, as it well might, conclude that it should, finally and upon the whole, be well with the righteous, and ill with the wicked: but it could not be determined upon any principles of reason, whether human creatures might not have been appointed to pass through other states of life and being, before that distributive justice should finally and effectually take place. Revelation teaches us, that the next state of things after the present is appointed for the execution of this justice; that it shall be no longer delayed; but the *mystery of God*, the great mystery of His suffering vice and confusion to prevail, *shall then be finished;* and He will *take to Him His great power and will reign*, by rendering to every one according to his works."--Butler, *Analogy*, i. ii. § 16, note.

CHAPTER VIII.

THE REVELATION OF THE LIFE TO COME.

THE revelation of Jesus Christ partook in great measure of the nature of the authentication or certification of truth. That is to say, He came to assure men of the truth of much which had been previously hinted at, and dimly perceived. His disclosure of the truth has enabled men to say, 'Now we are sure,' where before they could only say, 'It is probable.' The main truths which He authoritatively revealed had, in some degree, been anticipated before He came. By His coming and teaching, He verified such anticipations, and stamped them with His divine authority. Thus, our Lord's teaching was not so much the revelation of absolutely new truth, as the verification and development of the old. This is the case very specially with regard to the doctrine of the Life to Come.

The immortality of the soul is a truth of natural religion. If a belief in man's existence after death has not been universal, it has in all ages been very widely spread. Man has ever felt it impossible to imagine extinction.[1] The Buddhist's desire for such extinction is altogether an unnatural desire, and cannot seriously be held to contradict the common instinct of mankind. Man naturally feels that he can never lose his personality, never really die. And this natural expectation of a future life has been declared by Jesus Christ to be a true expectation.

i.

The resurrection of Jesus Christ from the dead is the great pledge which He has given man of his immortality. We may say that a life after death is an objective fact, of which mankind in Christ has already experience. The apostles bore witness that He lived again after His death on the cross. And it is a Christian doctrine that, as He lived after death, so shall we who are His. St. Paul declares the Christian belief in the words, "Now hath Christ been raised from the dead, the first-

---

[1] "It is evident that our *present* powers and capacities of reason, memory, and affection, do not depend upon our gross body in the manner in which perception by our organs of sense does; so they do not appear to depend upon it at all in any such manner, as to give ground to think, that the dissolution of this body will be the destruction of these our *present* powers of reflection, as it will of our powers of sensation; or to give ground to conclude, even that it will be so much as a suspension of the former."—Butler's *Analogy*, i. i. § 23.

The Revelation of the Life to come. 309

fruits of them that are asleep."[1] The firstfruits are the fruits to be followed by further fruits of a similar kind—the pledge and earnest of the coming harvest. The Christian doctrine of the resurrection of the body does not imply that the particles of our earthly bodies, which have dissolved in the grave and passed into various forms of natural life, will be brought together again; but that we 'in our same selves shall be reclothed in a spiritual body, which we shall recognize as our own body.' "It is sown a natural body; it is raised a spiritual body"[2]—this is the Christian doctrine.

The belief that death does not end all, but is to be succeeded by a future life, is assured by the resurrection and ascension of Jesus Christ, and by His positive teaching. There is perhaps hardly any subject upon which He more freely and frequently dwelt, than that of the life to come. He distinctly taught that death is not the end of life, but only an accident in life; and that the river of life flows on in the same course, which it took before it passed the cataract of death. In predicting a future state of happiness or misery for man, He proclaimed a truth of natural religion, that in the end virtue will meet its reward and vice its punishment. It is a matter of observation that in this life virtue rarely receives its full acknowledgment, and similarly that vice often goes

[1] 1 Cor. xv. 20. [2] Ibid. 44.

unpunished. It is in accordance with the dictates of reason and justice that there is a reckoning to come, when all this life's inequalities will be rectified, and every one shall get his due.

ii.

But Christ's disclosure of the truths of eternal reward or punishment in a future life, is much more than a revelation of the rectifying of the inequalities and injustices of earth. He taught that it is not simply because men have done so much good, that they will be everlastingly blessed; or because they have done so much evil, that they will be everlastingly condemned. Time bears no proportion to eternity; and good or evil temporally followed, cannot be deserving of eternal reward or punishment. Jesus Christ taught men that by doing good, they become good; and that by doing evil, they become evil. He taught men the solemn truth that the cultivation of good or evil habits, in the end, forms a good or evil character; and that settled character will determine the state of every man in the life to come.

> 'Sow an act, reap a habit :
> Sow a habit, reap a character :
> Sow a character, reap a destiny.'

It is in this light that He would have men consider the meaning of the sentence of everlasting acceptance or rejection, which He will

The Revelation of the Life to come. 311

one day pronounce upon every human being: "Come, ye blessed of my Father, inherit the kingdom prepared for you from the foundation of the world," or " Depart from me, ye cursed, into the eternal fire which is prepared for the devil and his angels."[1]

In the light of our experience of the effects of continued right or wrong doing upon the formation of settled character, the sentences of the last day are to be regarded as God's declaration of the ultimate issues of a line of good or evil conduct—His willing or unwilling assent to each man's deliberate choice. 'As you have followed good, you have become good, Come, ye blessed.' 'As you have followed evil, you have become evil, Depart, ye cursed.'

"It is a monstrous crime to teach that any are created by God such that they cannot escape the punishment of hell, or that any can be 'lost' simply because they did not know the truth of the Gospel, like the heathen; or because, like many in Christian countries, they had no real opportunity of knowing and serving God. We can be quite certain that God 'willeth all men to be saved,' and that, if not in this life, then beyond it, He will give the fullest chances of knowing and loving Him to each soul whom He has created. Again, it is quite without warrant that any have presumed to say that the majority of mankind, or any

[1] St. Matt. xxv. 34, 41.

particular proportion of mankind, will be finally lost."[1]

Surely, Christ's revelation of the life to come is a reasonable doctrine. For a great moral end, He plainly declares the inevitable result of a life rightly or wrongly lived on earth. Next to the constraining power of His awful sacrifice, revealing as nothing else could the true malice of evil, and the divine call to righteousness, what could more powerfully persuade men to shun evil and to follow good, than the solemn truth that as they choose, so shall they come to be for ever and ever?[2]

'Once to every man and nation comes the moment to decide,
In the strife of truth with falsehood, for the good or evil side:
Some great cause, God's new Messiah, offering each the bloom or blight,
Parts the goats upon the left hand and the sheep upon the right;
And the choice goes by for ever 'twixt that darkness and that light.'

iii.

It will form a fitting conclusion to our survey of the revelation of God, to consider the enormous influence which a right faith has upon

[1] Gore, *The Creed of the Christian*, p. 107.
[2] "The happiness which good men shall partake is not distinct from their Godlike nature. Happiness and holiness are but two several notions of one thing. Hell is rather a nature than a place, and heaven cannot be so well defined by anything without as by something within us."—qu. by MacColl, *Christianity in relation to Science and Morals*, p. 312.

The Revelation of the Life to come. 313

conduct and character. The words of Christ are, "This is life eternal, that they should know thee the only true God, and Him whom thou didst send."[1] Life eternal, according to Jesus Christ, is the outcome of the knowledge of the true God. If, as Pope has said, 'He can't be wrong whose life is right,' it is surely more true to say, 'He can't be right whose faith is wrong.' The purer and truer a man's creed, the purer and truer will be his life. "When belief waxes uncertain," says Carlyle, "practice becomes unsound." "A man's action," says Emerson, "is but the picture-book of his creed." The high moral excellence which is found so conspicuously in Christian times, is the fruit of the knowledge of the true God. It is a true faith which is the root and mainspring of a righteous life. As a man's creed is, so, if he be true to it, will his conduct be; and as his conduct is, so will his character become; and as his character is, so will his eternal destiny be. Therefore, we may say with confidence,

WHOSOEVER WISHES TO BE
IN A STATE OF SALVATION,
IT IS BEFORE ALL THINGS NEEDFUL
THAT HE SHOULD HOLD THE CATHOLIC FAITH.
AND THE CATHOLIC FAITH IS THIS:
THAT WE WORSHIP ONE GOD IN TRINITY,
AND TRINITY IN UNITY.

[1] St. John xvii. 3.

Appendix.

"We may, without incongruity, say that God does in a manner contrary to nature, what He does contrary to nature as we know it. For what we mean by 'nature' is this well-known and customary order, and it is when God does anything contrary to this, that His actions are called miracles or wonders. But as for that supreme law of nature, which is beyond the perception of men, either because they are impious, or because they are still weak in knowledge—against this, God no more acts than He acts against Himself. And God's spiritual and rational creatures, amongst whom are men, the more they become participators in that immutable law and light, the more clearly they can see what can happen and what cannot; and the further off, on the other hand, they are (from that divine law and light), so much the more are they astonished at what they are not accustomed to, in proportion as they are blind to what is coming."—St. Augustine, *contra Faust.* xxvi. 3.

"Miracle, in the sense of violation of law, is simply impossible, because law is the expression of the essential nature and perfection of God. It is as impossible for God to perform a miracle in this sense as it is for Him to lie, and for the same reason, viz., that it is contrary to His essential nature. In what sense, then, is a miracle possible? I answer, only as an occurrence or a phenomenon *according to a law higher than any we yet know.*"—Le Conte, *Evolution*, p. 356.

MIRACLES.

ONE of the most common objections to the Christian revelation is, that it is supported by, and involves a belief in, miracles; and that miracles, in the light of our advanced knowledge, are impossible. Renan prefaces his *Life of Jesus* with the words, " Miracles are things that never happen: only credulous people believe that they have seen them."[1] Kalisch, a writer of the same school, has said, "Miracles are both impossible and incredible; impossible, because against the established laws of the universe, and incredible, because those set forth by tradition are palpable inventions of unhistoric ages."[2] Such positive statements as these possess a strong fascination to some minds, appealing as they do to a rude common-sense.

I. OBJECTIONS TO MIRACLES EXAMINED.

Obj. 1. *Miracles do not happen now.*

It is true that there is much unreasonable credulity and superstition in the world, which

[1] Preface, p. xi.
[2] *Comment. on Leviticus*, Pt. i. p. 427.

ought in no wise to be encouraged. It is true that we do not see men about us who can turn water into wine, or heal incurable diseases by a touch, or calm the raging storm by a word, or restore the dead to life. We have no experience in common life of the operation of such powers, and therefore such an assertion as 'Miracles never happen,' appears to be practically true. And so men draw the inference that what does not happen now, never has happened, and never can happen.

But to deny the possibility of miracles on such grounds, is quite as unreasonable as it would be for the inhabitants of a tropical climate to deny the possibility of water becoming solid ice; because, in their experience, water always remains liquid. If the stones lying upon the beach were rational creatures, and a man was to say, 'I once saw a stone fly horizontally a hundred yards through the air,' the objection might be raised, 'Impossible, stones always lie on the ground, and never take such flights through the air.' But if the man stooped down, picked up a stone, and flung it far into the sea, the objection would at once lose its force.

But on this subject we shall speak later in this chapter.

Obj. 2. *Miracles are against Natural Law.*

The more serious objection is urged, that miracles are impossible, because they violate the fixed laws of nature. This objection is based on the assumption that we know all the laws of nature—a thing which the leading men of science would be slow to affirm.

Now, no intelligent Christian believes that miracles are a violation or interference with the laws of nature. "The miracle-working power," says Lotze, "whatever it may be, does not directly turn against the law to set aside its authority; but by altering the inner states of things, in virtue of its internal connection with them, it indirectly modifies the usual result of the law, whose validity it leaves intact and permanently turns to account."[1] St. Augustine, in the fourth century, wrote thus— "We say that all portents (i.e., wonders) are contrary to nature, but they are not so. For how is that contrary to nature which happens by the will of God, since the will of so mighty a Creator is certainly the nature of each created thing. A portent, therefore, is not contrary to nature, but contrary to what we know as nature."[2] St. Thomas Aquinas, the great theological teacher of the thirteenth century, took the same ground. He taught that the natural order depends upon God as its First Cause: that He can change the order existing in secondary causes as He wills, because He is not subject to it, but the order itself is subject to Him: that if God sometimes acts contrary

[1] *Microcosmus*, Vol. i. Bk. iv. Ch. iii. p. 451.
[2] *De Civ.* xxi. 8.

to the usual course of nature, He never acts contrary to the supreme and highest law: that a miracle is a wonder to all men, because its cause is concealed from all: that miracles are effects produced by God, the causes of which are altogether unknown to us.[1]

In the light of modern objections to the possibility of miracles, it is instructive to find these great Christian teachers of the fourth and thirteenth centuries, pointing out that the laws by which God governs the universe, are wide and far-reaching, that we only understand them in part, and that the course of nature is not independent of the will of God.

It is in accordance with a law of nature that a stone should lie on the ground, but if I pick it up and cast it into the air, I overcome the natural force of gravitation, by the intrusion of a new force; and this force is due to the action of the higher power of human will over lifeless matter. From the stone's point of view, its flight through the air is abnormal and unnatural: from my point of view it is perfectly natural. The true account is, that the natural force which governs the stone is not destroyed, but overcome by the superior power of a stronger force.[2] If man has power to intrude

[1] *Sum. Theol.* 1a. 105. 6. 7.
[2] "Continually we behold in the world around us lower laws held in suspense by higher, mechanic by dynamic, chemical by vital, physical by moral; yet we do not say, when the lower thus gives place in favour of the higher, that there was any violation of law, or that anything contrary to

upon, and alter the course of the laws which belong to matter, surely God is not more bound in regard to the laws of the universe at large. It is an unworthy conception of God, which would oblige Him to keep within the limits of mere law, and to conform His every action to ancient precedent. Such a conception would make Him "the slave of old modes of action, obliged to repeat Himself, and debarred by venerable custom from every form of activity that wears the aspect of innovation."[1]

"If God is personal, if His being is better expressed in human will and character than in mechanical motion and unconscious life, miracles with adequate cause are neither impossible nor unnatural. It is blind instinct which works on in monotonous uniformity where conditions are exceptional. It is rational character which from time to time will violate uniformity in the interest of rational consistency."[2]

II. THE RATIONALE OF MIRACLES.

1. *New Forces produce New Effects.*

To assert that miracles have from time to time been wrought, is only to say that at such times new forces, producing new and strange

nature came to pass; rather we acknowledge the law of a greater freedom swallowing up the law of a lesser."—Trench, *Miracles*, p. 17.

[1] Bruce, *The Chief End of Revelation*, p. 180.
[2] Gore, *Bampton Lectures*, ii. p. 46.

effects, have made themselves felt. At certain stages in the evolution of the world, the appearance of new forces has been freely admitted by scientific men. Mr. A. R. Wallace, in words previously quoted, points out that "there are at least three stages in the development of the organic world when some new cause, or power, must necessarily have come into action—the change from inorganic to organic, the introduction of sensation or consciousness, the existence in man of a number of his most characteristic and noblest faculties." And he adds, "These three distinct stages of progress from the inorganic world of matter and motion up to man, point clearly to an unseen universe—to a world of spirit, to which the world of matter is altogether subordinate."[1] If, on each of these three occasions, to which may be added a fourth—the creation of the inorganic world, a new force producing new phenomena exerted itself, which can only reasonably be attributed to divine intervention, why may not similar interventions on a lesser scale also have taken place? To say that miracles cannot happen because they never have happened, is to base an argument on false premisses; for miracles certainly have happened in the great crises of the evolution of the world. Viewed from below, each of the four manifestations of new force, to which we have referred, is super-

[1] *Darwinism*, pp. 474, ff.

natural, miraculous.[1] If, in working miracles, God acts contrary to nature, we can only mean that He acts contrary to nature as we know it.

From the Christian point of view, "the Spirit of God is the sovereign power, who commands the evolution of all things, and presides over the ordered and progressive movement of the universe. As He once intervened in chaos and matter to produce sentient being, as in animal life to produce thinking creatures, so was He to intervene among thinking creatures, in order that 'earth might give her fruit,' and that mankind might see the Saviour, the Holy One, the Son of God, blossom on the earth. The result of divine intervention had been till now only a creature; this time the result was infinitely great. God united Himself personally to His work; and as He had incarnated life in matter, sensation in life, thought in sensation, He now made Himself incarnate in mankind. The separate kingdoms are super-imposed on and enwrap

[1] "If we define nature as phenomena governed by physical and chemical laws and forces, then life becomes supernatural and miraculous—because higher than nature as we define it. If we reduce the phenomena of life to law, and include these also in our definition of nature, but limit it there, then the free, self-determined phenomena of reason become supernatural, because above our definition of nature. There may well be still other and higher modes of divine activity, the law of which we do not and may never understand. These are above our present definition of nature, and therefore to us supernatural or miraculous."—Le Conte, *Evolution*, pp. 356, 357.

each other: the kingdom of life is added to the kingdom of matter; the animal kingdom to the kingdom of life; the human kingdom to the animal kingdom; the kingdom of God had come, and the Son of God was made Man."[1] Here we find an adequate cause for the miracles which are recorded in the Gospels.

2. *The Miracles of the New Testament.*

The miracles of the New Testament receive their authentication in a belief in the Person of Jesus Christ. Men do not become Christians by believing in miracles, but by believing in a divine Person. We believe in miracles upon sufficient evidence, because we believe in Jesus Christ, the Incarnate God. Of the natural expectation that He should assert His divine power over the world and human life, and that He Himself should be the subject of miracles, we have already spoken at some length.[2] When once the primary miracles of the Incarnation and Resurrection are accepted, the whole of the New Testament miracles become easy of belief. The miracles wrought by the apostles and disciples, may be regarded as extensions of the power of the Incarnate Lord in the persons of His servants, and are thus reasonable and credible.

[1] Didon, *Life of Christ*, Vol. i. p. 32.
[2] See pp. 212, ff.

3. *The Miracles of the Old Testament.*

When we approach the subject of the miracles recorded in the pages of the Old Testament, we are on somewhat different ground. It is not the intention of the writer to treat with any attempt at fulness this branch of a great subject. To do so, would lie beyond the range and limits of the subject of the Christian revelation. But he may be permitted to make two observations.

First, that what seems impossible, or even puerile to modern minds, in the present state of intellectual advancement and illumination, was not necessarily so in the earlier stages of the mental development of mankind. We teach children the alphabet before we teach them to read. It is reasonable to suppose that God would, for adequate reasons, suffer that to happen in man's infancy, which would be unnecessary now.[1]

Secondly, that which appeared to be miraculous to men in unscientific and ignorant ages, may often have been due to causes which are now recognized as merely natural.[2] For ex-

---
[1] See Note, p. 331.
[2] At a meeting of the Victoria Institute, held June 17, 1895, Major-General Tulloch gave an account of that part of Egypt in which he lately carried out a War Office survey, and through which the route of the Israelites at the exodus was supposed to have lain. He stated that "the conformation of the country had somewhat altered since that event took place, 3,400 years ago, but what specially came under his notice was the action of a gale of wind, which had stopped all survey work on the borders of Lake Menzahleh,

ample, as Archbishop Trench remarks, " Many of the plagues of Egypt were the natural plagues of the land,—these, it is true, raised and quickened into far direr than their usual activity. In itself it was nothing miraculous that grievous swarms of flies should infest the houses of the Egyptians, or that flights of locusts should devour their fields, or that a murrain should destroy their cattle. None of these visitations were, or are, unknown in that land; but the intensity of *all* these plagues, the dread succession in which they followed on one another, their connexion with the word of Moses which went before, with Pharaoh's trial which was proceeding, with Israel's deliverance which they helped onward, the order of their coming and going, all these entirely justify us

in a few hours carrying the waters of the lake beyond the horizon, leaving all sailing vessels resting on the damp bed of the lake." The *Daily Graphic* of June 18, 1895, from which the above statement is quoted, goes on to say, "An interesting discussion ensued, and it was pointed out that wherever the passage of the Israelites took place, the possibility of water being influenced by wind to so great an extent was demonstrated."

In the light of this interesting statement we may conclude that some of the miracles recorded in the Old Testament, may have been simply natural occurrences brought to a supernatural height.

"If it is meant that miracles are wrought through the instrumentality of natural laws, partly or wholly unknown to us, ... we may at once admit that many alleged miracles both of Scripture and Church history *may* have occurred in this manner. The miracle, for instance, of 'the Thundering Legion' may have been the immediate result of ordinary atmospheric laws, coinciding with the prayers of the Christian soldiers."—H. N. Oxenham, *Essays*, p. 281.

in calling them 'the signs and wonders of Egypt,' even as such is evermore the scriptural language about them."[1]

As a similar instance, we may refer to the much misunderstood miracle recorded in Joshua x. Joshua's words, " Sun, stand thou still," signify literally, " Be silent." The natural meaning is, " Be darkened." What took place was most probably that, upon Joshua's command, the heavens were covered with dark menacing clouds. The Canaanites, against whom the Israelites were fighting, as sun-worshippers, would be filled with terror at the sign. As they turned and fled, there broke on them a violent hail-storm, which slew those who were out of reach of the Israelites.

In considering many of the occurrences named in the Old Testament, which were regarded as miraculous by those who beheld them, it is only reasonable to read such events from the ancient point of view, with a mind, as it were, divested of modern scientific knowledge.

NOTE ON THE MIRACLES OF THE OLD TESTAMENT.

"The sacred writers of the Jews never admitted for a moment that irrational distinction, which is purely modern, between what we choose to call the natural and the supernatural. Between the physical and the spiritual they did, indeed, constantly distinguish; but they habitually regarded all purely physical forces as servants of the One Supreme and Universal Mind. They were never shy of referring to the

[1] *Miracles*, p. 14.

use made of them, even in the most apparently miraculous events, however apparently inadequate are the causes sometimes mentioned, when considered in the light of mere physical explanations. Thus, inordinate rains, and, in addition, some great physical catastrophe, which is described under the striking formula of 'the breaking up of all the fountains of the great deep,' are the proximate and physical causes assigned by the writer of Genesis to that wide submergence of the land under the waters of the sea, which is known to us in the tradition of the Flood (Gen. vii. 11). Thus, again, the passage of the Israelites through the Red Sea in their flight from Egypt, is still more specifically connected with the employment of a purely physical cause — 'And the Lord caused the sea to go back by reason of a strong east wind all that night' (Exod. xiv. 21). Nor in the cases where the Hebrew writers do not mention any physical cause in connexion with the wonders which they relate, is it safe or even reasonable to assume that none such were used. Thus the arrest of a great river in the fulness of its flow, is a greater physical wonder than the temporary retirement of an arm of the sea from its accustomed shores. And yet the passage dry-shod of the Jordan-bed by the Israelites under Joshua, is narrated in the Old Testament without any allusion to any physical agency whatever to account for an event so strange. Nevertheless it is now known that a similar event, precisely, occurred again in the thirteenth century of our era, at the same place, and is explained by the Arabian historian who records it as having been due to the falling of a great mass of earth and gravel into the bed of the river, some miles above the point where its effects were seen."—The Duke of Argyll, *The Philosophy of Belief*, pp. 213, ff.

4. *The Moral Purpose of Miracles.*

In the writings of St. Athanasius,[1] and St. Augustine,[2] we find 'the best ancient rationale of miracles.' Both these great authorities teach that miracles were a merciful

[1] *de Incarn.* §§ 18. 19.
[2] *de Trin.* iii. 5; *Ennar. in Ps.* cx. 4.

provision to arrest the attention of the thoughtless. They held that where men were blind to see God's presence in the ordinary course of events, He interposed by signs calculated to strike the mind, or to provoke enquiry, so that they should say, This is the finger of God.

In modern times this ancient belief has found able exponents in Archbishop Trench,[1] and Mr. Gore. The latter author says,—

"A miracle is an event in physical nature which makes unmistakably plain the presence and direct action of God working for a moral end. God is always present and working in nature, and men were meant to recognize Him in the ordinary course of events, and to praise Him as they recognized Him. But in fact man's sin has blinded his spiritual eye, he has lost the power of seeing behind the physical order; the very prevalence of law in nature, which is

[1] "From the very circumstance that nature is thus speaking evermore to all, that this speaking is diffused over all time, addressed unto all men, that its sound has gone out into all lands, from the very constancy and universality of this language, it may fail to make itself heard. It cannot be said to stand in nearer relation to one man than to another, to confirm one man's word more than that of others, to address one man's conscience more than that of every other man. However it may sometimes have, it must often lack, a peculiar and personal significance. But in the miracle, wrought in the sight of some certain men, and claiming their special attention, there is a speaking to them in particular. There is then a voice in nature which addresses itself directly to them, a singling of them out from the multitude. It is plain that God has now a peculiar word which they are to give heed to, a message to which He is bidding them to listen."—*Miracles*, p. 12.

its perfection, has led to God being forgotten, His power depreciated, His presence denied. In a miracle then, or what Scripture calls a 'sign,' God so works, that man cannot but notice a presence which is not blind force, but personal will. Thus God violates the customary method of His action, He breaks into the common order of events, in order to manifest the real meaning of nature, and make men alive to the true character of the order, which their eyes behold. Miracles are God's protests against man's blindness to Himself, protests in which He violates a superficial uniformity in the interests of deeper law."[1]

As Christians, we do not regard miracles as mere marvels wrought for the sole purpose of astonishing men, neither do we regard them as mere credentials of revelation. We regard them as manifestations of divine power called forth by special circumstances, and for adequate ends. And these ends we hold to be *moral ends*.[2] The Incarnation, the Atonement, the Resurrection, the Gift of the Spirit, were the greatest of all possible miracles, and they were wrought for the attainment of immense moral ends. The rescue of man from sin and its consequences, through the birth and sacrifice of Jesus Christ; the deliverance from the lasting

---

[1] *Bampton Lectures*, ii. p. 45.

[2] "The antecedent improbability against a miracle being wrought by a man without a moral object, is apt to be confused with that of its being done by God with an adequate moral object."—Romanes, *Thoughts on Religion*, p. 180.

power of death, through His resurrection ; the restoration of mankind to fellowship with God, by the gift of the Spirit—these were the ends in view which fully justified God's miraculous intervention. The confirmation of belief in Jesus Christ as the deliverer of our race, the vindication of His righteousness in the face of the climax of iniquity—these surely were moral ends of overwhelming importance to all men in all ages, and were worthy of a display of miraculous power on the part of God.

Renan has said that "the chief event in the world's history is the revolution by which the noblest portions of humanity passed from the ancient religions comprised under the name of Paganism, to a religion based on the Divine Unity, the Trinity, and the Incarnation of the Son of God."[1] In contrasting the state of mankind under Pagan and under Christian influences, he must be blind indeed, who does not confess that the end attained, 'the chief event in the world's history,' justified the miraculous means adopted.

Let us not forget, too, that the miracles attributed to Jesus Christ were works of mercy and beneficence.[2] They were works which shew that hunger and thirst, disease and death, sin and imperfection, are things temporal, which in God's good time are destined to pass away. They were signs that the groaning and

[1] *Life of Jesus*, Ch. i. p. 1.
[2] See *The Chief End of Revelation*, pp. 168, 196.

travailing creation will in the end be delivered from the bondage of corruption, in which it now lies. They were signs that the time is coming, when the tabernacle of God will be with men in a more full and glorious manner than it is now; and that " He shall wipe away every tear from their eyes; and death shall be no more; neither shall there be mourning, nor crying, nor pain, any more: the first things are passed away:" and that " He that sitteth on the throne" shall "make all things new."[1]

NOTE.

"The moral element in miracles is both essential and predominant. There is always a natural relation between the acts, and those for whom or by whom they are wrought. The external phenomena which would in one age and to one people suggest the idea of the personal working of God, would not do so in another age and to another people. . . . That which on one occasion would be felt to be a personal revelation of God, might convey an impression wholly different at another. The miracles of one period or state of society might be morally impossible in another. It seems certain that knowledge limits faith, not indeed as diminishing its power, but as guiding its direction. For instance, when any particular physical phenomena are apprehended as subject to a clear law, which is felt to be a definite expression of the Divine Will, it is inconceivable that faith could contemplate an interference with them; not because it would be impossible, but because the prayer for such an interference would itself be disloyal. For example, it would be positively immoral for us now to pray that the tides or the sun should not rise on a particular day. . . . But as long as the idea of the physical law, which rules them, was unformed or indistinct, the prayer would have been reasonable, and (may we not suppose) the fulfilment also. We

[1] Rev. xxi. 4, 5.

cannot act when we feel that our influence is excluded; and may not the converse also be true? May not all things be possible for us which we firmly hold to be possible, if at least the result would be such as to convey as its whole and general effect, the idea of the personal action of God? An age records only what it believes; but in a certain sense also it does what it believes."—Bp. Westcott, *The Gospel of the Resurrection*, 4th ed. pp. 45, 46.

III. CONCLUSION.

To sum up what has been said: It is the Christian belief that there is One God who is Almighty, the Maker and Ruler of the universe. To doubt His ability to vary the natural and ordinary course of things by supernatural and extraordinary events, is to limit His Almighty power. A God who is not superior to the universe and its laws, is no God. 'A denial of the possibility of miracles is a denial of the possibility of God.' Thus, to confess, 'I believe in God the Father Almighty, Maker of heaven and earth,' is to acknowledge God's power to do as He wills in the universe which He has made. If God is Almighty, nothing can be impossible to Him, which does not contradict His moral nature. And the miracles recorded in Holy Scripture in no wise contradict His moral nature. On the contrary, they happened to secure great moral ends—the strengthening of faith, the punishment of iniquity, the awakening of repentance, and to serve high purposes in the redemption of mankind, and in the moral government of the world.

If God is the Author of nature, He it is who has given nature her laws, and who governs nature in accordance with law.[1] The authority which imposes a law, can also, for sufficient reason, supersede it, or change the course of its operation. "The one concession, that God governs the world according to natural laws, does not involve the other, that in every particular case the general law is applied. There are exceptions made in human legislation, where it is foreseen that a general enactment would bear too hard upon a particular case. So the Creator may foresee from eternity that in this case and that, an exception to the general course of nature will serve His purpose better than the maintenance of the uniformity; and He may decree that exception accordingly from all eternity."[2]

When we realize that the purpose of miracles is a moral purpose, we are prepared to believe

---

[1] "There is a fine passage on the relation of natural law to God, in Hooker's *Eccles. Polity*, Bk. i. Ch. iii. 2. 4., which concludes thus: "See we not plainly that obedience of creatures unto the law of nature is the stay of the whole world? . . . If it be demanded what that is which keepeth nature in obedience to her own law, we must have recourse to that higher law whereof we have already spoken. . . . It cannot be but nature hath some director of infinite knowledge to guide her in all her ways. Who the guide of nature, but only the God of nature? 'In Him we live, move, and are.' Those things which nature is said to do, are by divine art performed, using nature as an instrument."

[2] Boedder, *Natural Theology*, p. 423.

that, by the will of God, nature in His hands can become the ready instrument to the fulfilment of such an end. To a mind which has right thoughts of God, there is nothing antecedently improbable in miracles. The main question is one of historical fact, resting on adequate testimony. A man may never have dreamed a dream or seen an apparition, but he would be altogether unreasonable to discredit the united testimony of others whom he believed to be sane and honest men, and whose word he had no reason to doubt. For believers in God, the question is not, Can God work miracles? but, Has He done so? And the latter question is to be answered by an appeal to history and evidence. The historical fact that miracles have happened is as well, if not better, attested than multitudes of other facts in history, which are commonly accepted as true.

> "I say, that miracle was duly wrought
> When, save for it, no faith was possible.
> Whether a change were wrought i' the shows o' the world,
> Whether the change came from our minds which see
> Of shows o' the world so much as and no more
> Than God wills for His purpose,
> I know not; such was the effect,
> So faith grew, making void more miracles
> Because too much: they would compel, not help.
> I say, the acknowledgment of God in Christ
> Accepted by thy reason, solves for thee
> All questions in the earth and out of it."
>   Browning, *A Death in the Desert.*

"It seems pretty generally agreed among thoughtful men at present, that definite theories of inspiration are doubtful and dangerous. The existence of a human element, and the existence of a divine element, are generally acknowledged; but the exact relation of the one to the other it may be difficult to define."—Bp. Harold Browne, in Aids to Faith, *Inspiration*, p. 303.

"We must not regard, as so many do, the spirit of man as the passive amanuensis of the Spirit of God. Revelation to man must of necessity partake of the imperfections of the medium through which it comes. As pure water from heaven, falling upon and filtering through earth, must gather impurities in its course differing in amount and kind according to the earth, even so the pure divine truth, filtering through man's mind, must take imperfections characteristic of the man and of the age."—Le Conte, *Evolution*, p. 334.

"Sacred books may be said to be to religion what legal codes are to law. Law existed before codes of law, and religion existed before codes of religion."—Max Müller, *Natural Religion*, p. 563.

INSPIRATION.

IT was the ancient belief of the Hindoos that the earth was supported upon the back of an elephant, which in turn rested upon a tortoise. We may well suppose that enquiring minds went on to ask, But upon what does the tortoise rest? Such a question was surely neither unnatural nor inappropriate; but it found no answer. The present century has witnessed the rise of a school of teachers, who treat Christianity in a similarly illogical way, placing it upon an altogether wrong basis. For example, Mr. S. Laing does not hesitate to say, "Orthodox Christianity is based on revelation; what is revelation based on? On the Bible—the whole fabric depends on the belief that the Bible is an inspired record conveying a divine message from God to man."[1] We trust that readers of *The Natural Religion* have arrived at a different conclusion; and are prepared to acknowledge that there is another and more reasonable account to be given of the basis of Christianity, than 'revelation is based on the Bible.'

[1] *Modern Science and Modern Thought*, p. 355.

Inspiration, according to the same writer, "means that a certain book was not written, as all other books in the world have been written, by writers who were fallible, and whose statements and opinions, however admirable in the main and made in perfect good faith, inevitably reflected the views of the age in which they lived, and contained matters which subsequent ages found to be obsolete or erroneous, but that this particular book was miraculously dictated by an infallible God, and therefore absolutely and for all time true. But, as a chain cannot be stronger than its weakest link, if any one of these statements were proved not to be true, the theory of inspiration failed, and human reason was called on to decide by the ordinary methods, whether any, and if any, what parts of the volume were inspired and what uninspired. Now it is absolutely certain," continues Mr. Laing, "that portions of the Bible, and those important portions relating to the creation of the world and of man, are not true, and therefore not inspired."[1] Renan takes the same view of inspiration,—"If the Gospels are inspired books and true, consequently, to the letter, from beginning to end, I have been guilty of a great wrong in not contenting myself with piecing together the broken fragments of the four texts."[2]

[1] *Modern Science and Modern Thought*, p. 251.
[2] *Life of Jesus*, Preface, p. xi.

Inspiration.

In other words, it is assumed that Christianity depends upon the authority of the Bible, and that the authority of the Bible rests on the theory of verbal inspiration; and that if one statement in the Bible can be proved to be incorrect or inaccurate, the whole fabric of Christianity totters, and falls to the ground a shattered ruin. In view of these ideas, let us consider:

i. THE RELATION OF CHRISTIANITY TO THE NEW TESTAMENT.

No rightly instructed Christian holds that the Christian revelation is based on the Bible, or, more correctly speaking, on the New Testament. Christianity is not primarily derived from the New Testament, for the simple reason that Christianity existed, in its essential features and purest form, for some years before a page of the New Testament was written. The statement that the New Testament is the foundation of Christianity is as inaccurate as it is to say that the cross on the dome of St. Paul's is the foundation of the cathedral. It is an historical fact beyond all dispute that the New Testament was the product of the Christian Church, and not its foundation—its child, and not its parent.[1]

---

[1] St. Irenæus, the great representative in the second century of the principle of apostolic tradition, even puts before his readers the imaginary case, "Suppose the apostles had left us no Scriptures," and goes on to say, "should we

What are the facts in detail? They are these: The Christian revelation was given, not by means of *a book*, but in and through *a Person*. It is with Jesus Christ, and not with the written books of the New Testament, that Christianity stands or falls. The Christian revelation rests upon God's Self-disclosure in the Person of His Son, Jesus Christ. This disclosure was made to the apostles, and it was confirmed to them by the advent of the Holy Spirit, who came to guide them "into all the truth."[1] Thus the apostles possessed the fulness of the Christian revelation direct from the Revealer Himself, and from His Spirit, without the medium of any Christian writings. Their Master bade them "Go, and make disciples of all the nations, baptizing them into the name of the Father and of the Son and of the Holy Ghost: teaching them to observe all things whatsoever I commanded you."[2] And when Jesus Christ promised the apostles the aid of His Spirit, He left them free to carry out His command by preaching, by instruction, or by the aid of written documents,

---

not follow the order of tradition which they handed down into whose hands they entrusted the churches?"—iii. 4. 1. Similarly Professor Bruce, "I am so far from identifying Scripture and Revelation, that I conceive it possible that a revelation of God might be given in history without any written record coming into existence, the divine action in the world being left dependent for its record on oral tradition."—*The Chief End of Revelation*, Preface to 2nd ed. p. ix.

[1] St. John xvi. 13.   [2] St. Matt. xxviii. 19, 20.

Inspiration. 341

at their discretion. It is an historical fact that the first spread of Christian truth was due to living teachers, and not to their writings.

This state of things continued for some years, until the roots of the Christian faith were firmly fixed in the hearts and minds of converts to Christianity. The use of written teaching came later; it grew out of the wants of the existing Church, as we see in the epistles of the New Testament, and in the Revelation of St. John the Divine.[1] The idea of committing the oral Gospel narrative to writing took shape in order that the truths revealed by Christ and His Spirit to the apostles, and which they taught by word of mouth, might, after their deaths, be handed on to future ages.[2] There is distinct evidence that almost all, or at least large portions of the New Testament were written for the purpose of recalling what had been previously taught by word of mouth.[3] The earliest portions of what we know as the New Testament were certainly not written before the middle of the

---

[1] See Rev. i. 11.

[2] See 2 St. Peter i. 15.

[3] See St. Luke i. 1-4; 1 Cor. xi. 23; xv. 3; Gal. i. 6-8; Heb. v. 12; St. James i. 19; 2 St. Peter i. 12; iii. 1; 1 St. John ii. 21; Jude 3.

" The books of the New Testament bear upon the face of them the evidence that they were not meant for primary instruction; they were addressed to men who were already Christians, that is to say, men who as members of a definite society, the Church or the Churches, had already received oral instruction."—Gore, *Bampton Lectures*, vii. p. 189.

first century, and the whole was not completed until its close. As a consequence, complete copies of the New Testament, could not have been the property of any Christian community until the beginning of the second century at the very earliest. And even then, such complete copies of the volume, written slowly and laboriously, must have been, for a considerable period, rare possessions.

It is therefore impossible to maintain that orthodox Christianity is based on the Bible. Such a statement is a perversion of the plainest historical facts; and writers, who ground their assaults on Christianity on such inaccurate assertions, are not to be trusted. Christians, who are rightly instructed, believe that the New Testament documents contain a true and authoritative record of the Christian revelation in all its essential features, and that they fix and safeguard that revelation. They do not regard the New Testament as the basis of Christianity, "for other foundation can no man lay than that which is laid, which is Jesus Christ."[1] Christianity is founded upon a Divine Person, not upon the library of sacred books, which were written by men who were already Christians when they wrote them. Thus, as we have said, the real attack upon Christianity is made upon the Person of Jesus Christ, and the trustworthiness of the apostles as His witnesses.

[1] 1 Cor. iii. 11.

ii. The Inspiration of the Bible.

The second charge brought against the truth of Christianity is that the authority of the Bible rests on the theory of verbal inspiration, and that this inspiration relates to all subjects referred to in its pages, such as history, natural science, &c. The opponents maintain that if one link of the chain of reference to such subjects is broken, inspiration, as they understand it, has failed, the authority of the Bible is discredited, and the foundation of Christianity is overthrown. Although the Church, in her creeds and formularies, is not committed to the theory of verbal inspiration, it must be admitted that popular teaching has, to a considerable extent, countenanced it. But such teaching, however widely spread, is not authoritative; it does not represent the matured thought of the best teachers of our own day, who neither adopt it nor build anything upon it.

The following quotations from the writings of three of the greatest theologians of the nineteenth century, put the subject of inspiration in its truer light.

Bishop Westcott writes: "The purely organic theory of inspiration rests on no Scriptural authority, and, if we except a few ambiguous metaphors, is supported by no historical testimony. It is at variance with the whole form and fashion of the Bible, and is destructive of all that is holiest in man and highest in religion, which seeks the co-ordinate elevation of all our faculties, and not the destruction of any one of them. . . . The language of the Lawgiver, the Historian, the Prophet, the Psalmist, the Apostle, is characteristic of the position which each severally occupied. Even when they speak most emphatically *the words of the Lord*, they speak still as men living among men, and the eternal truths which they declare, receive the colouring of the minds through which they pass. . . . Everywhere there are traces of a personality not destroyed, but even quickened by the action of the divine power,—of an individual consciousness not suspended, but employed at every stage of the heavenly commission. Inspiration then, according to its manifestation in Scripture, is *dynamical* and not *mechanical*;[1] the human powers of the divine messenger act according to their natural laws, even when these powers are supernaturally strengthened. Man is not converted into a mere machine even in the hand of God."[2]

Cardinal Newman wrote: "In what way inspiration is compatible with that personal

---

[1] In 'dynamical' inspiration, the free power of the human mind is exercised, under spiritual influence, in uttering the divine message. In 'mechanical' inspiration, the message would be conveyed through the man as a mere machine, or speaking trumpet, in the hand of God.

[2] *Introduction to the Study of the Gospels*, 7th Ed. pp. 6, 13.

agency on the part of its instruments, which the composition of the Bible evidences, we know not; but if anything is certain, it is this,—that, though the Bible is inspired, and therefore, in one sense, written by God, yet very large portions of it, if not far the greater part of it, are written in as free and unconstrained a manner, and (apparently) with as little consciousness of a supernatural dictation or restraint, on the part of His earthly instruments, as if He had had no share in the work. As God rules the will, yet the will is free,—as He rules the course of the world, yet men conduct it,—so He has inspired the Bible, yet men have written it. Whatever else is true about it, this is true,—that we may speak of the history, or mode of its composition, as truly as of that of other books; we may speak of its writers having an object in view, being influenced by circumstances, being anxious, taking pains, purposely omitting or introducing things, leaving things incomplete, or supplying what others had so left. Though the Bible be inspired, it has all such characteristics as might attach to a book uninspired,—the characteristics of dialect and style, the distinct effects of times and places, youth and age, of moral and intellectual character; and I insist on this, lest I seem to forget (what I do not forget), that, in spite of its human form, it has in it the spirit and the mind of God." [1]

[1] *Tracts for the Times*, No. 85, p. 30.

Dr. Liddon wrote: "At first sight, and judged by an ordinary literary estimate, the Bible presents an appearance of being merely a large collection of heterogeneous writings. Historical records, ranging over many centuries, biographies, dialogues, anecdotes, catalogues of moral maxims, and accounts of social experiences, poetry, the most touchingly plaintive and the most buoyantly triumphant, predictions, exhortations, warnings, varying in style, in authorship, in date, in dialect, are thrown, as it seems, somewhat arbitrarily into a single volume. . . . But beneath the differences of style, of language, and of method, which are undeniably prominent in the Sacred Books, and which appear so entirely to absorb the attention of a merely literary observer, a deeper insight will discover in Scripture such manifest unity of drift and purpose, both moral and intellectual, as to imply the continuous action of a Single Mind."[1]

Inspiration in Holy Scripture is analagous to design in nature. A canal and a stream may run side by side. The canal, as the work of man, with its straight banks and rigid locks, represents the mechanical theory of inspiration, which the opponents of Christianity delight to represent as the true idea. The brook, winding its way down the valley, shallow here, deep there, now flowing round rocky corners, now overcoming obstacles in its way, now working

[1] *Bampton Lectures*, ii. p. 44.

a passage under the roots of trees, but always moving according to natural law, and therefore to design, represents the true and reasonable idea of inspiration. By such a method, God conveys infallibly to men the truth which He wills to reveal, and yet leaves them free to express it in their own words, through their own minds, and in accordance with the current ideas of their own times. And these ideas, as we know, were sometimes deep, sometimes shallow, sometimes accurate, sometimes inaccurate.

We need not shrink from admitting that there may be inaccuracies and discrepancies[1] in the Bible, as to historical or scientific fact; but such mistakes, where apparent, in no case touch essential truths, or affect the moral purpose of the revelation. To regard the Bible as 'a repository of scientific lore and miscellaneous information' is a huge mistake. We may safely say that inspiration was not given to teach men history or natural science, as, for example, astronomy or geology; because such knowledge may be gained by the use of the natural faculties. As Mr. Hugh Miller said: "While Scripture tells man all that is necessary to his wants and welfare as a religious creature, it does not communicate to him a single scientific fact which he is competent to find out for

---

[1] On the alleged discrepancies in the Gospels, see pp. 188, 189. Some of the inaccuracies in the sacred text are doubtless due to the mistakes of copyists.

himself."[1] Had the writers of the Bible, by inspiration, expressed themselves in the scientific terms in use in the nineteenth century, their language would, until recent times, have remained quite unintelligible. It seems to have been ordered that the Mosaic account of the creation of the universe should be derived from early documents or primitive traditions; and that it should describe things as they would have appeared to an eyewitness, had one been present, rather than as they would be more accurately described by scientific men of modern times. The latter method would have been both unnatural and inappropriate, and it would have given perpetual occasion for doubt in unscientific and ignorant ages.[2]

We admit that portions of the Old Testament, which have been commonly regarded as strictly historical and literal, may be really inspired allegory[3]—such, for example, as the

---

[1] *The Testimony of the Rocks*, p. 376.

[2] "There is no evidence that inspired men were in advance of their age in the knowledge of physical facts and laws. And plainly, had they been supernaturally instructed in physical knowledge, they would so far have been unintelligible to those to whom they spoke."—*Expositor's Bible*, Genesis, p. 5. See also, *The Chief End of Revelation*, pp. 7, 8.

[3] By allegorical language is meant a figurative as contrasted with a literal form of speech. In the allegory the thing signifying and that signified are blended together. For example, our Lord's words, "I am the true vine, etc." (St. John xv. 1, ff.), are throughout allegorical. "The allegory," says Archbishop Trench, "needs not, as the

early chapters of Genesis—a form of conveying moral and religious truth eminently suited to man in his infancy. The narrative contained in these chapters teaches that there is but One God, who made all things in their nature and use very good; that moral evil formed no part of His original work in creation; that it entered into our world through man's lack of trust in the goodness of God; that by yielding to it man lost his fellowship with God, and came to misery; that moral evil is to be resisted, and in the end will be cast out; that a great Deliverer would one day appear to rescue man, and crush the power of evil. "If we accept the view of many ancient writers that the scenery of the story is allegorical, it will not be because the pictorial setting is in any way unworthy." [1] If we realize that the true purpose of these early chapters of Holy Scripture is to teach morality, religion, theology, and not natural science, it must be admitted that, granting the narrative to be cast in the form of allegory, it admirably fulfils its end.[2]

---

parable, an interpretation to be brought to it from without, since it contains its interpretation within itself; and, as the allegory proceeds, the interpretation proceeds hand in hand with it, or at least never falls far behind."—*The Parables*, p. 9.

[1] Strong, *Manual of Theology*, p. 255.

[2] Upon this subject, Bishop Temple says, "These are not, and cannot be, lessons of science. They are worked out into the allegory of the Garden of Eden. But in this allegory there is nothing whatever that crosses the path of science, nor is it for reasons of science that so many great Christian thinkers from the earliest age of the Church down-

Or, again, we may regard some of the narratives of the Old Testament as representative. For example, the story of the deluge is the best account of an universal tradition, common to all races in all parts of the ancient world. That such a catastrophe actually happened is evident from the fact of its universal belief.[1] Here we have an instance

---

wards have pronounced it an allegory. The spiritual truth contained in it is certainly the purpose for which it is told."—*Bampton Lectures,* p. 185.

"A Latin writer, of the fifth or sixth century, who gives an interesting summary of the Catholic Faith, and is clearly nothing else but a recorder of accepted beliefs, after speaking of the origin and fall of man and woman, continues thus: 'These things are known through God's revelation to His servant Moses, whom He willed to be aware of the state and origin of man, as the books which he produced testify. For all the divine authority (i.e., the scriptural revelation) appears to exist under such a mode as is either the mode of history which narrates only what happened, or the mode of allegory in such sense that it cannot represent the course of history, or a mode made up of these two so as to remain both historical and allegorical.'"—Gore, in Lux Mundi, *Preface to 10th ed.* p. xxxii. See also Ibid. Appendix ii. p. 538, "But if an Irenæus, a Clement, an Athanasius, an Anselm could treat the record (Genesis) or part of it as rather allegorical than historical, we can use the same liberty."

[1] "The story of the Flood has no exclusive connection with the Hebrew people, except this, that although traditions of some such great catastrophe are so widely spread that they may almost be said to be universal, yet it is in the Hebrew literature alone that it assumes a character which even pretends to be historical. The Babylonish account looks very like a corrupted edition of the same story. The modern science of geology has, until very lately, almost assumed its purely mythical character, or, at least, that it represents nothing but the enormous exaggeration of some merely local inundation. And this has been assumed upon the ground that no physical cause is known,

of a great tradition used as the vehicle for spiritual teaching—that evil is not passed by in God's sight, but that it invokes His displeasure, and calls down punishment.

Whilst admitting all this, we may hold that Holy Scripture, like creation, is the work of God from beginning to end, that His hand is to be discerned everywhere, and yet that His hand is not like that of the builder with line and rule, spade and trowel, laying out and building up by contract. We need to make it clear that as neither matter, space, time, life, nor force, have any existence of themselves apart from God, and yet that He works through

or is conceivable, which could have produced the described effects. Gradually, however, in recent years, some geologists, of the highest rank in the science, (notably Sir Joseph Prestwich) have opened their eyes to see the presence of abundant physical evidence of the fact that amongst the most recent of all the causes which have determined the superficial phenomena of the earth's surface, there must have been, not indeed a universal deluge over the whole globe at any one time, but a transitory submergence of the land beneath the waters of the sea—a submergence, however, so wide in area as to include apparently the whole northern hemisphere down to the latitudes of the Mediterranean. . . . A submergence to the extent of, say, 2,000 feet would be more than enough to produce all the distinctive effects ascribed to the Deluge, and would nevertheless be absolutely invisible to a spectator stationed at a very small distance in space outside our planet. But the main point to be observed here is, that in the Hebrew theology even this catastrophe, with its tremendous effects on living things, is represented as having been brought about by physical causes, and that these again are shadowed forth under forms of language wonderfully adequate to cover and convey the largest conceptions of their possible nature."— The Duke of Argyll, *The Philosophy of Belief*, pp. 215, ff.

them all in a way not inconsistent with human free will, so it may be with His inspiration of Scripture. We are to regard inspiration not as the work of a human artificer, but as that of an Intelligent Divine Agent, carrying out His gracious purpose by means of imperfect human instruments.

> The Bible! That's the Book! The Book indeed,
> The Book of books:
> On which who looks,
> As he should do, aright, shall never need
> Wish for a better light
> To guide him in the night.
>
> It is the index to eternity.
> He cannot miss
> Of endless bliss,
> That takes this chart to steer his voyage by.
> Nor can he be mistook
> That speaketh by this Book.
>
> A Book, to which no book can be compar'd
> For excellence;
> Pre-eminence
> Is proper to it, and cannot be shar'd.
> Divinity alone
> Belongs to it, or none.
>
> Christopher Harvey, A.D. 1709.
> *The Synagogue, or the Shadow of the Temple.*

NOTE.

The following declaration on the Inspiration of Holy Scripture was recently put forth by certain eminent churchmen.

"i. By Inspiration is meant a special action of the Holy Ghost, varying in character and in degree of intensity, upon those writers from whom the Church has received

Inspiration. 353

the books included in the Canon of Scripture, by which those books were directed to certain divine purposes, and protected from all defects injurious to those purposes.

"ii. The main purpose of Holy Scripture is generally to reveal truths concerning God and man, and in particular to bear witness to our Lord Jesus Christ. It fulfils this latter purpose, as in other ways so specially, by being the record—(1) of the preparation for Christ's Incarnation by the selection and supernatural training of a chosen people; (2) of His manifestation when 'The Word dwelt among us'; (3) of the results of that manifestation, viz., the coming and presence of His Holy Spirit, the revelation of His mind in Christian doctrine, the building up of His Church on the foundation laid by and in Him, the communication of the fruits of His redemptive work, and the promise of His appearing and His kingdom.

"iii. The several books of the Old Testament were delivered to the faithful of the old covenant, to whom God had revealed Himself through the oral teaching of His messengers and prophets; and were retained as 'Holy Scriptures', 'able to make men wise unto salvation through faith which is in Christ Jesus,' when the several books which make up the New Testament were successively entrusted to faithful Christians, baptized and instructed in the Church of God, which is 'the pillar and ground of the truth.' The way in which Holy Scripture has been sometimes isolated, by the attempt to use it as the sole ground of faith, and without the precedent condition of belief in Christ and fellowship with His Church, has been the cause of much misconception and confusion.

"iv. The frequent reference made by our Lord to the Old Testament in support of His own claims, or in illustration of His teaching, is decisive in favour of its inspiration in the sense defined above.

"v. It is certain that all the words of our Lord were always the most perfect words for His purpose, and that the forms in which they have been recorded for us are those which are best adapted to the needs of the Church.

"vi. Since the Human Mind of our Lord was inseparably united to the Eternal Word, and was perfectly illuminated by the Holy Spirit in the discharge of His office as Teacher, He could not be deceived, nor be the source of deception, nor intend to teach, even incidentally, for fact what was not fact.

"vii. The divine revelation set forth in the Bible is progressive, and issues in the final manifestation in the New Testament of God's truth and will. The Bible, taken as a whole, possesses conclusive authority in matters pertaining to faith and morals.

"viii. The Church has never authoritatively formulated what she has received to hold concerning the scope and limits of the inspiration of Holy Scripture; and it may even be said that there has not been a complete unanimity of view among her accredited teachers in regard to some points connected with that scope and those limits."

GLOSSARY,

Giving the sense in which certain words, mostly unexplained in the text, are used in this work.

abnormal, out of due course or natural order.
aboriginal elements, the first or earliest forms.
acquiescence, assent to, agreement in.
adaptability, adaptation, suitableness, fitness.
adequate, sufficient.
adoption, the treating as one's own that which is not so naturally.
agent, one who acts.
agency, action.
alienation, a state in which the sense of fellowship is broken.
amelioration, improvement.
amœba, a minute creature.
analogue, a subject resembling another subject.
analogy, resemblance of relations, likeness.
annihilation, the bringing to nothing.
antagonism, opposition.
antagonist, a foe.
antedate, to date before the right time.
antecedently, previously.
anticipation, expectation.
arbitrary, tyrannical, inconsiderate.
atheist, a disbeliever in God's existence.
the Atonement, the act of Christ in making God and man at one.
attested, certified.
attributes, qualities of a person.
authenticated, duly attested, established as true.
authoritative, with a force which commands attention.
automata, self-moving figures.

barbarous, uncivilized, savage.
bias, inclination, tendency.

catholic, world-wide, universal.
causation, the act of causing or producing.
centrifugal, tending to fly off from a centre.
centripetal, tending to drive towards a centre.
character, the sum of good or bad qualities in a person.
characteristics, leading features or qualities.
circuitous, round about.
climax, the highest point or measure.
coercion, compulsion.
the Comforter, the Strengthener: a title of the Holy Spirit.
complex, not simple, complicated.
complexity, complication, a condition in which things are interwoven.
concentration, collection into one point.
concept, conception, an image or idea in the mind.
concession, a thing granted.
conformable, in accordance with.
conjecture, guess, supposition.
conscience, the voice of reason within, which points out duty.
consciousness, the knowledge of what passes in the mind.
consent, agreement.
consistent, in harmony with.
constraining, urging with force.
consummated, completed, perfected.
contemporaries, those living at the same time.
co-operation, the working together with.
corroboration, the act of strengthening or confirming.
counterpart, that which answers to another thing.
credible, possible of belief.
crude, imperfect, rough.
cumulative, taken together as a whole.

Deity, God.
degradation, the falling from a higher to a lower condition.
demonstration, proof beyond question.
depreciate, to lessen the value.
deterioration, the growing worse.
development, growth, progress from lower to higher.
deviation, the wandering from the right path.
dictates, directions, promptings.
dilemma, a difficult or perplexing position.
discrepancy, disagreement.
divers, different.
divine, pertaining to God.
dominant, ruling.
dormant, asleep, inactive.

earnest, a pledge.
educe, to draw out.
efficient, able to produce the result intended.
elements, first principles, rudiments.
embryo, the first rudiments or beginnings of a thing.
emotion, mental disturbance.
enactment, law.
energy, power, force.
environment, surroundings.
estrangement, separation of affection.
evil, that which ought not to be.
evolution, unfolding, growth
expansion, enlargement.
extension, the stretching out.
extinction, the putting out.

factors, agencies.
the Fall, the sin of our first parents.
filial, son-like.
free will, the power of acting or not acting as we choose, when action is possible.
fundamental, pertaining to foundations, primary.

generation, the begetting.
good, that which ought to be.
grace, a spiritual gift of God, which enables man to attain the true end of his being.
guarantee, pledge, warrant.

immanence, indwelling, abiding presence.
immortality, life which never dies.
immutable, that which cannot be changed.
inadequate, insufficient.
inanimate, lifeless.
the Incarnation, the act of God in becoming Man.
inconceivable, that which cannot be imagined.
inconsistent, contradictory.
incredulous, unbelieving.
individual, a single person.
inevitable, unavoidable.
inexorable, unyielding.
inextricably, that cannot be freed or disentangled.
inference, a conclusion drawn from an argument.
infinite, boundless, unlimited by time or space.
influx, a flowing in.
inherent, inherited, naturally belonging to.

inimical, hostile, unfriendly.
injunctions, commands.
innate, inborn.
inorganic, lifeless.
insistent, urgent.
inspiration, the action of the Holy Spirit on the mind of man.
instinct, natural feeling or impulse.
integrity, uprightness.
intelligible, capable of being understood.
interposed, placed between.
intervene, to step in between.
intuition, perception without explanation or proof.
investigation, searching enquiry.
involuntary, unwilling.
irrational, without reason.
irrevocable, that which cannot be recalled or reversed.
isolated, standing alone.

limitations, bounds.

malignity, malice, bitter enmity.
manifestation, making plain or clear.
material, pertaining to matter or substance, not spiritual.
mechanical, without will as a machine.
mediator, a go-between.
miracle, an unusual work of God, wrought to reveal a divine purpose, or to secure a moral end.
mission, special object in view, purpose.
mitigate, to lessen or modify.
molecular, pertaining to very minute particles of matter.
moral, pertaining to conduct.
morality, right conduct.
moral agent, one who can distinguish right from wrong, one capable of right action.
moral being, as applied to God, a Being whose actions are right and just.
moral end, a righteous purpose.
moral evil, evil committed by a free agent.
moral freedom, freedom as to conduct.
mystery, that which passes understanding.
myth, a fanciful story embodying some truth.

neutralize, to make of no effect.
'*norma vivendi,*' the rule of living or conduct.

objective fact, fact outside the mind which dwells upon it.
obliterate, to blot out.
ordinances, observances commanded.
organic, endowed with life.
organism, a living body.
original righteousness, the state of man before the Fall.

paganism, heathenism.
pantheist, one who believes that nature or the universe is God.
the Paraclete, the Advocate: a title of the Holy Spirit.
the Passion, the sufferings of Jesus Christ.
penal consequences, results by way of punishment.
'*per ardua et aspera*,' through difficulties and adversities.
precedent, that which has been done before.
perception, notion, idea.
permanent, lasting.
permission of evil, the allowing or toleration of evil.
persistence, abiding force or action.
perverted, turned from its true purpose.
phenomenon, an appearance of nature, an unusual effect.
philosophy, the science of truth in the natural order.
physical, belonging to the body or material things.
polygamy, marriage with more wives than one at the same time.
postponed, put off for a time.
postulate, something to be assumed or granted.
potential, existing in possibility.
prehistoric, previous to historical record.
preliminary, a preparatory step or condition.
prelude, an introduction.
premisses, propositions from which inferences are drawn, bases of argument.
preposterous, absurd.
prime, *primal*, *primary*, first, earliest, original.
primeval, *primitive*, belonging to the earliest times.
problem, a matter to be explained.
procession of the Spirit, the coming forth of the Spirit from the Father and the Son in eternity.
progenitor, one who begets, a forefather.
prohibition, a forbidding.
proneness, inclination, disposition.
propitiate, to render favourable.
protoplasm, the first matter of which organisms are formed.
protracted, lengthened out.

providence, the care of God in directing His creatures to their natural end.
punitive, by way of punishment.

radical, pertaining to the root or foundation.
rational, possessing reason, reasonable.
rationale, a reasonable account.
realize, to account as real.
reason, the power of understanding through the mind.
reasonable, in accordance with right reason.
reconciliation, renewal of friendship after disagreement.
recreation, the creating anew.
rectitude, uprightness.
the Redemption, the act of Christ in restoring man to God.
reiterated, repeated again and again.
reparation, the act of making amends.
revelation, uncovering, disclosure, the sum of truth in the order of grace or glory made known to man.
rudimentary, belonging to first principles, in an original or early state.

science, reasoned knowledge.
self-consciousness, the recognition of thoughts or actions as one's own.
self-determination, the exercise of one's own will.
sensation, impression made on the mind through the senses.
sentient, that perceives or feels.
simulate, to feign, to assume the appearance of.
species, a sort, kind, or class.
sphere, the scene of action or influence.
spontaneous, of its own accord.
stability, firmness.
stimulate, to urge onward.
subordinate, in a lower scale or position.
superhuman, more than human.
supernatural, above the ordinary course of nature.
supersede, to override or set aside.
superstition, belief in that which is false or without evidence.
supervision, the act of overseeing.
survival,, the act of outliving others.
symmetrical, in due proportion.

testimony, evidence.
theologian, a student or teacher of theology.
theology, the science of God or divine things.

Glossary.

toleration, the allowing that which is not approved.
tradition, teaching or opinion handed down.
transmission, the handing on from one to another.
truth, conformity of thought to fact or reality.
type, a kind, or order.

ultimate, final.
unfalteringly, without hesitation.
unique, singular.
unobtrusiveness, modesty.
unparalleled. unequalled.
untenable, that which cannot be held or defended

validity, soundness.
veracious, truthful.
verification, the act of proving to be true.
vicarious, acting in place of another.
vindicate, to justify.
violate, to outrage.
virtue, the habit of doing right.
vivid, lively, clear.
vivifying, life-giving.
voluntary, free.

the Word, a title of the Son of God.

INDEX TO AUTHORS.

Allman, 87
Andrewes, Bp., 250
Aquinas, St. Thomas, 5, 15, 245, 319
Argyll, Duke of, 50, 328, 351
Arnold, 223
Athanasius, St., 175, 328
Augustine, St., 5, 11, 49, 72, 74, 126, 139, 231, 234, 235, 286, 316, 319, 328

Bacon, 102, 121
Balfour, 90, 157
Bernard, St., 263
Blunt, 67
Boedder, 71, 74, 81, 160, 245, 248, 334
Browne, Bp., 336
Browning, 335
Bruce, 174, 241, 321, 331, 340, 348
Butler, Bp., iii., ix., 2, 42, 56, 60, 121, 147, 306, 308.

Carlyle, 127, 313
Carter, 142
Christlieb, 237
Chrysostom, St., 188, 239
Church, 301
Cicero, 11, 59, 62, 116, 120
Clement, Alex. St., 71
Clifford, 85, 90
Cobb, 33
Cocker, 112
Cowper, 135
Cox, 129, 130, 132, 135
Curteis, 29

Damascene, St. John, 59

Darwin, 71, 82, 85, 89, 92, 150
De Quatrefages, 24, 71
Didon, 324
Dixey, 154
Döllinger, 238, 260
Drummond, 89, 91, 101, 123, 140, 146, 151, 168
Du Bois-Raymond, 90

Eagar, 65, 66, 188
Ellicott, Bp., 54, 66, 70, 71, 78, 114, 115, 119, 120, 134, 138

Fisher, 44
Footman, 42, 181

Gladstone, 204, 294, 300
Goldziker, 34
Goodwin, Bp., 184, 186
Gore, 6, 33, 169, 172, 175, 177, 178, 186, 188, 195, 214, 215, 216, 217, 222, 228, 232, 236, 237, 238, 242, 256, 266, 275, 291, 299, 300, 312, 321, 329, 341, 350

Harrison, 31, 32
Harvey, 352
Holland, 186
Hooker, 334
Hugo, Cardinal, 58
Hutchings, 268, 286, 287
Huxley, 85, 87, 89

Ignatius, St., 217
Illingworth, 17, 18, 29, 34, 42, 44, 50, 54, 68, 76, 103, 104, 117, 121, 124, 146, 147, 153, 156, 166, 175, 212, 236

Irenæus, St., 191, 267, 339

Janet, 94

Kalisch, 317
Kant, 115
Keble, 173, 272

Lactantius, 72, 78
Laing, S., 24, 78, 88, 201, 204, 337, 338
Le Conte, 92, 164, 316, 323,
Lecky, 208 [336
Leo, St., 219, 250
Leontius of Byzantium, 13
Liddon, 38, 74, 105, 126, 129, 134, 165, 173, 181, 188, 193, 194, 196, 199, 200, 204, 207, 209, 210, 255, 256, 260, 277,
Locke, 42 [346
Lotze, 48, 49, 86, 299, 319
Luthardt, 54, 58, 120, 218, 257, 277
Lyttelton, 265, 268

MacColl, 46, 49, 146, 216, 312
MacDonald, 20
Manning, Cardinal, 180, 203
Mansel, 38
Martineau, 85
Maurice, 34, 182
McClean, 3
Mill, J. S., 102, 186
Miller, 142, 143, 347
Moore, Aubrey L., 47, 57, 81, 83, 85, 105, 107, 120, 247
Momerie, 136
Moule, 292
Mozley, J. B., 68, 172
Müller, Max, 4, 6, 7, 11, 15, 16, 21, 22, 24, 26, 30, 63, 174, 181, 239, 336
Mylne, Bp., 226

Newman, Cardinal, 6, 13, 160, 181, 344

Ottley, H. B., 188
 ,, R. L., 51, 112, 281
Oxenham, 326

Paley, 94, 101, 185 [274
Pascal, 57, 58, 109, 131, 195,
Pearson, Bp., 62
Plutarch, 62

Renan, 221, 317, 331, 338
Romanes, 57, 59, 78, 79, 83, 97, 170, 187, 203, 330
Ruskin, 10, 286
Russell, E. F., 294

Sanday, 188, 221
Smith, W., 35 [85, 104
Spencer, H., 22, 44, 78, 84,
Spenser, E., 94
St. George Mivart, 87
Stewart, 208
Stolz, 21
Strong, 349

Temple, Bp., 349
Tennyson, 256
Tertullian, 59, 128
Theophylact, 262
Thomson, Archbp., 263, 265, 269, 271, 278
Trench, Archbp., 33, 213, 321, 326, 329, 348
'Troglodyte,' 31, 249
Tulloch, 202
Tyndall, 85

Ullathorne, Bp., 126

Van Oosterzee, 59

Wace, 118 [283, 322
Wallace, 89, 92, 100, 140, 148,
Watson, Ellen, 58 [343
Westcott, Bp., 188, 300, 333,
Wilberforce, 250, 267
Wordsworth, 37

GENERAL INDEX.

Adam, 179, 298
Adaptation in nature, 98 ff.
Allegory, 348, 349
Ancestor-worship, 22, 24 ff., 64 ff.
Anthropomorphism, 28 ff., 125
Apostles, the, 229, 289, 296, 301, 324, 340
,, ,, testimony of, 185, 220 ff., 289
Apostolic succession, 300, 303
Atheism, 65, 66, 121
Atonement, the, 261 ff., 330

Baptism, 230, 231, 250, 258, 299
Belief in God universal, 14, 63 ff.
Buddhism, 72, 205, 308

Caffres, 65
Cause, the First, 45, 74, 77 ff., 95, 319
Causes, natural, 76 ff., 103
,, secondary, 78 ff.
Character, 155, 310 ff.
CHRIST, adaptation of teaching of, 201 ff.
,, authority of, 183, 194
,, characteristics of, as a teacher, 192 ff., 307
,, ,, ,, teaching of, 199 ff.
,, death of, 200, 203, 224
,, the Deliverer, 218, 330, 331
,, a divine Person, 190 ff.
,, an historical Person, 184
,, holiness of, 192 ff., 198, 219, 263, 280
,, influence of, 203 ff.
,, the Mediator, 261 ff.
,, miracles of, 212 ff., 324, 331
,, morality of teaching of, 199 ff.
,, passion of, 156, 248, 270, 272, 279
,, proofs of Divinity of, 191 ff.
,, revelation in, 176 ff., 183 ff., 340, 342
,, resurrection of, 200, 203, 220 ff., 280, 308, 309, 324, 330

General Index.

CHRIST, the Second Adam, 216, 266 ff., 295
,, self-assertion of, 195 ff.
,, supernatural elements in life of, 212 ff.
,, testimony to, 184 ff.
,, the Truth, 190, 301
,, virgin-birth of, 215 ff., 288
Christianity, 2, 5 ff., 169, 180, 201 ff., 208, 331, 337 ff.
,, relation to New Testament, 339
Church, the, 209 ff., 223, 295 ff.
,, a divine society, 211, 296
,, extension of the Incarnate Life, 295 ff.
,, humble origin of, 210
,, the organ of truth, 301 ff.
,, mission of, 295 ff.
,, progress of, 210, 211
,, the sphere of grace, 297 ff.
Communion, the Holy, 299
Conscience, 114, 119, 120, 164, 173, 248
Creation, 45, 74 ff., 104 ff., 131 ff.
Creeds, the, 232

Death, 142 ff., 152, 307 ff.
Degradation, 17, 64, 67, 69, 274
Deluge, the, 350
Delusion, 35, 40
Design in nature, 95 ff.
Development, 4, 23, 34, 39, 81 ff., 105 ff., 170, 307
Dualism, 129, 130
Duty, 114, 115

Epistles of St. Paul, the, 187, 221
Evidence, cumulative, 60, 109, 225
Evil, moral, 127 ff., 143, 218, 243, 248, 261 ff.
,, origin of, 126 ff.
,, physical, 141 ff., 241
Evolution, 69, 81 ff., 104 ff., 161, 168, 213

Faith, 56 ff., 161, 162
Faith and practice, 312, 313
Fall, the, 275 ff., 298
Fetichsm, 66
Free will, 119, 131 ff., 311, 312
Future life, 2, 157, 307 ff.

GOD, conceptions of, 16, 18, 23, 28 ff.
,, Fatherhood of, 239 ff.

General Index.

God the Holy Trinity, 68, 229 ff., 313
,, immanent in nature, 80 ff., 105 ff., 246
,, a Moral Being, 2, 113 ff., 127 ff., 156, 166, 173, 253
,, personality of, 39 ff., 112, 113, 117 ff., 166, 321
,, providence of, 76, 81, 108, 244 ff.
,, relation to man, 240 ff.
,, seen in man, 23 ff., 173
,, seen in nature, 3, 11 ff., 35, 74 ff., 172
,, a Spirit, 30
,, unity of, 229, 232
Gospels, the, 186 ff.
,, discrepancies in, 188
,, genuineness of, 188
Grace, 5, 6, 280, 297 ff.

Heathen, the, 178, 179, 311
Hero-worship, 27

Identity, 41 ff.
Illusion, 32 ff.
Immortality, 22, 24, 157, 307 ff.
Incarnation, the, 138, 156, 177, 202, 204, 208, 212, 214, 231, 248, 250, 279, 287, 296, 298, 324, 330
Inspiration, 337 ff.
Intuition, 15, 54, 58 ff., 165

Jews, the, 18, 123, 167, 175, 209, 229, 232, 240, 286

Law in nature, 96, 164, 246, 252 ff., 318 ff.
Life, origin of, 86 ff.
Life to come, the, 2, 157, 307 ff.
Livingstone, 148
Love, 48 ff., 122, 124, 132 ff., 234 ff.

Man, dignity of, 117, 191, 250
,, immortality of, 22, 24, 157
,, moral nature of, 114 ff., 130 ff., 173
,, personality of, 41 ff., 112, 122, 236
,, primitive, 17, 18, 20, 36, 76, 168, 170, 171, 274, 325
,, relation to God, 249 ff.
,, ,, fellows, 257
Mankind, a race, 266 ff., 298
Mind in animals, 91, 92
,, origin of, 88 ff.

General Index.

Miracles, 212 ff., 224, 317 ff.
,, of CHRIST, 212 ff., 324, 331
,, as evidence, 212, 213, 324, 330
,, moral purpose of, 328 ff.
,, of New Testament, 324
,, objections to, 317 ff.
,, of Old Testament, 325 ff.
,, rationale of, 321 ff.
Monotheism, 67
Moral evil, 127 ff., 143, 218, 243, 248, 261 ff.
,, freedom, 118, 131 ff.
,, law, 114 ff., 173, 199 ff.
Myth, 32 ff., 180

Napoleon I., 206
Nature, adaptation in, 98 ff.
,, order in, 96
,, unity of, 75
'Natural,' 12, 327
Natural law, 96, 164, 246, 252 ff., 318 ff.
,, selection, 102 ff.
New birth, 219

Obedience, 118, 132 ff.
Origin of evil, 126 ff.
,, life, 86 ff.
,, mind, 88 ff.

Pain, animal, 143 ff.
,, human, 152 ff.
Personality of God, 39 ff., 112, 113, 117 ff., **166, 321**
,, man, 41 ff., 112, 122, **236**
Physical evil, 141 ff., 241
Polytheism, 67, 232
Prayer, 251 ff.
,, effects of, 255 ff.
,, objections to, 252 ff.
Probability, 56
Prophets, 164, 167, 174
Providence, 76, 81, 108, 244 ff.

Reason, 13, 54 ff., 109, 161, 162, 179
'Religion,' 11
Religion, supernatural, 4 ff.
,, universal, 63 ff.
Resurrection of the body, 309

General Index.

Retribution, 2, 117, 152 ff., 310 ff.
Revelation, 2, 3, 13, 14, 18, 40, 68, 121 ff., 161, 165 ff., 183, 232, 307, 337 ff.
,, in CHRIST, 176 ff., 183 ff., 340, 342
,, primeval, 17, 18, 67, 69, 168

Sacraments, 281, 299 ff.
Satan, 141, 271
Scriptures, the Holy, 3, 6, 13, 28, 84, 85, 108, 135, 141, 232, 337 ff.
,, ,, Inspiration of, 343 ff.
Self-consciousness, 38, 43 ff., 59, 81, 112, 131
Sermon on Mount, 200, 207
Sin, 118, 152, 200, 218, 243, 248, 261 ff.
,, actual, 278 ff.
,, original, 218, 273 ff.
Solar system, 101
SPIRIT, THE HOLY, 283 ff., 301, 330
,, ,, a divine Person, 230
,, ,, and the Incarnation, 219, 287, 288
,, ,, the Life-giver, 285, 291, 292, 323
,, ,, in man, 164, 179, 281, 286, 292
,, ,, in the Church, 296 ff.
,, ,, in nature, 285
,, ,, procession of, 232, 233
,, ,, in prophets, 286, 287
'Supernatural,' 12, 214, 327
Superstition, 2, 66 ff.

Theism, 66, 97
Theology, 161 ff.
Tradition, 3, 6, 13, 18, 25, 340
TRINITY, THE HOLY, 68, 229 ff., 313

Universe, creation of, 75 ff., 131, 133, 246 ff.

Will, 58, 80, 118

www.ingramcontent.com/pod-product-compliance
Lightning Source LLC
Chambersburg PA
CBHW072130220426
43664CB00013B/2198